MU2MT3 Introduction to Music Therapy

Academic Year: 2019/20

Term:

Day/Evening: Evening

Instructor: Rachael Finnerty

Email:finnerr@mcmaster.ca

Office: TSH 432

Phone: 905 512 4416

Website:www.musictherapyacademy.com

Office Hours: By Appointment

Course Objectives:

This course offers an introduction to the literature and professional practice of music therapy with an emphasis on the diversity of music therapy applications such as bio-medical, psychoanalytical, behavioural and rehabilitation. Music therapy interventions and approaches will be highlighted through music therapy articles, readings & guest speakers. Knowledge of the profession of music therapy, its diversity of client groups, music therapy interventions and approaches will be assessed through multiple-choice quizzes, a midterm and a final exam.

Textbooks, Materials & Fees:

An Introduction to Music Therapy Courseware 2019-2020

Method of Assessment:

Quiz 1 Avenue 4%	Quiz 2 Avenue 4%	**Mid-Term** Room to be Assigned Class 6 35%	Quiz 3 Avenue 4%	Quiz 4 Avenue 4%	Quiz 5 Avenue 4%	Accumulative **Final Exam** 45%

Policy on Missed Work, Extensions, and Late Penalties:

15minutes are allotted for each quiz. Each quiz is 15 questions. A missed quiz will be graded as 0. The lowest quiz grade will be dropped for each student (it will become 15/15). The quiz must be completed within the allotted time. No exceptions will be made. An MSAF is not required for the first quiz missed.

McMaster Student Absence Form (MSAF)

This is a self-reporting tool for undergraduate students to report absences DUE TO MINOR MEDICAL SITUATIONS that last up to 5 days and provides the ability to request accommodation for any missed academic work. Please note, this tool cannot be used during any final examination period. You may submit a maximum of 1 Academic Work Missed request per term. It is YOUR responsibility to follow up with your Instructor immediately (NORMALLY WITHIN TWO WORKING DAYS) regarding the nature of the accommodation. If you are absent for reasons other than medical reasons, for more than 5 days, or exceed 1 request per term, you MUST visit your Associate Dean's Office/Faculty Office). You may be required to provide supporting documentation. This form should be filled out immediately when you are about to return to class after your absence.

Please note the following policies

Academic Dishonesty

You are expected to exhibit honesty and use ethical behaviour in all aspects of the learning process. Academic credentials you earn are rooted in principles of honesty and academic integrity.

Academic dishonesty is to knowingly act or fail to act in a way that results or could result in unearned academic credit or advantage. This behaviour can result in serious consequences, e.g. the grade of zero on an assignment, loss of credit with a notation on the transcript (notation reads: 'Grade of F assigned for academic dishonesty'), and/or suspension or expulsion from the university.

It is your responsibility to understand what constitutes academic dishonesty. For information on the various types of academic dishonesty please refer to the Academic Integrity Policy, located at www.mcmaster.ca/academicintegrity

The following illustrates only three forms of academic dishonesty:

1. Plagiarism, e.g. the submission of work that is not one's own or for which other credit has been obtained.
2. Improper collaboration in group work.
3. Copying or using unauthorized aids in tests and examinations.

Email correspondence policy

It is the policy of the Faculty of Humanities that all email communication sent from students to instructors (including TAs), and from students to staff, must originate from each student's own McMaster University email account. This policy protects confidentiality and confirms the identity of the student. Instructors will delete emails that do not originate from a McMaster email account.

Modification of course outlines

McMaster University reserves the right to change or revise information contained in course outlines in extreme circumstances. If a modification becomes necessary, reasonable notice and communication with the students will be given with an explanation and the opportunity to comment on changes. It is the responsibility of students to check regularly their primary email account via their @mcmaster.ca alias and course websites.

Topics and Readings:

- Overview of the profession of Music Therapy.
- Theoretical Foundations of Music Therapy
- Music Therapy Models, Assessments and Evaluations
- Music Therapy Interventions; Song writing, Pre-composed Music and Improvising
- Music Therapy with specific populations such as; Mental Health, Palliative Care, Acquired Brain Injury, Dementia, Autism and Rehabilitation, Parkinson's.

Class 1-	Class 2 –	Class 3 –	Class 4 –
Overview of Music Therapy + WebinarLink Courseware p.167-180	History of Music & Wellness History of Music Therapy Courseware p.1-8 +PowToon Resource	Approaches/ Models Music Therapy Neurologic Music Therapy -Guest Speaker, Annilee Baron) Courseware p.141-156 p.181-195 + WebinarLink	Songwriting as Music Therapy intervention Music Therapy & Acquired Brain Injury Guest Speaker Kristen Anderson Courseware p.25 - 34 + WebinarLink
Class 5- Pre-composed music as a Music Therapy intervention Music Therapy & Dementia Courseware p.35-46	**Class 6-** **MidTerm** Room to be Assigned **7-8pm**	**No Class** Reading Week	**Class 7-** Improvising as a music therapy intervention Music Therapy & Autism Spectrum Disorder Guest Speaker (Annilee Baron) Courseware p.9-24 & p.47-74

Class 8- Music Therapy and Mental Health Guest Speaker Aimee Berends ✹ Courseware p.75- 92 + WebinarLink	Class 9- Music Therapy & Palliative Care ✹ Courseware p.93-110	Class 10- Nov 12&13 Music & Culture ✹ Community Music Therapy ✹ P.111-120	Class 11- Nov 19&20 Music Therapy Research & NICU Guest Speaker – SingIt Girls Courseware p.131-140 +WebinarLink
Class 12 Nov 26&27 Music Therapy & Parkinson's Disease & Pain Perception Courseware p.121-130 & 157-166	Class 13 Dec 3&4 Review for Final Exam – **Classes 1-12**	**Accumulative Final Exam** Organized through the exams office	

Other Course Information:

Class attendance is an important factor in understanding the material. **iClickers** are not mandatory, however opportunities to engage using **iClickers** in answering questions about the material will be provided in class.

Final grades are rounded to closest whole number (76.7 = 77). Final grades will reflect your accomplishments. Grades will not be adjusted/raised because you need a higher grade to apply for graduate school. However, if you have any questions about quizzes, midterm, or final exam material, the Instructor will happily meet with you to discuss any concerns about specific questions.

Music 2MT3

TABLE OF CONTENTS
& ACKNOWLEDGEMENTS

    PAGE

Music Therapy: Historical Perspective   1
   Davis, W. B. and Gfeller, K. E
     An Introduction to Music Therapy: Theory and Practice, Davis, W.B. et al.
     © 2008 American Music Therapy Association
     Reprinted with permission.

Basic Therapeutic Methods and Skills   9
   Wigram, T.
     Improvisation: Methods and Techniques for Music Therapy Clinicians,
     Educators and Students, Wigram, T.
     © 2004 Jessica Kingsley Publishers
     Reprinted with permission.

Songwriting to Explore Identity Change and Sense of Self-concept Following   25
Traumatic Brain Injury
   Baker, F. et al.
     Songwriting: Methods, Techniques and Clinical Applications for Music
     Therapy Clinicians, Educators and Students, Baker, F. & Wigram, T., eds.
     © 2005 Jessica Kingsley Publishers
     Reprinted with permission.

Music Therapy with the Elderly   35
   Aldridge, D.
     Music Therapy Research and Practice in Medicine. From Out of the Silence,
     Aldridge, D.
     © 1996 Jessica Kingsley Publishers
     Reprinted with permission.

Preverbal Communication Through Music to Overcome a Child's Language Disorder   47
   Oldfield, A.
     Case Studies in Music Therapy, Bruscia, K.E. ed.
     © 2006 Barcelona Publishers
     Reprinted with permission.

Individuals with Autism and Autism Spectrum Disorder (ASD)   55
   Adamek M. S. et al.
     An Introduction to Music Therapy: Theory and Practice, Davis, W.B. et al.
     © 2008 American Music Therapy Association
     Reprinted with permission.

Performance in Music Therapy: Experiences in Five Dimensions   75
     Jampel, P. F.
       <u>Voices: A World Forum for Music Therapy</u>, 11.1
       © 2011 VOICES:A World Forum for Music Therapy
       Reprinted with permission.

Music Therapy in Hospice and Palliative Care   93
     Walker, J. and Adamek, M.
       <u>An Introduction to Music Therapy: Theory and Practice</u>, Davis, W.B. et al.
       © 2008 American Music Therapy Association
       Reprinted with permission.

Collaborative Work: Negotiations between Music Therapists and Community Musicians   111
in the Development of a South African Community Music Therapy Project
     Oosthuizen, H. et al.
       <u>Voices: A World Forum for Music Therapy</u>, 7.3
       © 2007 VOICES:A World Forum for Music Therapy
       Reprinted with permission.

Music Therapy in Parkinson's Disease   121
     García-Casares, N.
       <u>Journal of the American Medical Directors Association</u>, 19.12
       © 2018 Elsevier Science
       Reprinted with permission.

Music Therapy Self-Care Group for Parents of Preterm Infants in the Neonatal   131
Intensive Care Unit: A Clinical Pilot Intervention
     Roa, E.
       <u>Medicines</u>, 5.134
       © 2018 Multidisciplinary Digital Publishing Institute (MDPI)
       Reprinted with permission.

Excerpts from A History of the Music Therapy Profession   141
     Hyrniw Byers, K.
       <u>A History of the Music Therapy Profession: Diverse Concept and Practices</u>,
       Hyrniw Byers, K.
       © 2016 Barcelona Publishers
       Reprinted with permission.

Excerpts from Biomedical Foundations of Music as Therapy   157
     Taylor, D.
       <u>Biomedical Foundations of Music as Therapy</u>, Taylor, D.
       © 2010 Barton Publications
       Reprinted with permission.

Excerpts from Music Therapy Treatment Process
Davis, W. B. and Gfeller, K. E
<u>An Introduction to Music Therapy: Theory and Practice</u>, Davis, W.B. et al.
© 2008 American Music Therapy Association
Reprinted with permission.

CHAPTER

MUSIC THERAPY: HISTORICAL PERSPECTIVE

William B. Davis
Kate E. Gfeller

CHAPTER OUTLINE
  MUSIC THERAPY IN PRELITERATE CULTURES
  MUSIC AND HEALING IN EARLY CIVILIZATIONS
  USES OF MUSIC IN ANTIQUITY: HEALING RITUALS
  MUSIC AND HEALING IN THE MIDDLE AGES AND RENAISSANCE
  MUSIC THERAPY IN THE UNITED STATES
    18th-Century Writings on Music Therapy
    Literature from the 19th Century
    Music Therapy in 19th-Century Educational Institutions
    Early 20th-Century Music Therapy
  THE DEVELOPMENT OF THE MUSIC THERAPY PROFESSION

Scholars from diverse disciplines, including anthropology, psychology, musicology, and physiology, have long questioned why music has been in our behavioral repertoire for thousands of years (Hodges, 1996; Winner, 1982). Music has no apparent survival value, yet it has been an important part of all cultures, past and present. Music has been called "the universal language" and "the greatest good that mortals know." Throughout recorded time, it has been credited with the power to "solace the sick and weary" and to express unspoken emotions (Stevenson, 1967). It is remarkable that music has claimed such a valued role throughout history. This chapter will discuss the role of music in preliterate cultures, the relationship between music and healing during the advent of civilization, the early practice of music therapy in the United States, and the development of the music therapy profession.

MUSIC THERAPY IN PRELITERATE CULTURES

Preliterate societies are those which possess no system of written communication. Early nomadic people banded together in small groups for survival and eked out a living as hunters and food gatherers. They had no agriculture, political structure, or permanent housing. These small groups developed distinct customs and rituals that set them apart from other similar groups. We can only speculate about the musical component of prehistoric life, but we can gain some clues by studying how music is used in preliterate cultures that exist today. This knowledge helps us to understand human response to music and provides some background about the close relationship between music and healing (Nettl, 1956).

Members of preliterate cultures generally believe they are controlled by magical forces and surrounded by an evil, unpredictable environment. To remain healthy, they feel compelled to obey a complex set of regulations that protect them from the hostile forces of nature and their fellow human beings. They perceive magic as an integral part of a healthy and peaceful life (Sigerist, 1970).

Members of preliterate cultures believe in the power of music to affect mental and physical well-being. Music is often connected with supernatural forces. For example, among certain preliterate societies, the songs used in important rituals are thought to have come from superhuman or unearthly sources (Merriam, 1964; Sachs, 1965). These songs, with their unexplainable powers, are used for entreating the gods and in all activities requiring extraordinary assistance, such as in religious or healing rites.

In some preliterate societies, an ill person is viewed as a victim of an enemy's spell. He or she is blameless and thus enjoys special treatment from the group. In other societies, however, it is believed that a person suffers illness to atone for sins committed against a tribal god. As long as the afflicted member continues to contribute to the well-being of the family and community, status does not change. If the person becomes too ill to uphold social responsibilities, he or she is considered an outcast and ostracized. In these cultures, the cause and treatment of disease is primarily determined by the "medicine man," who often applies elements of magic and religion in order to exorcise the malevolent spirit or demon from the patient's body. The type of music used is determined by the nature of the spirit invading the body.

Because of slightly different concepts of disease among preliterate societies, the role of the musician/healer and style of music vary. In most instances, the tribal musician/healer holds a place of importance within society. It is this person's duty not only to determine the cause of the disease, but also to apply the appropriate treatment to drive the spirit or demon from the patient's body. Sometimes, music functions as a prelude to the actual healing ceremony. Drums, rattles, chants, and songs may be used during the preliminary ritual and also throughout the actual ceremony (Sigerist, 1970). It is important to note that the musician/healer usually does not act alone. Preliterate societies recognize the power of the group and include family and society members in the ritual. Healing séances or choruses provide spiritual and emotional support in order to facilitate a quick recovery (Boxberger, 1962). As noted earlier, we must speculate about the customs of preliterate societies from ancient times. If, as many scholars believe, that current practices among contemporary preliterate societies offer a "window" into the past, then is likely that music was an important part of healing ceremonies very early in human history.

MUSIC AND HEALING IN EARLY CIVILIZATIONS

The hunters and food collectors of preliterate cultures predominated for about 500,000 years. The advent of agriculture 8,000–10,000 years ago led to a more stable existence, the growth of larger populations, and the rise of civilization. Civilization is characterized by the evolution of written communication, the growth of cities, and technological achievement in areas that include science and medicine. It is a way of life for a large group of people living in a more or less permanent alliance with a particular set of customs and view of nature. The first civilizations appeared between 5000 and 6000 B.C. in an area that is now Iraq and became firmly established by 3500 B.C. Music played an important part in "rational medicine" during this time as well as in magical and religious healing ceremonies.

USES OF MUSIC IN ANTIQUITY: HEALING RITUALS

With the advent of civilization, the magical, religious, and rational components of medicine began to develop along separate lines. In ancient Egypt (c. 5000 B.C.), these elements existed side by side, but healers generally based a treatment philosophy on only one. Egyptian music healers enjoyed a privileged existence, due to their close relationship with priests and other important government leaders. Egyptian priest-physicians referred to music as medicine for the soul and often included chant therapies as part of medical practice (Feder & Feder, 1981).

During the height of the Babylonian culture (c. 1850 B.C.), disease was viewed within a religious framework. The sick person suffered as penance for sins committed against a god and was viewed by society as an outcast. Treatment, if offered, consisted of religious ceremonies to placate the offended deity (Sigerist, 1970). Healing rites often included music.

Music was regarded as a special force over thought, emotion, and physical health in ancient Greece. In 600 B.C., Thales was credited with curing a plague in Sparta through musical powers (Merriam, 1964). Healing shrines and temples included hymn specialists, and music was prescribed for emotionally disturbed individuals (Feder & Feder, 1981). The use of music for curing mental disorders reflected the belief that it could directly influence emotion and develop character. Among the notables of Greece who subscribed to the power of music were Aristotle, who valued it as an emotional catharsis; Plato, who described music as the medicine of the soul; and Caelius Aurelianus, who warned against indiscriminate use of music against madness (Feder & Feder, 1981).

By the 6th century B.C., rational medicine had almost completely replaced magical and religious rites in Greece. Although a minority still attributed illness to supernatural powers, the majority supported rational investigation into the causes of disease. For the first time in history, the study of health and disease was based on empirical evidence (Sigerist, 1970).

The predominant explanation of health and disease became the theory of the four cardinal humors. This theory was described by Polybus, son-in-law of Hippocrates, in his treatise, "On the Nature of Man," circa 380 B.C. The four humors were blood, phlegm, yellow bile, and black bile, and each element contained a unique quality. Good health was the result of maintaining a balance among the four humors, whereas an imbalance of two or more elements led to illness. Sick individuals were considered to be inferior. With only slight modification, this theory influenced medicine for the next 2,000 years, becoming most important during the Middle Ages.

MUSIC AND HEALING IN THE MIDDLE AGES AND RENAISSANCE

Although much of the splendor of classical Greece was lost during the Middle Ages, this time period (c. 476–1450 A.D.) represents an important connection between antiquity and the present. After the fall of the Roman Empire, Christianity became a major force in Western civilization. The influence of Christianity prompted a change in attitudes toward disease. Contrary to earlier thinking, a sick person was neither inferior nor being punished by gods. As Christianity spread throughout Europe, societies began to care for and treat their sick members. Hospitals were established to provide humanitarian care to people with physical ailments. Sufferers of mental illness, however, were not as fortunate. Mentally ill people were believed to be possessed by demons and were often incarcerated and abused (Boxberger, 1962).

Although Christian beliefs heavily influenced attitudes toward disease during the Middle Ages, the practice of medicine was still based on the theory of the four humors developed during Greek civilization. This framework also provided the basis for the role of music in treating illness. Numerous statesmen and philosophers believed in the curative powers of music, including Boethius, who claimed that music either improved or degraded human morals. Cassiodorus, like Aristotle, viewed music as a potent type of catharsis, whereas St. Basil advocated it as a positive vehicle for sacred emotion. Many believed hymns to be effective against certain unspecified respiratory diseases (Strunk, 1965).

During the Renaissance, advances in anatomy, physiology, and clinical medicine marked the beginning of the scientific approach to medicine. Despite developments in the laboratory, however, treatment of disease was still based on the teachings of Hippocrates and Galen and a sophisticated interpretation of the four humors. During this period, there was some integration of music, medicine, and art. For example, it was not unusual to find writings, such as those of Zarlino (a musician) and Vesalius (a physician), that touched on the relationship between music and medicine (Boxberger, 1962).

Music during the Renaissance was not only used as a remedy for melancholy, despair, and madness, but also prescribed by physicians as preventive medicine. Properly dispensed music was recognized then, as it is today, as a powerful tool to enhance emotional health. For those who could afford the luxury of attending live performances, music helped to maintain a positive outlook on life. Optimism was particularly important during this time, because Europe was being ravaged by epidemics that sometimes decimated entire villages (Boxberger, 1962).

During the Baroque period (1580–1750), music continued to be linked with the medical practice of the day, based as before on the theory of the four humors. In addition, the theory of temperaments and affections by Kircher (1602–1680) provided a fresh viewpoint on the use of music in the treatment of disease. Kircher believed that personality characteristics were coupled with a certain style of music. For example, depressed individuals responded to melancholy music. Cheerful people were most affected by dance music, because it stimulated the blood (Carapetyan, 1948). Thus, it became necessary for the healer to choose the correct style of music for treatment. Supporting the use of music to treat depression, Burton, in his *Anatomy of Melancholy*, stated that "besides that excellent power it hath to expel many other diseases, it is a sovereign remedy against Despair and Melancholy, and will drive away the Devil himself" (Burton, 1651). Other writers, such as Shakespeare and Armstrong, also included numerous examples of music as therapy in their plays and poems (Davis, 1985).

By the late 18th century, music was still advocated by European physicians in the treatment of disease, but a definite change in philosophy was underway. With increased emphasis on scientific medicine, physicians and scientists began to investigate scientifically supported explanations for illness, rather than religious or superstitious explanations. Consequently, the use of music to "soothe" the gods would no longer be consistent with contemporary views on illness and healing. While many aspects of medicine from that time period would be viewed through contemporary eyes as naive or simply wrong, there was important progress regarding scientifically based medical treatment. During this time period, music was relegated to special cases and applied by only a few physicians who viewed treatment from a holistic (multitherapeutic) framework. The belief that music influenced mood was one way in which music was considered relevant to medical practice at this time. This shift in medical practice and the role of music within healing practices were evident during the growth and development of music therapy in the United States.

MUSIC THERAPY IN THE UNITED STATES

The practice of music therapy in the United States has a long, storied history. Although music therapy as a profession became organized only in the 20th century, music has been used in this country to treat physical and mental ailments since the late 18th century.

18th-Century Writings on Music Therapy

The earliest known reference to music therapy in the United States was an unsigned article in *Columbian Magazine* in 1789. The article, entitled "Music Physically Considered," presented basic principles of music therapy that are still in use today and provided evidence of music therapy practice in Europe. Mainly using the ideas of Descartes (a French philosopher), the anonymous author developed a case for using music to influence and regulate emotional conditions. An interesting conclusion drawn by the author was that a person's mental state may affect physical health. The author also asserted that music, because of its effect on emotions, was a proven therapeutic agent. One other important point in this article was the author's advice that the skilled use of music in the treatment of disease required a properly trained practitioner. This advice is as pertinent now as it was in 1789 (Heller, 1987).

Another article published during this period was entitled "Remarkable Cure of a Fever by Music: An Attested Fact." This article was published in 1796 in the *New York Weekly Magazine*. The anonymous author described the case of an unnamed French music teacher who suffered from a severe fever. After nearly two weeks of constant distress, a concert was performed at the patient's request. His symptoms reportedly disappeared during the performance but returned upon its conclusion. The music was repeated throughout the man's waking hours, resulting in the suspension of his illness. In two weeks' time, the music teacher recovered completely.

Both authors based their conclusions of the music's effectiveness on anecdotal rather than scientific evidence. Such claims lack credibility by today's standards, but these articles suggest that some practitioners during the 18th century were interested in using music in medical treatment. At that time, medical care was crude and often dangerous, so a gentle treatment like music therapy was likely welcomed by the public, who often suffered at the hands of the unregulated medical profession (Heller, 1987).

CHAPTER 4

Basic Therapeutic Methods and Skills

There are many different therapeutic methods that are applied in music therapy when using improvisation. Bruscia (1987, p.533) began with a description of 64 'clinical techniques' and with the increasing volume of published literature on music therapy over the last 12 years, further techniques and methods used in therapy have been reported (Codding 2000, 2002; Pedersen 2002; Staum 2000; Wigram and Bonde 2002; Wigram and De Backer 1999a, 1999b; Wigram, Pedersen and Bonde 2002).

Therapy methods can either be used intentionally (or intuitively) in therapy work with clients or they can be the objects of analysis when reflecting on a period of free-flowing improvisation to explore what was actually happening. It is not usual for music therapists to pre-plan exactly the method they might use, unless they are working in an activity-based model, or with a structured assessment procedure. In improvisational music therapy, particularly, the model requires an adaptive and flexible response to the way the client begins to make music. There can be a certain degree of planning based on the assessment that has taken place and an estimation of the client's needs and the objectives of therapy that will promote certain techniques above others. However, it is more typical that improvisational music making occurs, and within that music making intuitive judgements about therapeutic method are made based on the 'here and now' experience. Music therapists don't remain exclusively attached to one musical technique or therapeutic method for a set period of time, and might fluctuate between a number of different methods (as well as musical techniques) over the course of a single improvisation.

This chapter presents, discusses and exemplifies certain specific methods that are commonly used in music therapy, in order to provide methods within which the musical techniques that have been described in the previous chapter can be applied.

It is very useful to practise these techniques together with another person, first of all playing the experience and subsequently responding to the musical production of another. Each technique will include a musical illustration, complemented by an example on the CD.

4.1 Mirroring, imitating and copying

Mirroring and *imitating* are frequently used as empathic techniques where the music therapist intends to give a message to the client that they are meeting them exactly at their level and attempting to achieve synchronicity with the client. Bruscia has described the technique of mirroring as 'synchronising' – doing what the client is doing at the same time'. I define mirroring in a similar way but with a slightly broader explanation, in order to suggest to clinical practice that mirroring involves more than just musical behaviour:

> *Mirroring: Doing exactly what the client is doing musically, expressively and through body language at the same time as the client is doing it. The client will then see his or her own behaviour in the therapist's behaviour.*

This can only be achieved musically, where the client's music is both simple enough and predictable enough for the therapist to anticipate how to mirror exactly what the client is doing. This also applies to the physical behaviour of the client. In order for the mirror to be exact, the therapist may also need to pay attention to using a very similar instrument as the client in order to achieve a mirrored response. However, it is possible to accomplish mirroring by using a different instrument. Example 17 on the CD gives an illustration where the therapist can use the piano almost as a drum while the client plays on a drum.

CD17: Mirroring – client on drum + therapist on piano

'Close enough' mirroring is a technique where the therapist is doing almost exactly the same as the client but due to technical reasons cannot copy exactly. For example, this would work very well where the client is randomly playing notes on a metallophone and the therapist mirrors that by playing as near an imitation as possible at the same time, achieving the direction of the melody and the general contour of the melody without necessarily matching exact notes.

Conceptually, we can see the identities of the participants in mirroring (client and therapist) in a very symbiotic relationship, where they become fused and undivided. Figure 4.1 illustrates the place of the therapist and client inside two circles where the integration of one circle into another represents the closeness of the material.

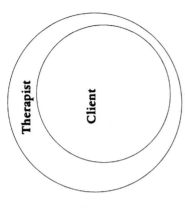

Figure 4.1: Musical closeness in mirroring

Imitating or copying are also empathic methods of improvisation and imitating has been defined by Bruscia as 'echoing or reproducing a client's response after the response has been completed'. This relies on the client leaving spaces in the music for the therapist to imitate what he or she is doing. It should be used quite specifically, and caution needs to be exercised as imitating or copying a client's production might appear as though you were either teasing or patronizing the client. While mirroring and copying are relatively simple methods, they can also be quite confronting to a client, and can be risks, for example, with clients with paranoia or thought disorder for whom this method may excite irrational fears. This approach needs to be used sensitively and appropriately. Nevertheless, it is a therapeutic strategy to help a client to be aware that musically you are echoing and confirming what they have done.

4.2 Matching

I regard *matching* is one of the most valuable of all the improvisational methods that can be applied in therapy. It is, in my approach, a typical starting point to work together with the client musically, from which a number of other therapeutic strategies or methods emerge. It is also an empathic method, as the music produced by the therapist in response to the client confirms and validates their playing and their emotional expression.

I have defined the term to be quite inclusive:

IMPROVISATION

Matching: Improvising music that is compatible, matches or fits in with the client's style of playing while maintaining the same tempo, dynamic, texture, quality and complexity of other musical elements (Wigram 1999a).

To achieve a 'match' in musical terms means that the therapist's music is not identical to the client's, but is the same in style and quality. Therefore the client experiences that the therapist's music 'fits together and matches' his or her own production.

Conceptually, we can begin to see the two separate identities of the participants (client and therapist) in their musical relationship, where they are together, congruent and matched musically, but with some individual differences that show emerging separateness. Figure 4.2 shows two circles separating, representing the matched material but separating identities of the therapist and client.

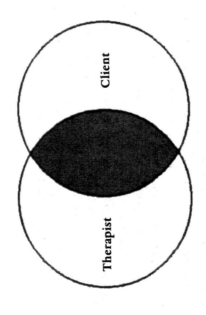

Figure 4.2: Musical connections in matching

Bruscia does not include matching as a term, but incorporates the idea into a definition of reflecting. Pavlicevic (1997) has referred to it in her book *Music Therapy in Context* giving a different conceptual understanding. She thinks of matching as 'partial mirroring where, for example, the client plays a definite and predictable musical pattern, and the therapist mirrors some, but not all, of the rhythmic components' (p.126).

My experience and use of matching in therapy is more as an equal, complementary style of playing together, as illustrated in Figures 4.3, 4.4 and 4.5, and demonstrated in CD18, CD19 and CD20. The CD examples start with the 'client' playing, and show how the therapist joins in, matching the music of the client. In the first examples (Figure 4.3 and CD18) the rhythmic style of the client is revealed as short, quite stable rhythmic patterns in a regular pulse. As the improvisation develops, the

BASIC THERAPEUTIC METHODS AND SKILLS

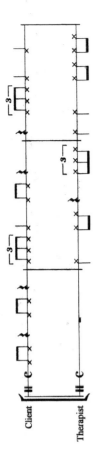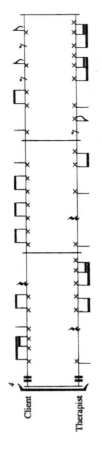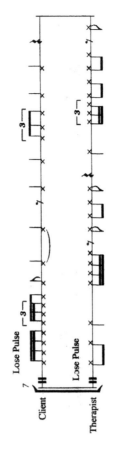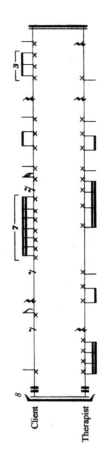

Figure 4.3: Matching: client on bongos, therapist on conga

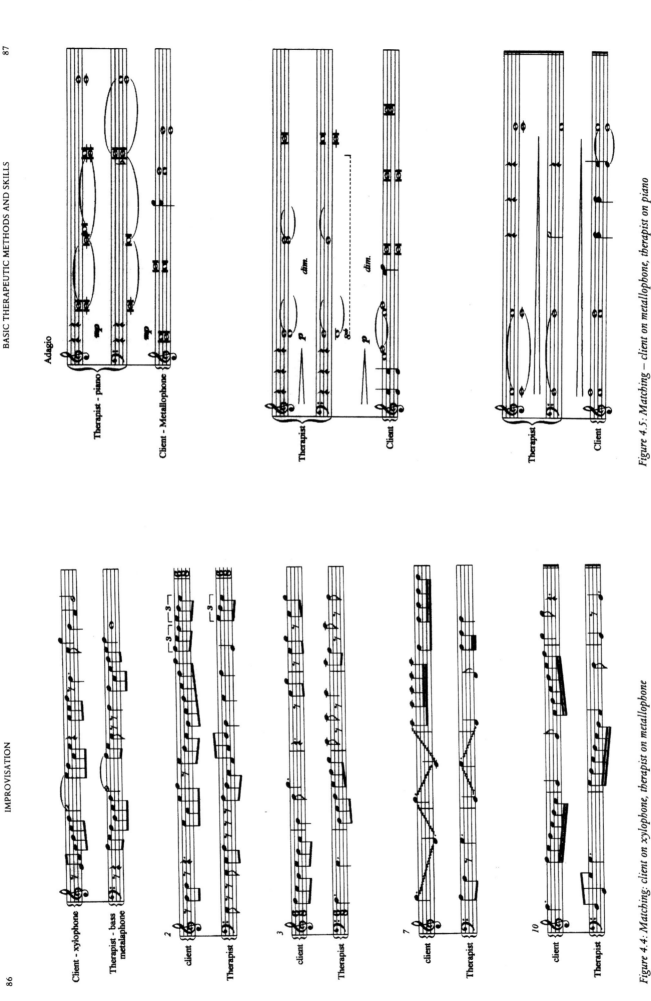

Figure 4.4: Matching: client on xylophone, therapist on metallophone

Figure 4.5: Matching – client on metallophone, therapist on piano

style changes with a loss of any sense of pulse in the client's playing, and the therapist can be heard to adapt and sustain matching.

CD Example 18: Matching – client on bongos, therapist on djembe

In the next examples (Figure 4.4 and CD19) melodic matching is illustrated. Here the emphasis is on style of the melody, in particular phrase lengths, step-wise or large interval movement and tonality. The client's material changes as the example goes on, and the therapist can also be heard to adapt to this change.

CD Example 19: Matching – client and therapist on melodic instruments

Finally, Figure 4.5, CD 20 gives an example where the therapist (piano) uses chords to match with a client (metallophone) who is playing sustained, two-tone sounds, without any sense of rhythmic or harmonic direction. In the therapeutic process of matching it is very important to stay true to the client's music, and not attempt to modify, change or manipulate. At this stage of therapeutic intervention, using the matching method, therapeutic directions or 'solutions' are not the primary objective, and may emerge later. The engagement, close to the tradition and goal of client centred therapy, is to offer 'unconditional positive regard' in the form of acceptance and matching.

CD Example 20: Client on xylophone, therapist on piano

Matching exercises

The CD has two examples of a person playing that provide an opportunity to practise the therapeutic method of matching. The first part of the process in matching is to listen to and analyse the musical components of a client's production, also taking into account their level of expression in their body and their face. However, as these examples are presented on CD, the latter information is not available and one needs solely to consider the musical elements.

Table 4.1 identifies the musical elements for these two examples in order to clarify the type of music the therapist should produce to match and empathize with the client's material.

Table 4.1 Structured matching exercises

Example	Style	Rhythm	Dynamic	Tonality
1 (CD21)	Folk	4/4 regular	Soft and slow	Pentatonic
2 (CD22)	Jazzy	Irregular	Wide range	Atonal

4.3 Empathic improvisation and reflecting

Mirroring, *copying* and *matching* involve a more technical exercise of creating a musically congruent response to the client, attending primarily to the balance and salience of musical elements, as well as body language and expression. *Empathic improvisation* and *reflecting* require a response that is more specifically connected to the emotional state of the client.

Empathic improvisation

This is difficult to illustrate in a book or on a CD. It involves a therapeutic method that was first applied by Juliette Alvin where, typically at the beginning of a session, she would play (on her cello) an improvisation that empathically complemented the client's 'way of being'. In practice this means taking into account the client's body posture, facial expression, attitude on this particular day and previous knowledge of their personality and characteristics, and playing something to them that reflects a musical interpretation of their own way of being at that moment. It was intended by Alvin as a very empathic technique, not attempting in any way to change the client's feelings or behaviour, but simply to play them to the client without any hidden manipulation of their feelings. If a client comes into the therapy room agitated and upset, this mood can easily be incorporated into an empathic improvisation; the therapist is not trying to ameliorate or reduce the degree of distress which the client is currently experiencing but merely to play it back to them as a supportive and empathic confirmation.

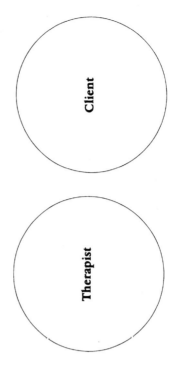

Figure 4.6 Two separate circles, representing separate musical identities, but with emotional empathy

Reflecting

This technique is well documented in Bruscia's 64 techniques and he defines it as 'Matching the moods, attitudes, or feelings exhibited by the client' (Bruscia 1987, p.540)

In reflecting, unlike mirroring, copying or matching, the therapist's music might be quite different from the client's as the purpose of this therapeutic technique is to understand and reflect back the client's mood at that moment, rather than be a more technical reflection of their music. However, there needs to be congruence in mood or emotional expression between the therapist's music and the client's music otherwise the method would cease to have any empathic effect.

Conceptually, we can see two separate identities of the participants in reflecting (client and therapist), in a relationship where they are separated musically, yet still congruent emotionally. Figure 4.6 illustrates the separation of the therapist and client circles.

CD23 demonstrates a client playing in a random, rather directionless rhythm on percussion instruments (drum and cymbal). Note that the therapist allows a short time to pass before beginning to reflect musically and empathically. This is an important part of the process:

Listen to the client's music before giving a response.

I frequently find myself reminding students in training and therapists under supervision that reflecting on your experience of the client's music is essential to be sensitive in response. There are sometimes patterns or characteristics that can help both in deciding the therapeutic method of response and the musical 'style'. The response the therapist gives in CD23 reflects the aimless and random style of the client's playing, using melody and harmony.

CD Example 23: Reflecting example 1 – therapist on piano, client on drums and cymbal

In the next example, the client presents a very different picture while playing the piano. Feelings of anger and frustration are present in the sharp, bunched chords the client is playing. There is an underlying sense of pulse, with accents and sudden changes in dynamics to reinforce the apparent irritation of the client. The therapist reflects these feelings with a melodic line on the xylophone.

CD Example 24: Reflecting example 2 – therapist on xylophone, client on piano

Two exercises are now presented on the CD, with the client playing piano in the first and temple blocks in the second. While these examples do not allow the reader to understand the actual emotional state or feelings exhibited by the client, they can be used by imagining what they could be, based on the music that is presented and trying to find a way to frame a response that is an empathic reflection of the music.

Exercise: Using CD25 and CD26, listen to each example for a few seconds, establishing in your mind the possible emotional state or mood of the music ('client'), and then allow your own emotional state to be affected by the music you are listening to. When you have become sensitive to the mood or emotion present in the music you are listening to, and your own emotional reaction to it, begin to play that emotional reaction on another instrument, reflecting the feelings that are present in the music, and present in yourself.

CD Example 25: Reflecting exercise 1 – client on piano
CD Example 26: Reflecting exercise 2 – client on temple blocks

4.4 Grounding, holding and containing

Grounding, holding and containing are all therapeutic methods that are extremely useful when applied with clients who have a very random or floating way of playing, and way of being. It is helpful where the client appears or sounds unconnected to their music, or the music lacks any stability, direction or intentionality. I have defined the process of grounding as:

Grounding: Creating a stable, containing music that can act as an 'anchor' to the client's music.

Examples of specific musical techniques that can be used in grounding include:

- strong octaves or fifths in the bass of the piano;
- steady pulsed beats on a bass drum;
- strong chords of a stable tonal nature using typically dominant and tonic chords;
- a simple ostinato.

Rhythmic grounding

Rhythmic grounding is a very useful way of providing a foundation to something the client is doing. Bruscia defines it as 'Keeping a basic beat or providing a rhythmic foundation for the client's own improvising' (Bruscia 1987).

An important aspect of rhythmic grounding is that it is not necessary to impose a meter on the client's rhythmic musical production. In fact, it can be quite constraining and directive to take the client's musical production and establish a specific meter such as 4/4 or 3/4 for what they are doing. Music can be pulsed but meterless, and quite often becomes more dynamic by the variable use of accentuation within a stable pulse. Another important aspect is to intervene with a stable and secure melodic or rhythmic pattern, quite often limiting your playing where a client's playing is rather full and complex. The process of limiting in the therapist's music is to provide a stable and understandable ground, and avoid adding to the potentially chaotic complexity of the client's improvisation (Figure 4.7).

CD27 is an example of a client playing randomly on the xylophone, where the therapist then joins in on a drum and establishes a rhythmic ground to the client's music. You will hear the client begin to 'entrain' to the therapist's rhythmic ground and stabilize his or her own music accordingly.

CD Example 27: Example of rhythmic grounding – client on xylophone, therapist on a drum

Exercise: The next example on the CD (CD28) is a person playing a xylophone. Try to listen for any rhythmic patterns in the person's music, and then introduce a rhythmic ground. Remember, the faster or more complex the client's music, the more stable and limited must be the musical ground of the therapist. As this is an exercise requiring you to play with a CD example, potential for the person playing on the CD to 'adapt' to the therapist's grounding is clearly not expected. However it is a good exercise to practise finding ways of developing *matching into grounding.*

CD Example 28: Rhythmic grounding exercise client on xylophone

Tonal grounding

Tonal grounding is a process where one establishes a tonal bass which acts as a foundation or 'anchor' to the client's music if it is predominantly melodic or harmonic and is wandering around. I define this as:

Tonal grounding: Providing an octave, fifth or harmonic chord in the bass that is congruent with, and tonally grounding for, the client's music.

Bruscia defines this as tonal centring – 'providing a tonal centre, scale, or harmonic ground' (Bruscia 1987, p.535).

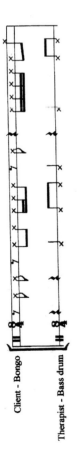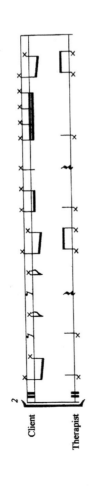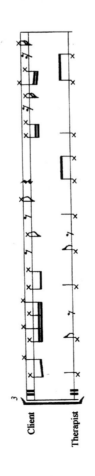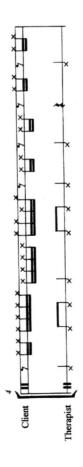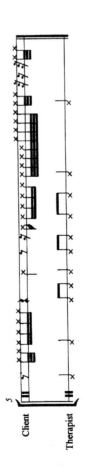

Fig 4.7: Rhythmic grounding – client and therapist on bongos and bass drum

The musical example (Figure 4.8) illustrates this; a client plays a rather random, directionless melody on a metallophone which develops into repetitive patterns of falling thirds. The therapist intervenes with a tonal ground in the piano.

CD Example 29: Example of tonal grounding – client on glockenspiel, therapist on piano

Exercise: CD30 provides an exercise where a person plays music on a piano and as a duet partner you can work in the bass to provide some tonal centre for this. The technique involves analysing the type of music the person is playing and seeing if it falls within a key, or if a ground tone could be used as a tonal centre. For example, if the client is playing mainly the white notes of the piano, A minor, D minor and C major could be used as keys to provide a tonal centre. If the client is playing on the black notes, E flat minor and F sharp major can be used as the keys to provide the tonal centre (pentatonic).

CD Example 30: Tonal grounding – moving from diatonic to pentatonic

Harmonic grounding

Tonal grounding can be extended to *harmonic grounding*. This tends to involve either tonal harmonies (as in the two-chord improvisation) or pentatonic harmonies. As an extension to the use of fifths and octaves for tonal grounding, try using the CD30 exercise to engage with harmonic grounding.

Combined tonal and rhythmic grounding

Rhythmic grounding and *tonal grounding* can be combined to establish an even more secure musical foundation for a client. A good example of this would be to use a drone bass accompaniment figure to provide such a combined grounding foundation (Figure 4.9). The style could be given a 6/8 Celtic flavour by some suggestions from the therapist in the accompaniment, and then the harmonic ground can be enhanced with chordal structures (CD31).

CD 31 shows how the therapist maintains stability in the piano.

CD Example 31: Combined rhythmic and tonal grounding – client on piano, therapist also on piano

Holding and containing

Holding and containing are quite similar therapeutic methods. Basically, I employ holding as a therapeutic method and process where one provides a musical anchor to

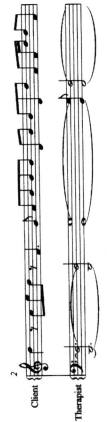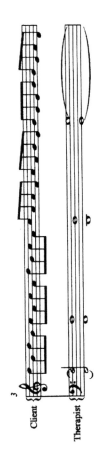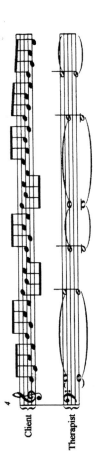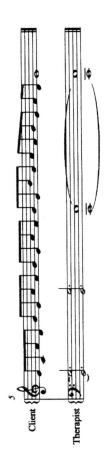

Figure 4.8: Example of tonal grounding – client on metallophone and therapist on piano

a client who is ungrounded in his or her playing and whose music is random and without direction. Consequently techniques such as tonal grounding/tonal centring are going to be helpful in order to provide that anchor. It works well to use simple harmonic accompaniments as a holding 'tool' where the use of sustained sounds without attempts at interactive or dynamic music making provides the containing frame. The therapist's music would typically be slow, sustained and very stable. However, at the same time it doesn't have to force a pulse or a meter on the client for it to be good enough music for holding. Therefore I define holding as:

Holding: Providing a musical 'anchor' and container for the client's music making, using rhythmic or tonal grounding techniques.

Bruscia offers a different definition of holding, one that is more expanded to include the wider concept of the 'musical background', and also includes the concept that the technique contains the feelings of the client: 'as the client improvises, providing a musical background that resonates the client's feelings while containing them' (Bruscia 1987, p.536)

Containing implies a different process where the client's music is quite chaotic and may also be quite loud. Therapeutically, the client needs to be allowed to be chaotic, noisy, exaggerated (a good example would be an out-of-control child having a 'musical/emotional' tantrum). The therapist provides a musical container for the client's music, playing strongly and confidently enough to be heard by the client. One musical idea that can work well in therapy is to play at opposite ends of the piano with strong, stable octaves (CD32). Many other types of music could act as a container for the client's music, but it needs to be structured music that provides a pattern.

CD Example 32: Containing: Chaotic music contained by the therapist – client on cymbals, drums and xylophone, therapist on piano

4.5 Dialoguing

Music is a marvellous medium for engaging in different types of conversation or dialogue between two or more people. It is even possible, of course, to have a dialogue with oneself musically! I have not found a definition for *Dialoguing* in its application in music therapy as either a musical technique or a therapeutic method, although there are terms that describe some of the processes involved in making or developing a dialogue. I define dialoguing in the following way:

Dialoguing: A process where therapist and client/clients communicate through their musical play.

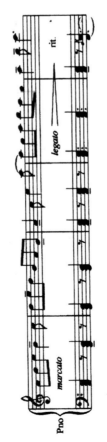

Figure 4.9: Combined rhythmic and tonal grounding – client on piano and therapist on piano ground, even when there are mismatches in the harmony between the client's 'jumping around' melody and the drone ground

There are two main forms of dialogue, which I define as follows:

Turn-taking dialogues: Making music together where the therapist or client(s) in a variety of ways, musical or gestural, can cue each other to take turns. This 'turn-taking' style of dialogue requires one or other to pause in their playing and give space to each other.

Continuous 'free-floating' dialogues: Making music in a continuous musical dialoguic exchange – a free-floating dialogue. Here participants (therapist(s) and client(s)) play more or less continuously and simultaneously. In their playing musical ideas and dynamics are heard and responded to, but without pause in the musical process.

To liken a dialogue to a conversation is probably the nearest and most understandable way of describing this process. Consequently, one can imagine that just as in a conversation, there are a number of ways in which the dialogue can progress:

1. Therapist and client(s) take turns to play, taking over immediately from each other.
2. Therapist and client(s) take turns to play with pauses in between 'statements'.
3. Therapist or client(s) interrupt each other.
4. Therapist and client(s) 'play at the same time' (talk at the same time) as each other.
5. Client(s) make(s) long statements; therapist gives 'grunt' or 'ah-ha' responses of very short phrases.
6. The therapist's musical style in the dialogue is very empathic (similar) to the style of the client(s) (or vice versa).
7. The therapist's playing in the dialogue is very oppositional/confrontational to the client(s) (or vice versa).

Ways to promote dialogue

Musical dialogues don't necessarily occur automatically or naturally in improvisational music making. In fact, some clients find it extremely difficult to engage in dialogues, either because they can't follow or respond to normal turn-taking exchanges (typical in autistic clients), or because they talk so much that they don't stop for long enough to listen to what somebody else has got to say (this can be typical in clients with Asperger's syndrome).

Before explaining more specific techniques for promoting dialogue, there are two clearly defined therapeutic techniques proposed by Bruscia that can be utilized:

Interjecting – waiting for a space in the client's music and filling in the gap.

Making spaces – leaving spaces within one's own improvising for the client to interject his/her own materials (Bruscia 1987, p.535).

Using these two methods naturally leads one into dialoguing and initiates the 'conversation' or 'argument' style of improvisational music making, where the playing together becomes directly communicative. Many clients may not understand or pick up the signals that help nurture dialoguing, and this can be helped through modelling. Modelling is a method that can be applied to many of the previously described musical and therapeutic techniques, and many of those yet to be discussed. Bruscia's definition of modelling is:

Modelling – presenting or demonstrating something for the client to imitate (1987, p.535).

This provides us with a quite specific (and clearly directive) method which is most useful where that type of direction is needed. I would like to suggest an extended and broader definition here in order to explain that something more than purely imitating occurs:

Modelling: Playing and demonstrating something in a way that encourages the client to imitate, match or extend some musical ideas.

In the music making that goes on in music therapy there are subtle or obvious ways of promoting the initiation, development and progression of a dialogue. These involve either musical cues or gestural cues.

Musical cues

- Harmonic cues: indicating that you are coming to the end of some musical 'statement' by playing either a perfect or plagal cadence (or even an interrupted cadence). The harmonic modulation in a musical statement can also sound like a question.
- Rhythmic cues: playing a rhythmic pattern that closes, following which it is obvious that there is a space or playing a rhythmic pattern that is symmetrical and therefore gives a clear indication of closure (also allowing space for a client to play next).
- Melodic cues: playing in ascending phrase, a phrase that indicates the end of a pattern, etc.

- Dynamic and timbre cues: there are many types of dynamic cues that could indicate a space for developing a dialogue. Accents help to establish a punctuation point; making a crescendo on a phrase to a climax indicates a point of stopping; making an accelerando to a point of stopping also indicates a pause which allows a space for somebody to say something; staccato playing following some legato playing may also indicate something coming to a conclusion.

Gestural cues

Given that musical cues can be rather subtle and are not necessarily attended to, especially by clients who enjoy making a lot of noise and playing continuously, it may be necessary to model the dialogue idea through giving a gesture. The idea is to indicate a space where you would like the client to start playing (or continue playing) on their own in order to develop the dialogue. Therefore you can introduce some of the following ideas:

- Show you have stopped playing in some way, by taking your hands from the instrument or 'freezing' at the instrument so that you are not moving at all and looking as if you are waiting for the client to stop before you can play again (very effective with children when they catch on to the idea as it gives them a strong sense of being 'in control'!)
- Turn to look at the client and take your hands off the instrument.
- Use eye referencing to indicate that you are going to play and then eye reference the instrument to encourage the client to play.
- Point and indicate whose turn it is to play.
- Use physical prompts, either to encourage somebody to start playing, or to encourage them to stop playing:

Starting to play:

- nudging behind the elbow;
- supporting under the elbow;
- supporting under the wrist;
- taking a hand and helping a client to play.

(This is a graduated list of responses from a very gentle prompt to a hand-over-hand modelling.)

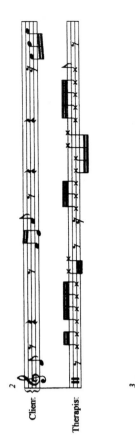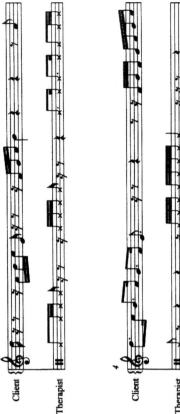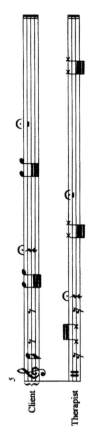

Figure 4.10: Example of Dialoguing – client on xylophone, therapist on congas

Stopping playing:

- putting the hand out in a stop position;
- reaching over and almost touching the hand of the client;
- reaching over and holding the beater or instrument that the client is using to play for a short time;
- reaching over and stopping the client playing physically by holding their hand; taking an instrument away while you interject a short phrase and then handing the instrument back.

(This is a graduated list ranging from gestural cues to physical direction.)

Figure 4.10 illustrates an emerging dialogue beginning with a client playing on a xylophone, without pulse, and shows how the therapist gently interjects, makes spaces for the client, then uses rhythmic patterns to develop the dialogue.

CD Example 33: Dialoguing 1 – client on metallophone, therapist on xylophone

The techniques described above range from subtly to strongly directive. Direction in some form is sometimes necessary in order to build up, through modelling, the process of musical dialoguing or turn-taking. I am often asked how one can develop communicative musical dialogue with clients who have perseverative and repetitive playing, who seem to be unable or unwilling to leave any space in their musical production to allow a dialogue to develop. The ideas described above are typical in the techniques I have found helpful to model, initiate and develop dialogue. However, one also needs to take into consideration the instrument chosen and the physical playing style. Clients who play repetitive pulses on drums may do so because the motor movement (also described as sensory motoric playing) is what they are interested in doing, and there is little or no musical or communicative intentionality. All the above techniques may prove futile in the face of such playing, and changing instruments may be the best way to break down obsessive patterns of playing and introduce dialogue.

Phrasing, interrupting, pausing and talking at the same time

Having begun to develop dialogue, the patterns that emerge can sound more and more like a conversation when attention is paid to phrasing, interrupting, pausing and talking at the same time. Phrase lengths vary – especially where one person is doing most of the talking, and the other is merely acknowledging or confirming with an 'uh-huh' response. So, in musical dialogue, these patterns of conversation can increasingly represent the prosody and phrasing of speech, with accents, inflec-

Figure 4.11: Example of conversational dialogue using variable phrasing, continued on next page

tion, interruptions and sometimes even talking at the same time. In the process of dialoguing – whether through a rhythmic or a melodic exchange – the potentials of varied phrasing will add significantly to the communicative character of the dialogue.

Figure 4.11 illustrates this, and CD Example 34 shows how all the dynamic aspects of interpersonal communication can be present in a musical dialogue. Given that music therapy is a medium through which 'communication' takes place through musical exchange, dialoguing is a very important and valuable technique to support and engage a client.

In the real world, communication and dialogue between people can frequently turn into a heated debate, perhaps even an argument. Polite turn-taking gives way to interrupting, increasing accents, 'rude' sounds, shouting, losing tempers – everything a good healthy argument should have! CD34 illustrates the musical dynamic of dialogue that becomes an argument, and as music therapy allows people to say something in music (in an argument) that would be unacceptable in words, this is a valuable tool in therapy work to draw out emotional attitude and affect.

CD Example 34: Dialoguing 2: Conversations and arguments! Therapist on xylophone, client on African split drum and djembe

Continuous 'free floating' dialogues

When working with clients who play quite continuously, repetitively, perhaps even obsessionally, and have difficulty in stopping to listen, the therapist's option is to try to promote or engage with the second type of dialogue method described above – the continuous 'free-floating' dialogue. Here, the therapist can listen to and echo musical ideas, themes, motifs and dynamic patterns of the client, attempting to build up a dialogue of musical ideas within an ongoing improvisation.

It cannot be compared with a conventional conversation, where turn-taking is a typical element. In the free-floating dialogue, the musical genre of opera is represented, where two (or more) people can be simultaneously contributing to an exchange, sometimes singing about two different things at the same time, yet with a necessary musical connection through melody or harmony. It happens frequently in improvisations, and this kind of instantaneous reciprocity and shared understanding builds up between client(s) and therapist, and acts as a framework for communicative experiences. The subtlety of this type of interaction is such that it is not always possible to be aware of how it is happening while it is going on, and only with later audio or video analysis can one recognize the presence of a subtle and developing dialogue. CD35 gives an example of just such a dialogue, where the therapist uses

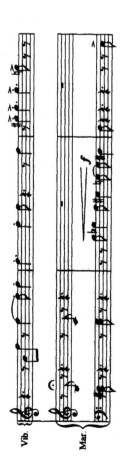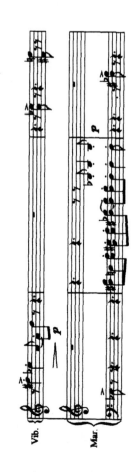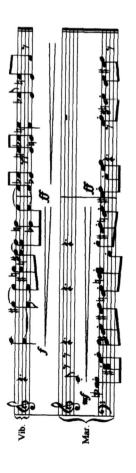

Figure 4.11: Example of conversational dialogue using variable phrasing, continued

the xylophone to match, and then dialogues with a client's continuous playing on a drum.

CD Example 35: Dialoguing 3: continuous 'free-floating' dialogue – therapist on piano, client on xylophone

4.6 Accompanying

Accompanying is one of the most useful and important of the supportive techniques in improvisational music therapy. I often recommend its use when one has established a framework for clients to use or where a client is particularly autonomous and wants to take a soloist's role in the music making.

I define the therapeutic method of accompanying as:

> *Accompanying: Providing a rhythmic, harmonic or melodic accompaniment to the client's music that lies dynamically underneath the client's music, giving them a role as a soloist* (Wigram 2000b).

Accompanying is a frequently used method for joining in with a client's music where the message one is giving is of support and empathy. The definition refers specifically to the idea that the music lies 'dynamically underneath', and this typifies the quality of 'accompanying' and gives it strength as a supportive music. If the client plays *f* then the accompaniment is going to be *mf*. If the client plays above middle C in the tonal range, the accompaniment can be placed lower, although it is possible to work with a bass lead and an accompaniment in the higher register.

Accompaniment style music, certainly on the piano, needs to have certain characteristics:

- to be simple and repetitious;
- to be a short rhythmic or harmonic sequence that is sustained;
- to continue in a stable way despite some changes in the client's music;
- to be sensitive to pauses or small developments in the client's music.

Typically, accompaniments can be (either tonal or atonal) um-cha-cha (3/4 waltz) style or um-cha-um-cha (2/4 and 4/4 common time) style. Figure 4.12 gives us an example of this type of accompaniment, in both a tonal and an atonal frame. The 2-chord improvisation that was exemplified in Chapter 3 is a good sequence to use for an accompanying style, as is the Spanish 2–8-chord sequences that will be explained in Chapter 6 under frameworking techniques.

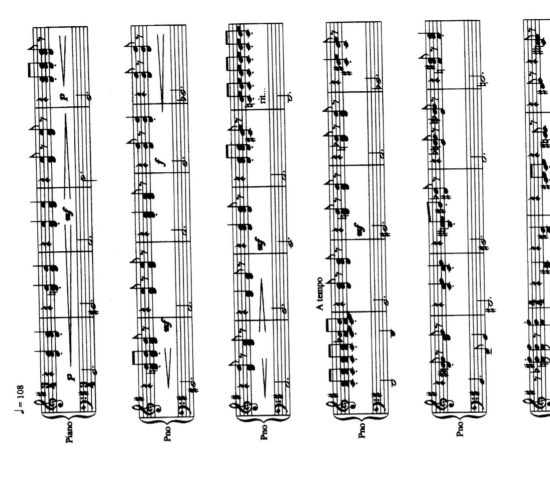

Figure 4.12: Example of 3/4 and 4/4 accompaniment style using tonal and atonal frame, continued on next page

CD36 gives an illustration of a client starting to play randomly on a **xylophone and glockenspiel** while the therapist introduces an accompaniment style using (at first) two chords to support it, then developing some accompaniment effects.

CD Example 36: Accompanying – client on xylophone and glockenspiel, therapist on piano

Most of these accompaniment methods can be equally effective on guitar or other harmonic instruments (harmonica, accordion, autoharp, organ, synthesizer). Purely rhythmic accompaniments can also be generated, and are especially effective in providing a supportive frame. The most important characteristic of this therapeutic method to remember is your supportive role, allowing the client to take the lead, playing more softly, with stability and repetitious motifs of figures, and perhaps with a thinner, sparser texture.

Exercises: Try making different types of accompaniments to the following styles of playing using the examples on the CD with which to work:

CD Example 37: Accompaniment exercise 1 – a wandering treble melody by a client on a piano where they play first of all only on the white keys and secondly only on the black keys

CD Example 38: Accompaniment exercise 2 – a client playing an accented, rhythmic and pulsed melody on xylophone and metallophone, that breaks out of meter halfway through

CD Example 39: Accompaniment exercise 3 – a client playing some rhythmic patterns on a drum

In all three exercises try formulating accompaniments using different instruments such as piano, guitar or drums/percussion.

4.7 Summary and integration

These are some basic therapeutic methods that need to be practised in order to acquire both the technical and therapeutic skills to use them. As can be seen, they start to incorporate the musical techniques that are adapted to fit the intention of the method. The exercises suggested in Chapters 3 and 4 are designed to allow the reader a chance to practise these methods using either piano or other instruments. Many of these musical techniques and therapeutic methods will be revisited in later chapters because improvisation is not undertaken with clients through isolated methods, but through a sequence (sometimes fast-moving) of different methods and musical techniques.

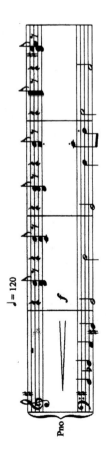
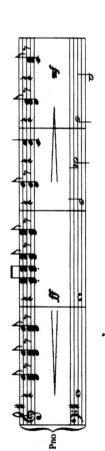
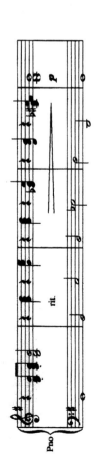
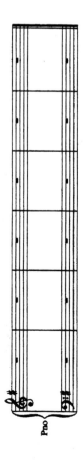

Figure 4.12: Example of 3/4 and 4/4 accompaniment style using tonal and atonal frame, continued

The last part of this chapter is therefore concerned with the integration and sequential process of linking together these methods to illustrate how one can move through a therapeutic sequence of events with a client. As has been stated earlier, *matching* is a logical and empathic place to start with a client. However, in therapy we don't approach our clients with some predetermined plan of intervention, at least not in improvisational music therapy. The spontaneous experience, adapting and responding on a moment-by-moment basis to the interactive process, requires us to maintain a free-flowing flexibility in the application of therapeutic method.

The last example, illustrated only as audio example CD40, shows how one might move through three or more methods in an improvisational interaction with a client.

Matching $\longrightarrow$ Accompanying $\longrightarrow$ Dialoguing $\longrightarrow$ Containing $\longrightarrow$ Matching

The client is playing a xylophone, and begins with rhythmic, melodic fragments. The therapist matches, and the engagement begins. As the client grows more confident, the therapist takes the role of accompanist. A little further on, the therapist takes an initiative by making spaces and interjecting, and introduces the idea of dialoguing. The client works with this, but as the dialogue builds up dynamically to an argument, the therapist adapts to a containing approach. As the client's music loses some of its intensity and energy, the therapist follows and returns to a final empathic section of matching.

CD Example 40: Example of integrating therapeutic method and musical technique

So far, the techniques and methods recommended for both practising and developing within an improvisational model for use in clinical work have concentrated on identifying specific techniques using musical parameters and therapeutic method. Most of the examples and the exercises recommended have involved a form of improvisation where the music is spontaneously created, using some simple play rules.

Frequently, when working with musical material, one wants to develop a style of improvisation that fits something that the client may be doing or to create a particular type of musical frame for some specific purpose. I call this method of work 'frameworking'. In addition, we are constantly faced with the need to find ways of making changes in the music, making a transition from playing in one way to playing in another way. The development of these transitions is a critical part of music therapy skills (and in fact is used very widely by musicians, composers and others to connect together different types of music).

In order to move to the next stage of the process of developing improvisation skills, I will describe and give examples of both frameworking and transitions and then explain a number of exercises that can be used to develop these methods.

6

Songwriting to Explore Identity Change and Sense of Self-concept Following Traumatic Brain Injury

Felicity Baker, Jeanette Kennelly and Jeanette Tamplin

Rehabilitating physical, cognitive and communication functioning following Traumatic Brain Injury (TBI) is an intensive, exhausting and highly emotional task for children, adolescents and adults. Successful rehabilitation relies on clients maintaining high levels of motivation. This is often difficult to achieve, however, when emotional responses to the trauma have an adverse impact on the client's levels of motivation. Over the past 12 years, the authors have successfully employed songwriting interventions with children, adolescents and adult TBI clients to facilitate the adjustment process and to help maintain their motivation for therapy. This chapter will outline the approaches we used in conducting therapeutic songwriting with TBI clients. We first highlight the specific adjustment issues faced by TBI clients to provide a sense of the complexity of dealing with these clients' adjustment processes. Included in this chapter is an explanation of some of the cognitive impairments typically acquired by TBI clients and, more importantly, their impact on the adjustment and songwriting process. Following this, our protocol for writing songs with clients is outlined and this is illustrated through two case examples – one with a late adolescent client and the other with a paediatric client.

Confronting and adjusting to change

Traumatic brain injury is often the outcome of a sudden and unexpected event which results in damage to the brain. Given the unexpected hospitalization and threats to independence, it is not surprising that clients experience emotional crises and often undergo a lengthy adjustment phase. Clients have to adjust and cope with significant life changes that involve accepting many losses: loss of independence and functioning, loss of control, loss of former body, loss of financial status, loss of many roles, loss of future hopes and dreams, and loss of ability to participate in preferred leisure activities.

Several theories have emerged about how and when adjustment occurs and what variables influence the process. Wright (1960) viewed adjustment to disability in terms of it reflecting the interaction between a person's value system, level of emotional maturity and acceptance of self, and mental health status. Olney and Kim (2001) suggest adjustment is a staged process which includes:

- the response to the initial impact
- defence mobilization
- the initial realization
- a period of retaliation
- reintegration and adjustment which is characterized by confidence, contentment and satisfaction.

Adjustment involves the formation of an identity that integrates all aspects of the self, as well as an understanding at multiple levels of the meanings and implications disability has on the person's life. Major themes arising from such processes include: how individuals describe their difficulties; how they cope with specific limitations; and how they manage their identity and integrate their identity as a person with a disability into a cogent sense of self.

With specific reference to TBI, Simpson, Simons and McFadyen (2002) propose that the major challenge faced by people after TBI is reaching an understanding of exactly how the injury has affected their cognitive and psychosocial abilities. They experience an uncertainty about the full impact of the TBI throughout the period of recovery, rehabilitation and longer-term adjustment. The full impact of the injury may remain 'hidden' for some time.

TBI clients may be long-term patients and it is not unusual for them to be cared for within the hospital ward for up to two years. There are two distinct periods within the recovery period when clients are most vulnerable and confronting adjustment issues:

Stage 1 The first period usually occurs as they approach the stage of rehabilitation where progress begins to slow and there is a growing realization that a full recovery is becoming less likely.

Stage 2 The second period of vulnerability occurs between 6 to 12 months after discharge. On initial discharge, there is excitement about leaving the hospital and returning home. However, as this excitement wears off and the reality of long-term life changes is contemplated, boredom and depression may ensue.

Appropriately timing the inclusion of this method into therapy programmes with this population is crucial, and it is at these particular two phases of recovery from TBI where songwriting interventions can be especially valuable. Clinicians need to consider the appropriate timing in which to encourage reflection and adjustment through songwriting. The music therapist has an ethical duty to safeguard the emotional well-being of clients by not raising issues of which the client is not yet aware or emotionally ready to deal with. When client recovery is active, full participation in rehabilitation is essential. During this important phase of treatment, music therapists also need to make a clinical decision as to whether exploring adjustment issues are appropriate at that time. Reflecting and reviewing one's situation can lead to temporary crises when moments of insight occur and this may be detrimental to a client's treatment programme. More appropriate is the inclusion of self-reflection through songwriting when the client's rehabilitation is being hampered by negative emotional responses. In this situation, a client needs to work through these issues in order to maintain motivation for continued therapy.

Exploration through song

Coping and adjusting to trauma has been promoted within our therapy programmes by facilitating client exploration of thoughts, feelings and reactions to their acquired injury through songwriting. In analysing the lyrics of 82 songs written by clients with TBI, several themes emerged within the songs which could be directly related to aspects of patient adjustment to injury. These have been detailed in a number of our recent publications (Baker, Kennelly and Tamplin in press[a], in press[b], in press[c]). In particular, clients described feelings about, and responses towards, their present situation including the distress and pain involved in the hospitalization process and the feelings of isolation, dependency, helplessness and anger associated with their current situation. Many clients voiced concerns about how their physical and cognitive impairments caused others to view them, thus articulating confronting and painful issues related to body image (Charmaz 1995). Positive experiences were also included within songs, particularly experiences related to memories about, and reflections upon, significant others. When connecting with the positive aspects of the past and those people who were or had been playing an important role within their life, clients were able to grieve losses; a necessary step in the adjustment process. These losses may include loss of role within family, school, workplace and social circle; loss of cognitive, communication and physical function; loss of identity; and loss of financial security. The expression of past experiences also facilitates some relief from the overwhelming and often negative feelings related to their present situation. Grappling with the uncertainty of the future was also voiced within a number of the songs written by clients.

Communication impairments: inhibitors of adjustment

Language and communication impairments greatly inhibit the songwriting process and the therapeutic process. Clients with TBI may demonstrate a range of communication impairments including aphasia, dyspraxia and dysarthria:

- *Aphasia.* Neurological damage causing aphasia leads to impairments in word-finding and language. Clients with aphasia or dysphasia know what they want to say but can't find words or language necessary to communicate and express themselves accurately.
- *Dyspraxia and/or Dysarthria.* Neurological damage causing dyspraxia and/or dysarthria leads to impairments in articulating speech. Here, clients may be unable to clearly articulate the words chosen to express their thoughts and feelings. It may take lengthy periods of time to understand what the client is saying due to the need for repetition or the length of time required to articulate a message (due to initiation problems or fatigue).

When neurological damage results in an inability to verbally articulate or where speech is not the most efficient means of communication, alternative devices or strategies to communicate are used. Holding long, detailed discussions with clients about their situation may be beyond their abilities and the time frame of a session. Further, these clients often fatigue easily. Clinicians need to be aware that a client may not be accurately expressing the full range of their feelings due to these limitations.

Cognitive impairments: inhibitors of adjustment

Adjustment to disability involves understanding, exploring, responding and working through a range of loss and grief issues and forming a new identity. As outlined by Wright (1960), in a non-brain-injured person this staged process is dependent upon a person's value system and their level of emotional maturity. Therefore, the process of adjustment is inherently different for children than for adults. Further, the process is dependent upon various intellectual processes, implying that the greater the cognitive impairment, the more difficult the process of adjustment is. In particular, a client with a TBI may display a combination of cognitive impairments which directly affect and complicate the process of adjustment.

Poor insight is a common problem in clients with TBI. A client may be unaware of their impairments or the implications of their impairments. Consequently, adjusting to changed circumstances is challenging when a client is unable to perceive impairments. For example, a mother might continuously express a desire to go home and attend to the daily needs of her children. However, she has difficulty connecting her physical impairments, such as her inability to walk, with her inability to carry out specific tasks required in her parenting role.

Short-term memory problems impact on the therapeutic songwriting process. Clients may have difficulty resolving issues when unable to recall exploring these issues on previous occasions. They may raise the same issues at the beginning of each session without recalling sessions when the issue was previously raised. The therapist needs to be sensitive to the emotional intensity of the clients' self-expression as they may believe that they are talking about these experiences for the first time. Surprisingly, many clients with severe memory deficits can recall songs that they are writing in therapy from session to session. Often they will not recall the song if asked about it, but will spontaneously sing and recall the words of the song when it is sung. This reinforces the strong link in the brain between music and emotion and its value in helping clients recall experiences and participation in earlier sessions. This assists the client to move through the stages in the adjustment process.

The process is further complicated by gaps in long-term memory whereby clients may have difficulty recalling details they wish to include in the songs they are writing. For example, one client had a memory gap for the year prior to his accident. Within this time period, his wife had given birth to his baby and consequently he was unable to recall this important event in his life.

Additional cognitive problems found during the adjustment phase are:

- poor concentration
- poor attention
- limitations in planning and organization skills
- limitations in problem-solving, initiation, and abstract thinking
- inability to learn new information
- perseverative tendencies.

All these difficulties may impede the adjustment process. Some of these problem areas are further addressed in the next chapter, by Baker.

Introducing songwriting as an intervention

There are many different methods of approaching the songwriting process when focusing on emotional expression and adjustment issues for clients with a TBI. Some approaches are more appropriate than others for clients with particular needs and preferences. Often the clinician chooses the most appropriate way to introduce the songwriting process for a particular client, based on an assessment of cognitive functioning. It may be difficult for a client with cognitive difficulties to understand and remember a range of options for how to approach songwriting. To avoid confusing the client and to maintain the therapeutic aim of the songwriting intervention (i.e. assisting the adjustment process), it may be more appropriate for the clinician to be more directive in the process. The clinician might ask the client to express an idea and then immediately provide an example of how this idea may be represented as a song line. The client is provided with immediate feedback as to how the song will be created. The clinician may be able to use previously gained information about the client's musical preferences and use the intensity of emotion expressed by the client as a guide for how to represent the lyrics musically. For example, angry lyrics could be supported by loud, driving chords, or grief may be represented by a gentle accompaniment of slow arpeggiated chords. In this way, the client and clinician work together, 'unravelling' the song in the moment.

For clients with fewer cognitive difficulties, a range of options for how to begin the song may be presented and the client is able to choose the approach with which they feel most comfortable. Many clients don't feel confident with music composition and need to be supported and guided through the early stages of the song creation process. This may involve discussion of the potential therapeutic benefits of writing a song, including:

- identifying and externalizing emotions
- communicating to loved ones
- self-motivation and encouragement
- simply telling their story.

Songwriting can create an alternative way to approach reality and may precipitate a change in thinking. It also encourages and promotes growth and self-awareness (Glassman 1991).

In some cases it may be appropriate to play an example of a song that another patient has written (after consent has been given) to illustrate the process and result.

Many patients feel most comfortable starting with lyric creation. In this case, the clinician may ask the patient if they would prefer to use the music to a song which they already know or like and write new lyrics (song parody), or whether they would like to create a completely new song. It is often necessary to reassure a patient that the therapist is able to provide as much musical support and guidance as necessary in the composition of the music, should they choose to write an original song. Providing the opportunity for choice throughout the songwriting process is imperative as it allows the client to have as much creative control as possible. Empowerment is particularly important for patients with a TBI as much of their lives are beyond their control, which may lead to the development of an external locus of control (Fenton and Hughes 1989).

When to introduce songwriting into therapy

The songwriting process is rarely started in the first music therapy session when addressing emotional and adjustment issues for patients with a TBI is a main goal of therapy. In many cases, a patient who has been attending music therapy for some time may begin to explore these issues as more insight into their situation develops or as a discharge date draws closer and the reality of ongoing disability sets in. For a patient who is already involved in a music therapy programme, the move into songwriting can be a natural progression. The rapport developed over time between the client and therapist provides an environment of trust and support. In addition, the therapist may develop greater insight into a patient's personality and key issues over time, as result of working together during the rehabilitation process. For a patient who is newly referred to music therapy specifically to address emotional and adjustment issues, often the first session is used to develop rapport, discuss musical tastes, allow the client to tell their story and build a sense of trust. To introduce songwriting in this first session may often be too confronting and scary for the new client; however, it may be appropriate to talk about the songwriting process, present different options for how to write a song and discuss possible song topics or themes. This then allows the client time before the next session to prepare mentally and emotionally to write a song. For some clients, however, it may be appropriate to begin the song in the first session, particularly in the case of frontal lobe damage and where memory problems and other cognitive issues are present. Similarly, in a situation where issues arise during the therapy session for a client, it may be appropriate to 'strike while the iron is hot', and capture ideas as they are presented, rather than delay the process until the next session. It can also be useful for the client to take away some record of a song's progress at the end of a session. This may be in the form of a written copy of the song ideas and/or lyrics or a recording of the unfinished song so that he or she can prepare new ideas or changes between sessions.

Beginning a new song: lyric creation

The most common way to start writing a new song is to brainstorm ideas and record these on paper. This may often follow a period of discussion where the client is encouraged to talk about issues that are important or troubling and express their feelings about these issues. The client is then encouraged to select a topic or theme that has arisen out of this discussion from which ideas for lyrics may be generated. This process, entitled Therapeutic Lyric Creation (TLC), often follows a fairly standard format and has been developed over time by the authors:

Stage 1 Generate a range of topics to write about.

Stage 2 Select a topic for further exploration.

Stage 3 Brainstorm ideas directly related to the chosen topic.

Stage 4 Identify the principal idea/thought/emotion/concept within the topic (which functions as the focus of the chorus).

Stage 5 Develop the ideas identified as central to the topic.

Stage 6 Group related points together.

Stage 7 Discard the irrelevant or the least important points.

Stage 8 Construct an outline of the main themes within the song.

Stage 9 Construct the lyrics for the song.

In building client confidence with songwriting, it is often most appropriate to start with this general brainstorming of thoughts and ideas. This allows the flow of ideas to begin and expression is not impeded by the need for lyrical structure yet. In spite of a client's ability (or non-ability) to write, it is often best if the therapist scribes the ideas as this allows the client to talk freely and without interruption to the thought process. The therapist should take care to transcribe what the client says verbatim, so as to preserve the integrity and authenticity of the client's ideas. These ideas may be reworded or reorganized later on in the process to fit into a lyrical structure. The therapist should also provide the appropriate degree of support to facilitate the client's expression of ideas. This may consist of asking questions about statements that the client has made or asking the client to expand on certain statements. It is also therapeutically important for the therapist to validate and encourage clients in their expression of significant personal issues. For clients who have difficulty with initiation, this initial process may be more productive if the therapist takes the role of an interviewer and asks the client key questions about issues which have been highlighted as being significant. For example, a client may make a statement such as 'I hate being in hospital', but have difficulty explicating why he or she hates it, or providing more information about his or her emotional responses. In this situation, the therapist may ask open-ended questions such as 'what is it, in particular, about being in hospital that you dislike?' or 'describe to me what it's like for you to be here'.

Fill-in-the-Blank and Song Parody Techniques

Alternatively, a Fill-in-the-Blank Technique (FBT) using a familiar song may be adopted. This technique has been previously described in the literature (Freed 1987; Goldstein 1990; Robb 1996). A song that the client relates to may be used and adapted to make it more personally relevant. For example, a song by Moving Pictures could be adapted and presented as follows:

What about me? It isn't fair
I've had enough
Now get me out of here
Can't you see? I want to be free
But every day I'm stuck in here.

Here, clients complete the lyrics by including words or phrases that were brainstormed earlier in the process. This technique provides more structure for clients who may have difficulty expanding and organizing simple ideas. It can also provide direction for the lyrics and may serve as a beginning point for a client who is having trouble getting started.

Song Parody Technique (SPT) uses the music of a pre-composed song whereby the lyrics of the original song are completely replaced by client-generated lyrics. In many cases, a combination of these two techniques is employed.

In our clinical experience, SPT and FBT are the most commonly chosen and adopted methods with paediatric patients. Due to their developmental stage, many paediatric patients have not developed an individual music identity separate from their peers. Therefore, they are drawn to specific popular songs and musical artists. The very nature of this technique avoids the need for paediatric patients to make decisions about musical elements which may be too abstract for them at this developmental stage. This may be further compounded by impaired cognitive functioning as a result of a TBI.

Song Collage Technique

Another technique, which can be helpful for clients who have difficulty identifying or articulating their emotions, is the use of Song Collage Technique (SCT). This technique involves the client looking through music books or the lyric sheet within CD covers and selecting words or phrases from pre-composed songs that stand out, or have personal significance to them. The therapist facilitates this process by presenting a selection of songs which he/she considers contain meanings or descriptions of situations with which the client may resonate or identify. In these situations, identifying with the messages of other songs can enhance this therapeutic process. The clients can then add ideas to these words and phrases and reorganize or reword them into their own song lyrics.

The collection of words and phrases is similar to the brainstorming process mentioned earlier. In a similar way, like ideas are then grouped together and reordered to suit the client's preferences. The therapist encourages and supports the client in changing any necessary words, expanding ideas and adding phrases to link the different points within the song.

Use of Rhyme Technique

The use of rhyming lyric patterns herein termed the Use of Rhyme Technique (URT) can be employed to create structure in a song. The therapist should make a decision whether or not to introduce this option based on the client's cognitive abilities. If a client is able to generate lists of words that rhyme with key words which they have included, then this technique is a good way to expand and organize song ideas, for example sad/bad/mad/glad/dad.

If a client writes a song line such as 'being here just makes me sad', a list of words rhyming with sad (bad, mad, glad, dad, had) can be generated and one of these words that fits in with a previously brainstormed idea can be used, or the rhyming word can be used to generate a new idea. For example, 'being here just makes me sad, but I'll take the good with the bad', or 'being here just makes me sad, but I remember the good times that I've had'. Depending on the clients' cognitive abilities, the therapist may suggest phrases using the rhyming words that the clients have generated or the therapist may generate a list of rhyming words and ask the clients which word they relate to most and ask them to create the next phrase ending with this word.

Music composition

Often the music is created after at least some of the lyric creation has been completed. This is generally because many clients attending music therapy are not musicians themselves and feel most comfortable with the lyric creation part of the songwriting process. It is important to build the clients' confidence with a task with which they are more comfortable before introducing a more challenging or demanding task. The specialized skills of the music therapist are employed in explaining the music creation process and involving the clients in this process to the greatest degree possible. At the start of the songwriting process, clients are given the option of writing their own music, or using the music to a familiar song of their choice to which to write their own lyrics (SPT).

SPT is useful when clients feel daunted by the idea of writing music for their song, or when clients have difficulty conceptualizing how to structure a lyrical line without music. The use of pre-composed music can provide this sense of structure and gives the client guidelines for how many words or syllables for a line and how many lines for a verse or chorus. For some clients this sense of a familiar structure provides a feeling of security; however, for others it may be too limiting. It can sometimes be difficult to try to fit an idea for a lyrical line into the musical structure of a pre-composed song line. In some cases the integrity of clients' ideas may be better preserved if they do not have to change an idea in order to fit it into an existing rhythmic or melodic structure. Clients are then able to write lyrics freely and the music is composed to meld with the structure of the lyrics.

Musical genre and style

A good place to start the music creation is with the clients' preference for musical genre. This ground is familiar to most people, musicians and non-musicians alike. Most clients are able to state which genres of music they like or listen to, and if they cannot, the therapist can often determine this by asking the clients which artists or bands they like. It is important for the therapist to use language that the client can understand in order to promote maximum control and ownership of the music. It is often useful to ask questions about genre preference in relation to specific artists. For example, 'Do you want the music for your song to sound like a Metallica song or a Ben Harper song?'

Once the genre has been selected, different accompaniment styles can be presented for the client to choose between. These ideas may be improvised on an instrument by the therapist or trialled using an electronic keyboard accompaniment program or computer software. The choice of instrumentation is often determined by genre preference. For example, it is very difficult to create authentic sounding hip hop music using only an acoustic guitar. For this style of music, the use of computer software with recorded samples and loops and/or keyboards with pre-programmed accompaniments may be more appropriate. If a guitar is used, different accompaniment styles such as finger picking, pizzicato chords or strummed chords may be presented and different stylistic ideas, such as reggae or bossanova rhythmic patterns, power chords, standard blues riffs or use of a slide, offered as appropriate. Using a piano or electronic keyboard, arpeggios, octaves or chords may be presented as accompaniment options. The ideas for harmonic progressions are often best presented by the therapist as improvised passages, unless the client is musically proficient. Most clients will be able to identify aurally which harmonic progressions they like or think fit best with the feel of their song.

If the client is happy to sing in order to work out melody lines, then this is the next step in the song creation process. However, in our experience, even those clients who enjoy singing often don't feel confident or comfortable in using their voice to compose melody lines. The most common method we have found for melody composition is for the therapist to provide melody options for the client to listen to and choose between. The client is also encouraged to make independent decisions about the direction of the melody line; for example, 'Do you want the end of this line to go up or down?' Providing maximum opportunity for the client to contribute to the music composition ensures greater ownership of the completed song. Similar questions in terms of the range of dynamics and tempi to be used may also be asked to the client when completing the songwriting process.

Applications of the song post-recording

A recording and written transcription of the completed song is given to the client following completion of the lyrics and music. The song may be recorded on cassette tape, or for a better quality recording, a minidisc recording can be downloaded onto a computer and burnt onto a CD. These recordings serve as a record of the therapeutic songwriting process and can be used by clients to validate their emotional journey.

Some songs may be used:

- to communicate messages to loved ones
- to record positive past memories and experiences
- for self-motivation and encouragement during difficult times
- to affirm and encourage other clients who may be experiencing similar difficulties.

Sometimes when working with children, picture books including photos of children, their family, home and friends can also be incorporated with the final transcription of the song so as to provide a more visual/pictorial image of the song created.

Case example: A filthy song – genre to match emotional intensity

Sam was a young man aged 19 when he was referred for music therapy. He had received a severe traumatic brain injury resulting from a train accident. There was uncertainty surrounding the circumstances of the accident and whether it was an attempted suicide. Sam was very physically disabled as a result of his brain injury. His speech was severely dysarthric and consequently difficult to understand. His legs had both been broken in the accident, and he had high muscle tone resulting from the brain injury that caused him a lot of pain in physiotherapy. In addition to these physical issues, Sam also had severe cognitive and behavioural issues that affected his ability to participate in his rehabilitation. He was an angry young man, with limited insight into his disabilities and need for rehabilitation. Prior to music therapy intervention, his therapy sessions were often cancelled or ended prematurely due to non-compliance or aggression. As Sam's rehabilitation progress was being hindered by his negative emotional responses and behaviour, he was referred to music therapy for emotional expression and communication needs. The opportunity for self-reflection and expression through songwriting was considered appropriate as Sam needed to work through these issues in order to maintain motivation for continued therapy.

The songwriting process was not introduced into music therapy sessions until Sam had participated in music therapy for some time and rapport between the music therapist and Sam had been established. This foundation of trust and openness led Sam to feel comfortable talking with the music therapist about his feelings. This process of rapport building was further enhanced through making music with Sam which he enjoyed and to which he related. The music therapist introduced the concept of songwriting to Sam as a potential vehicle through which he could express and capture his emotional processes. Sam had a strong emotional connection to music and therefore he was responsive to this idea. He had a particular love of heavy metal music and this was the genre he wished to use for his song.

Sam's first song was written over three sessions, and evolved very much spontaneously rather than as a reorganization of the generated ideas. In brain storming, Sam's ideas were mostly phrases full of emotional intensity. Prior to his accident Sam was studying acting and his song lyrics reflected his artistic temperament. His ideas flowed quickly and remained largely unchanged in the final version of the song. As this song was very cathartic in nature, it was important to retain the ideas in their original form to capture the intensity of emotion expressed. This is the final version of his song lyrics. The name of the place where he lives has been omitted for confidentiality.

A filthy song

Chorus
I feel like shit, I hate it here
I miss my friends, wish they were near
I feel so bad, I want to walk again like I used to do
I love my dad because he believes in me.

Verse 1
I hate this place it bores me to tears
And I feel like nothing in this universe
I hate this place I'm sick of it
Want to escape from this hell hole that I'm in
I want to go home....

Chorus

Verse 2
I was riding on a train one day
Going home to X where I've lived all my life
Both my legs were broken, they were hanging out the door
Of the train, then I passed out and I don't remember anything after that
Then I woke up here in hell.

Incorporating Sam's preference for heavy metal music and the intense negative emotions that he was expressing, a range of musical ideas and options for accompaniment style were presented for him to choose between. Sam selected minor chords to start both the verse and chorus as well as major–minor chord shifts (e.g. A major to A minor) at points within the song which may have reflected the intensity of sadness and anger he was experiencing. This contrast of emotions was also represented through a change in accompaniment style. The lyrics in the chorus expressed sadness and apathy and were represented musically through a melodic and sparse vocal line. The verses expressed anger and frustration and this was represented by a change in tonality, a more driving strumming style and an increase in dynamics. The melodic range was limited to four semitones and the use of a shifting C and C# creating musical tension and lack of change. A bridge of six bars between each verse and chorus was created using previously unused chords to express a new depth of emotion. In this part, the melody line finishes on the highest pitch within the song as if to emphasize the importance of this particular line.

This first song that Sam wrote in music therapy clearly expressed many emotional responses that he was experiencing, including loss, grief, anger, boredom and love. In it he also tells his story, the story of his accident, injury and hospitalization experience. The finished song was then recorded and the final version of the song is illustrated in Figure 6.1.

Sam wrote several songs in music therapy over the course of his inpatient rehabilitation programme. His second song explored fears of life after death and past antisocial drug-taking behaviour. The next song in his process focused on the physical pain and frustration of undertaking rehabilitation, specifically physiotherapy. It also addressed issues of body image. The final song written in his process addressed issues of the future, particularly going home and the desire for a relationship. Songwriting became a medium to document his adjustment process.

Sam's songs had other therapeutic applications in that he was able to listen to the recordings of the finished songs for self-motivation and validation of his emotions.

Case example: 'Wannabe' like a Spice Girl – song parody and musical identity

Sally was almost aged 12 when she was involved as a pedestrian in a motor vehicle accident where she sustained multiple traumas, including a severe head injury. As Sally progressed through PTA she received joint music therapy and speech pathology sessions which focused on two main areas: dysarthria and language difficulties. Her cognitive difficulties included memory impairment, psychomotor slowing, impaired problem-solving, rigid thinking and impaired social judgement. Sally was unmotivated to participate in most therapy sessions. Therefore a referral for individual music therapy sessions was made to address her emotional needs including self-expression and adjustment to hospitalization.

Music therapy assessment revealed that Sally enjoyed listening to and playing music. She had previously learnt the piano and the clarinet at school and enjoyed listening to a variety of age-appropriate popular music, particularly the Spice Girls. To address the need for self-expression, songwriting was offered to Sally and she chose to use song parody as her preferred method. She was excited about the idea of producing her own songs and chose to use the music of a popular Spice Girls song 'Wannabe' to which to write her own lyrics. This demonstrates that song parody, in particular the use of current popular songs, is the preferred method of songwriting with this age group.

Sally appeared to have little difficulty in creating ideas for lyrics, but her dysarthria adversely affected her ability to articulate her intended speech

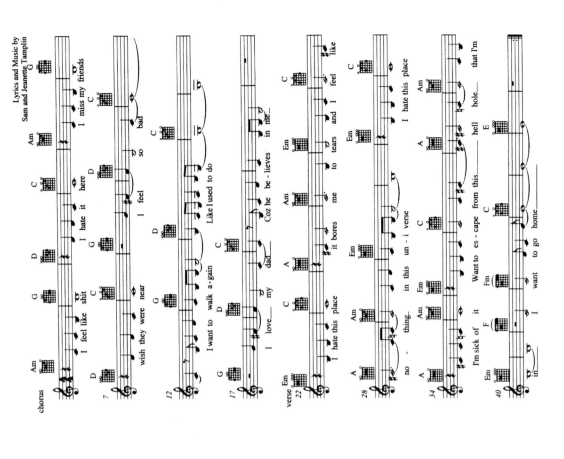

Figure 6.1 Final version of 'A filthy song'

clearly. Sally's mother was more familiar with Sally's way of speaking and was present for most sessions. Her mother was able to assist Sally if she was experiencing difficulties in articulating her thoughts and ideas. Based on clinical experience with this population, the music therapist offered Sally a selection of subject choices for her song – family, home and hospital. Sally chose to write about her experiences in hospital, which included relationships with staff members and descriptions of negative aspects of her hospital experience.

The use of song parody provided the necessary structure and predictability of melody and rhythm to aid the organization of her ideas into a lyrical format. Sally was always quick to remind the music therapist if her lyrics were not interpreted accurately. Sally was often excited during this songwriting process and often wanted to perform actions to the songs while in her wheelchair. During these times she would often need to be reminded to remain focused on the songwriting activity. These are the lyrics to the final version of Sally's song.

Naughty nurses

Verse 1

I'll tell you what I want what I really really want
I want to get out of this dumb stupid hospital
I hate medicine medicine makes me feel sicker
Except for Baclofen

Chorus

If you want to be so naughty you've got to be like Tracey
Tracey is my favourite and she is the best
Christine and Rebecca, they're my favourites too
But hospital is so smelly 'cause I think it is

Verse 2

I'll tell you what I like what I really really like
I like Sam because she does OT with me
and then there's Prue 'cause I just like her
There's no real reason I just like her

She was promised an opportunity to videotape her performance of the completed song with actions included.

Before Sally was discharged she expressed a need to write a 'going home' song. During these final therapy sessions she would often speak of being excited about leaving hospital and because this date was so close to Christmas and her twelfth birthday, there were so many family events, holiday activities and of course presents to which to look forward. This resulted in another song parody being created using yet another Spice Girls song, 'Stop Right Now'. This song spoke of her family members, events to which she was looking forward and also the desire to walk again. Both of these song parodies were video-recorded and presented in booklet form together with pictures of Sally and her family which she was then able to take home and share with family and friends.

While these were the only two songs that Sally wrote during her rehabilitation, each song parody described two significant moments in her life – her own experience of being in hospital and also preparations for the future and returning home. Song parody provided Sally with the opportunity to express a variety of emotions, thoughts and feelings which not only assisted her adjustment to hospital but also to her future as she returned home to begin a new life.

Conclusions

This chapter has primarily addressed the therapeutic rationale for introducing songwriting to TBI clients. Songwriting can facilitate the expression of emotions and assist in the movement towards emotional adjustment. Some of the more relevant and effective therapeutic techniques used when writing songs with TBI clients have been outlined. In particular, techniques such as song parody, fill-in-the-blank, song collage and the use of rhyme can be appropriate strategies to manage the cognitive deficits with which these clients may present. At the same time these techniques can be used to encourage the creation of lyrics which express feelings. In writing song lyrics, clients have opportunities to explore their own reactions to the issues addressed within the song. This is a vital step in coming to terms with the trauma that they have experienced and the short- and long-term implications of this trauma that have so adversely impacted upon their lives.

The chapter has also highlighted the importance of creating genres of music that are appealing to the client. We have particularly emphasized the attention to detail in the selection of the accompaniment style for a client's song. The use of samples, loops and pre-programmed accompaniment styles within music software programs and modern electric keyboards can be used effectively to create genre-specific effects. When using guitar accompaniment, it is important to talk with the client about how they want the song to sound and experiment with different guitar strumming and picking styles (bossanova, reggae, ballad, hard rock, etc.) to create the feel and genre for the song that is desired.

Music therapists working in rehabilitation must be flexible, creative and adaptive in their therapeutic approach to songwriting. The techniques presented in this chapter need to be at the fingertips of the informed therapist in order to facilitate clear clinical decision-making about the method of presentation. This, in turn, offers maximum choice and control over the song creation process to the TBI client, in a manner appropriate to their level of need.

CHAPTER NINE

Music Therapy with the Elderly

We have seen in the previous two chapters that it is possible to build a bridge between music therapy understandings and art therapy understandings, between music therapy and medicine. Furthermore, I have proposed a way in which we can analyse how music therapists construct their clinical understandings regarding the way that patients play. This chapter continues in the same vein, addressing the pressing problem facing modern Western society of dementia in the elderly. First, the scene is set in terms of the problem of dementia within the broader health care community. Then, a music therapy understanding is presented that compares the problem as it is seen in individual therapy. We will read that music therapy has something significant to offer in terms of treatment in what is often regarded as a hopeless problem. Indeed, as we will see in the next chapter, which deals with music therapy with HIV and AIDS patients, the diagnosis of the disease and the reactions of both patients and practitioners to such a diagnosis often compound the negative aspects of the disease itself. A form of therapy that introduces some element of hope, when grounded in a reality that all parties can agree upon, is an important step forward in treating such chronic problems.

Dementia is an important source of chronic disability, leading to both spiralling health care expenditure among the elderly and a progressive disturbance of quality of life for the patient and his family. In the United States of America the cost of institutional care for patients with dementia is estimated at over $25 billion a year (Steg 1990). If 4 per cent to 5 per cent of the North American elderly population suffer from dementia, then 1.25 per cent of the total population are suffering with the problems of severe dementia. Other estimates of the same population suggest that 15 per cent of those over the age of 65 will have moderate to severe dementia with projections to 45 per cent by the age of 90 years (Odenheimer 1989). Current estimates are that over 60 per cent of those cases of dementia result

from Alzheimer's disease (Kalayam and Shamoian 1990). With anticipated increases in the population of the elderly in Europe,[1] it is timely to find treatment initiatives in the Western world which will ameliorate the impact of this problem.

Dementing illnesses, or acquired cognitive disorders, have been recognized for centuries, but little progress was made in specific diagnoses until the evolution of the nosological approach to disease and early clinical descriptions of neurosyphilis and Huntington's chorea in the 1800s. Such descriptions were further supported by concurrent understandings that suggested the influence of the brain on behaviour. The first histopathological characterizations of cognitive disorders were enabled by developments in the optical microscope. Thus, Alzheimer (1907) was able to see the neuronal degeneration and senile plaques in the brain of a 55-year-old woman with progressive memory impairment, and identify the disease which today bears his name.

While cognitive impairment is evident from behaviour, and neurohistopathy can recognize neuronal degeneration, the diagnosis of Alzheimer's disease is prone to error[2] and authors differ as to the difficulty of making a precise diagnosis (Odenheimer 1989; Steg 1990). In the early stages of the disease the symptoms are difficult to distinguish from those of normal aging, a process which itself is poorly understood. To date there exist no normative established values of what cognitive impairment or memory loss are, or what neurochemical and neurophysiological changes accompany normal aging. It is therefore extremely difficult to establish criteria for determining abnormal changes from a normal population, and the researcher/clinician must in part rely upon within-the-subject designs to indicate progressive deterioration.

A second source of error in diagnosing Alzheimer's disease is that it is masked by other conditions (see Table 9.1). Principal among these conditions is that of depression, which itself can cause cognitive and behavioural disorders. It is estimated that 20 per cent to 30 per cent of patients with Alzheimer's disease will have an accompanying depression (Kalayam and Shamoian 1990), thereby compounding diagnostic problems further.

---

1 Between 23 per cent and 25 per cent of the national populations aged over 65 by the year 2040 (Aldridge 1990).
2 Estimated in a range from 10 per cent to 30 per cent error in the general medical population (Steg 1990).

Table 9.1 Differential diagnosis of Alzheimer's disease

Differential diagnosis of Alzheimer's disease

Multi infarct dementia and other forms of cerebrovascular disease
Parkinson's disease
Progressive supranuclear palsy
Huntington's disease
Central nervous system infection
Subdural haematoma
Normal pressure hydrocephalus
Multiple sclerosis
Seizure disorder
Brain tumour
Cerebral trauma
Metabolic disturbance
Nutritional deficiency
Psychiatric disorder
Substance abuse or overmedication

Clinical Descriptions of Dementia

The clinical syndrome of dementia is characterized by an acquired decline of cognitive function which is represented by memory and language impairment. While the term dementia itself is used widely to describe cognitive impairment it is specifically applied in medical literature to two conditions: dementia of the Alzheimer's type (DAT) and multi-infarct dementia.

The course of Alzheimer's disease is one of progressive deterioration associated with degenerative changes in the brain. Such deterioration is presented in a clinical picture of episodic changes and a pattern of particular cognitive failings which are variable (Drachman *et al.* 1990). Mental status testing is one of the primary forms of assessing these cognitive failings, which include short- and long-term memory changes, impairment of abstract thinking and judgement; disorders of language (aphasia), and difficulty in finding the names of words (anomia); the loss of ability to interpret what is heard, said and felt (agnosia); and an inability to carry out motor activities, such as manipulating a pen or toothbrush, despite intact motor function (apraxia). When such clinical findings are present then a probable diagnosis can be made; a more definite diagnosis depends upon tissue diagnosis (see Table 9.2).

Table 9.2 Diagnostic evaluation of dementia

Diagnostic categories

Complete medical history
Mental status examination
Complete physical and neurological investigation (including investigation for infection of central nervous system if suspected)
Complete blood count and blood chemistry tests (including vitamin B12 levels)
Thyroid function tests
Serology for syphilis
Computerized tomography (CT) or magnetic resonance imaging (MRI), electroencephalography (EEG), or positive emission tomography (PET) scanning

While dementia of the Alzheimer's type begins after the age of 40, and is considered to be a disease of the elderly, the influence of age on prognosis is not as significant as the initial degree of severity of the problem when recognized (Drachman *et al.* 1990). Disease severity, as assessed by intellectual function, appears to be the most consistent predictor of the subsequent course of the disease, particularly when accompanied by a combination of wandering and falling, and behavioural problems (Walsh, Welch and Larson 1990). However, the rates of decline between sub groups of patients are variable and a patient's rate of progression in one year may bear little relationship to the future rate of decline (Salmon *et al.* 1990). Some authors (Cooper, Mungas and Weiler 1990) suggest that an as yet unproven factor, other than declining cognitive ability, may also play a part in the associated abnormal behaviours of anger, agitation, personality change, wandering, insomnia and depression which occur in later stages of the disease.

Clearly Alzheimer's disease causes distress for the patient. The loss of memory and the accompanying loss of language, before the onset of motor impairment, mean that the daily lives of patients are disturbed. Communication, the fabric of social contact, is interrupted and disordered. The threat of progressive deterioration and behavioural disturbance has ramifications not only for the patient themselves, but also their families, who must take some of the social responsibility for care of the patient, and the emotional burden of seeing a loved one becoming confused and isolated.

Assessment of dementia

A brief cognitive test, the Mini-Mental State Examination (Folstein, Folstein and McHugh 1975), has been developed to screen and monitor the progression of Alzheimer's disease. The test itself is intended for the clinician to assess functions of different areas of the brain, and is based upon questions and activities (see Table 9.3). As a clinical instrument it is widely used and well validated in practice (Babikian *et al.* 1990; Beatty and Goodkin 1990; Eustache *et al.* 1990; Faustman, Moses and Csernansky 1990; Gagnon *et al.* 1990; Jairath and Campbell 1990; Summers *et al.* 1990; Zillmer *et al.* 1990). As a bedside test the MMSE is widely used for testing cognition and is useful as a predictive tool for cognitive impairment and semantic memory (Eustache *et al.* 1990) without being contaminated by motor and sensory deficits (Beatty and Goodkin 1990; Jairath and Campbell 1990).

Table 9.3 Mini-Mental State Examination

Item	Component	Score
Orientation for time	year, season, month, date and day	5
Orientation for place	state, county, city, building and floor	5
Registration	Subject repeats 'rose', 'ball' and 'key'	3
Attention for calculation	Serial subtraction of 7 from 100 or spell 'world' backward	5
Recall	'Rose', 'ball' and 'key'	3
Naming	Pencil and watch	2
Repetition	No ifs, ands, or buts	1
Three-stage verbal command	Take a piece of paper in your right hand, fold it in half, and put it on the floor	3
Written command	Close your eyes	1
Writing	A spontaneous sentence	1
Construction	Two interlocking pentagons	1
Total		30

Source: after Folstein, Folstein and McHugh (1975).

Elderly patients scoring below 24 points out of a possible total score of 30 are considered as demented. However, this scoring has been questioned on the grounds of its cut-off point of 24 as the lower limit, particularly for early dementia (Galasko *et al.* 1990); and that it is influenced by education (Gagnon *et al.* 1990). Poorly educated subjects with less than eight years of education may score below 24 without being demented.

Further criticisms of the Mini-Mental State Examination (MMSE) have been that it is not sensitive enough to mild deficits, but it could be augmented by the addition of a word fluency task and an improvement in the attention–concentration item (Galasko *et al.* 1990). In addition, the MMSE seriously underestimates cognitive impairment in psychiatric patients (Faustman, Moses and Csernansky 1990). An important feature neglected by the MMSE is that of 'intention' or executive control (Odenheimer 1989), which refers to the ability of the patient to persevere with a set task, to reach a set goal or to change tasks.

The items which the MMSE fails to discriminate (minor language deficits), or neglects to assess (fluency and intentionality), however, may be elicited in the playing of improvised music. A dynamic musical assessment of patient behaviour, linked with the motor co-ordination and intent required for the playing of musical instruments used in music therapy, and the necessary element of interpersonal communication, may provide a sensitive complementary tool for assessment.

We see in Table 9.4 how medical elements of assessment can find their correlates in musical parameters. As we have seen in the chapter related to bowel disease, both languages share similar terms, and it is possible to build a conceptual bridge between two forms of practice. By doing this neither practice is reduced to the other, but we do have a valuable conceptual tool for proposing commonalities in the practice. We can take all the elements demanded in a medical assessment and translate those into terms that are applicable for music therapy and demonstrate its applicability to medical practice. Conversely, we can translate what happens in music therapy and demonstrate its applicability to medical practice. What is important to take from the music therapy assessment is that the idea of intention (which is behavioural as much as it is cognitive) can be demonstrated in an activity that offers a situation in which intentionality can be achieved. The problem with assessment tests is that they are so often reduced that they become unnatural and totally divorced from the context of the person's life. How we behave in laboratories and consulting rooms is often somewhat different from our behaviour in our own homes and with friends. Music therapy, too, is no natural context; but embedding an assessment of intentionality within the context of musical playing is less clumsy, and more flexible, than a specific test.

understand speech he was no longer capable of the co-ordination required to lead a major orchestra. While his mind, he reports, was full of musical ideas, he could not set them down (Dalessio 1984). Eventually his intellectual functions and speech deteriorated until he could no longer recognize his own music.

However, the responsiveness of patients with Alzheimer's disease to music is a remarkable phenomenon (Swartz et al. 1989). While language deterioration is a feature of cognitive deficit, musical abilities appear to be preserved. This may be because the fundamentals of language, as we have seen in previous chapters, are musical, and prior to semantic and lexical functions in language development.

Although language processing may be dominant in one hemisphere of the brain, music production involves an understanding of the interaction of both cerebral hemispheres (Altenmiller 1986; Brust 1980; Gates and Bradshaw 1977). In attempting to understand the perception of music there have been a number of investigations into the hemispheric strategies involved. Much of the literature considering musical perception concentrates on the significance of hemispheric dominance. Gates and Bradshaw (1977) conclude that cerebral hemispheres are concerned with music perception and that no laterality differences are apparent. Other authors (Wagner and Hannon 1981) suggest that two processing functions develop with training where left and right hemispheres are simultaneously involved, and that musical stimuli are capable of eliciting both right and left ear superiority (Kellar and Bever 1980). Similarly, when people listen to and perform music they utilize differing hemispheric processing strategies.

Evidence of the global strategy of music processing in the brain is found in the clinical literature. Morgan and Tilluckdharry (1982) tell how singing was considered to be a welcome release from the helplessness of being a patient, allowing thoughts to be communicated externally. Although the 'newer aspect' of speech was lost, the older function of music was retained. Berman (1981) suggests that recovery from aphasia is not a matter of new learning by the non-dominant hemisphere but a taking over of responsibility for language by that hemisphere. The non-dominant hemisphere may be a reserve of functions in case of regional failure. If singing gives a glimpse of this brain plasticity, then music therapy has a potential for working with dementia patients.

Little is known about the loss of musical and language abilities in cases of global cortical damage, although the quality of response to music in the final stages of dementia is worth noting (Norberg, Melin and Asplund 1986). Any discussion is necessarily limited to hypothesizing, as there are no

Table 9.4 Features of medical and musical assessment

Medical elements of assessment	Musical elements of assessment
continuing observation of mental and functional status	continuing observation of mental and functional status
testing of verbal skills, including element of speech fluency	testing of musical skills; rhythm, melody, harmony, dynamic, phrasing, articulation
cortical disorder testing; visuo-spatial skills and ability to perform complex motor tasks (including grip and right–left co-ordination)	cortical disorder testing; visuo-spatial skills and ability to perform complex motor tasks (including grip and right–left co-ordination)
testing for progressive memory disintegration	testing for progressive memory disintegration
motivation to complete tests, to achieve set goals and persevere in set tasks	motivation to sustain playing improvised music, to achieve musical goals and persevere in maintaining form
'intention' difficult to assess; but considered important	'intention' a feature of improvised musical playing
concentration and attention span	concentration on the improvised playing and attention to the instruments
flexibility in task switching	flexibility in musical (including instrumental) changes
mini-mental state score influenced by educational status	ability to play improvised music influenced by previous musical training
insensitive to small changes	sensitive to small changes
ability to interpret surroundings	ability to interpret musical context and assessment of communication in the therapeutic relationship

Music and Dementia

Late in adult life, at the age of 56, and after completing two major concertos for the piano, Maurice Ravel, the composer, began to complain of increased fatigue and lassitude. Following a traffic accident his condition deteriorated progressively (Henson 1988). He lost the ability to remember names, to speak spontaneously and to write (Dalessio 1984). Although he could established baselines for musical performance in the adult population (Swartz et al. 1989). Aphasia, which is a feature of cognitive deterioration, is a complicated phenomenon. While syntactical functions may remain longer, it is the lexical and semantic functions of naming and reference which begin to fail in the early stages. Phrasing and grammatical structures remain, giving an impression of normal speech, yet content becomes increasingly incoherent. These progressive failings appear to be located within the context of a semantic and episodic memory loss illustrated by the inability to remember a simple story when tested (Bayles et al. 1989).

Musicality and singing

Musicality and singing are rarely tested as features of cognitive deterioration, yet preservation of these abilities in aphasics has been linked to eventual recovery (Jacome 1984; Morgan and Tilluckdharry 1982), and could be significant indicators of hierarchical changes in cognitive functioning. Jacome (1984) found that a musically naive patient with transcortical mixed aphasia exhibited repetitive, spontaneous whistling, and whistling in response to questions. The patient often spontaneously sang without error in pitch, melody, rhythm and lyrics, and spent long periods of time listening to music. Beatty (Beatty et al. 1988) describes a woman who had severe impairments in terms of aphasia, memory dysfunction and apraxia, yet was able to sight read an unfamiliar song and perform on the xylophone which is to her was an unconventional instrument. Like Ravel (Dalessio 1984), and an elderly musician who could play from memory (Crystal, Grober and Masur 1989) but no longer recalled the name of the composer, she no longer recalled the name of the music she was playing.

Swartz and his colleagues (Swartz et al. 1989, p.154) propose a series of perceptual levels at which musical disorders take place:

(1) the acoustico-psychological level, which includes changes in intensity, pitch and timbre

(2) the discriminatory level, which includes the discrimination of intervals and chords

(3) the categorical level which includes the categorical identification of rhythmic patterns and intervals

(4) the configural level, which includes melody perception, the recognition of motifs and themes, tonal changes, identification of instruments, and rhythmic discrimination; and

(5) the level where musical form is recognized, including complex perceptual and executive functions of harmonic, melodic and rhythmical transformations.

In Alzheimer's patients it would be expected that while levels (1), (2) and (3) remain unaffected, the complexities of levels (4) and (5), when requiring no naming, may be preserved but are susceptible to deterioration.

It is perhaps important to point out that these disorders are not themselves musical; they are disorders of audition. Only when disorders of musical production take place can we begin to suggest that a musical disorder is present. Improvised musical playing is in a unique position to demonstrate this hypothetical link between perception and production.

Rhythm is the key to the integrative process, underlying both musical perception and physiological coherence. Barfield's (1978) approach suggests that when musical form as tonal shape meets the rhythm of breathing there is the musical experience. External auditory activity is mediated by internal perceptual shaping in the context of a personal rhythm. When considering communication, rhythm is also fundamental to the organization and co-ordination of internal processes, and externally between persons (Aldridge 1989, 1989a, 1991d).

Music Therapy and the Elderly

Much of the published work concerning music therapy with the elderly is concerned with group activity (Bryant 1991; Christie 1992; Olderog Millard and Smith 1989) and is generally used to expand socialization and communication skills, with the intention of reducing problems of social isolation and withdrawal, to encourage participants to interact purposefully with others, assist in expressing and communicating feelings and ideas, and to stimulate cognitive processes, thereby sharpening problem-solving skills. Additional goals also focus on sensory and muscular stimulation and gross and fine motor skill preservation (Segal 1990).

Clair (1990, 1991; Clair and Bernstein 1990, 1990a) has worked extensively with the elderly and found music therapy a valuable tool for working in groups to promote communicating, watching others, singing, interacting with an instrument, and sitting. Her main conclusions are that although the group members deteriorated markedly in cognitive, physical, and social capacities over an observation period of 15 months, they continued to participate in music activities. During the 30-minute sessions the group members consistently sat in chairs without physical restraints for the duration of each session, and interacted with others regardless of their deterioration. This was the only time in the week when they interacted with others (Clair and Bernstein 1990a). Indeed, for one 66-year-old man was it the sensory stimulation of music therapy that brought him out of his isolation such that he could participate with others, even if for a short while (Clair 1991).

Wandering, confusion and agitation are linked problems common to elderly patients living in hostels or special accommodation for Alzheimer's patients. A music therapist (Fitzgerald Cloutier 1993) has tested singing with an 81-year-old woman to see if it helped her to remain seated. After 20 singing sessions, the therapist read to the woman to compare the degree of attentiveness. While music therapy and reading sessions redirected the woman from wandering, the total time she sat for the music therapy sessions was double that of the reading sessions (214.3 mins vs 99.1 mins), and the time spent seated in the music therapy was more consistent than the episodes when she was being read to. When agitation occurs in such elderly women, then individualized music therapy appears to have a significantly calming effect (Gerdner and Swanson 1993). In terms of reducing repetitive behaviour, musical activity also reduces disruptive vocalizations (Casby and Holm 1994).

The above conclusions are supported by Groene (1993). Thirty residents (aged 60-91 years) of a special Alzheimer's unit, who exhibited wandering behaviour, were randomly assigned either to mostly music attention or to mostly reading attention groups, where they received one-to one attention. Those receiving music therapy remained seated longer than those in the reading sessions.

One of the central problems of the elderly is the loss of independence and self-esteem, and Palmer (1983, 1989) describes a programme of music therapy at a geriatric home designed to rebuild self-concept. For the 380 residents, ranging from those who were totally functional to those who needed total care, a programme was adapted to the capacities and needs of individual patients. Marching and dancing increased the ability of some patients to walk well; and for the non-ambulatory, kicking and stamping to music improved circulation and increased tolerance and strength. Sing-along sessions were used to encourage memory recall and promoted social interaction and appropriate social behaviour. (Palmer 1983, 1989). It was such social behaviour that Pollack (Pollack and Namazi 1992) reports as being accessible to improvement through group music therapy activities It is the participative element that appears to be valuable for communication, and the intention to participate that is at the core of the music therapy activity, which we will see in the following section.

Music therapy has also been used to focus on memory recall for songs and the spoken word (Prickett and Moore 1991). In ten elderly patients, whose diagnosis was probably Alzheimer's disease, words to songs were recalled dramatically better than spoken words or spoken information. Although long-familiar songs were recalled with greater accuracy than a newly presented song, most patients attempted to sing, hum, or keep time while the therapist sang. However, Smith (1991) suggests that it is factors such as tempo, length of seconds per word, and total number of words that might be more closely associated with lyric recall than the relative familiarity of the song selection.

In a further study of the effects of three treatment approaches, musically cued reminiscence, verbally cued reminiscence, and music alone, on the cognitive functioning of 12 female nursing home residents with Alzheimer's disease, changes in cognitive functioning were assessed by the differences between pre- and post-session treatment scores on the Mini-Mental State Examination. Comparisons were made for total scores and sub-scores for orientation, attention, and language. Musically cued and verbally cued reminiscence significantly increased language sub-section scores and musical activity alone significantly increased total scores (Smith 1986).

Music therapy with an Alzheimer's patient

Nordoff-Robbins music therapy is based upon the improvisation of music between therapist and patient (Nordoff and Robbins 1977). The music therapist plays the piano, improvising with the patient, who uses a range of instruments. This work often begins with an exploratory session using rhythmic instruments, in particular the drum and cymbal; progressing to the use of rhythmic/melodic instruments such as the chime bars, glockenspiel or xylophone; developing into work with melodic instruments (including the piano); and the voice. In this way of working the emphasis is on a series of musical improvisations during each session, and music is the vehicle for the therapy. Each session is audiotape-recorded, with the consent of the patient, and later analyzed and indexed as to musical content.

In the case example below music therapy is used as one modality of a comprehensive treatment package. The patient is seen on an outpatient basis for ten weekly sessions. Each session lasts for 40 minutes. She is unable to find her way on public transport and is brought to the hospital by her son.

Edith was a 55-year-old woman who came to the hospital for treatment. Her sister had died of Alzheimer's disease, and the family were concerned that she too was repeating her sister's demise as her memory became increasingly disturbed. She began playing the piano for family, friends and acquaintances at the age of 40, although without any formal studies, and, given this interest, music therapy appeared to have potential as an intervention adjuvant to medical treatment.

The patient was referred initially to the hospital when she, and her son, became aware of her own deteriorating condition, although the disease was in its early stages. At home she was experiencing difficulties in finding clothing and other things necessary for everday life. She could not cook for herself anymore and was unable to write her own signature. While wanting to speak, she experienced difficulty in finding words. It may be assumed that given the family background and her own understanding of her failings, the cognitive problem was exacerbated by depression.

Characteristics of the musical playing

RHYTHMIC PLAYING

In all ten sessions Edith demonstrated her ability to play, without the influence of her music therapist, a singular ordered rhythmic pattern in 4/4 time using two sticks on a single drum. This rhythmical pattern appeared in various forms and can be portrayed as seen in Figure 9.1. Example 1.

A feature of her rhythmical playing was that in nearly all the sessions, during the progress of an improvisation, the patient would let control of the rhythmic pattern slip such that it became progressively imprecise, losing both its form and liveliness. The initial impulse of her rhythmical playing, which was clear and precise, gradually deteriorated as she lost concentration and ability to persevere with the task in hand. However, when the therapist offered an overall musical structure during the course of the improvisation, the patient could regain her precision of rhythm. It could well be that to sustain perception an overall rhythmical structure is necessary, and it is this musical gestalt, that is, the possibility of providing an overall organizing structure of time, which fails in Alzheimer's disease.

The patient reacted quickly to changes in time and different rhythmic forms, and incorporated these within her playing. Significantly, she reacted fluently in her playing to changes from 4/4 time to 3/4 time, often remarking, 'Now it's a waltz...'. With typical well-known rhythmical forms, e.g. the Habaner rhythm, in combination with characteristic melodic phrases, she laughed, breathed deeply and played with stronger, more thoughtful intent.

These rhythmical improvisations, using different drums and cymbals, were played in later sessions on two instruments together. The patient had no difficulty in controlling and maintaining her grip of the beaters. Similarly she showed no difficulty in co-ordinating parallel or alternate handed

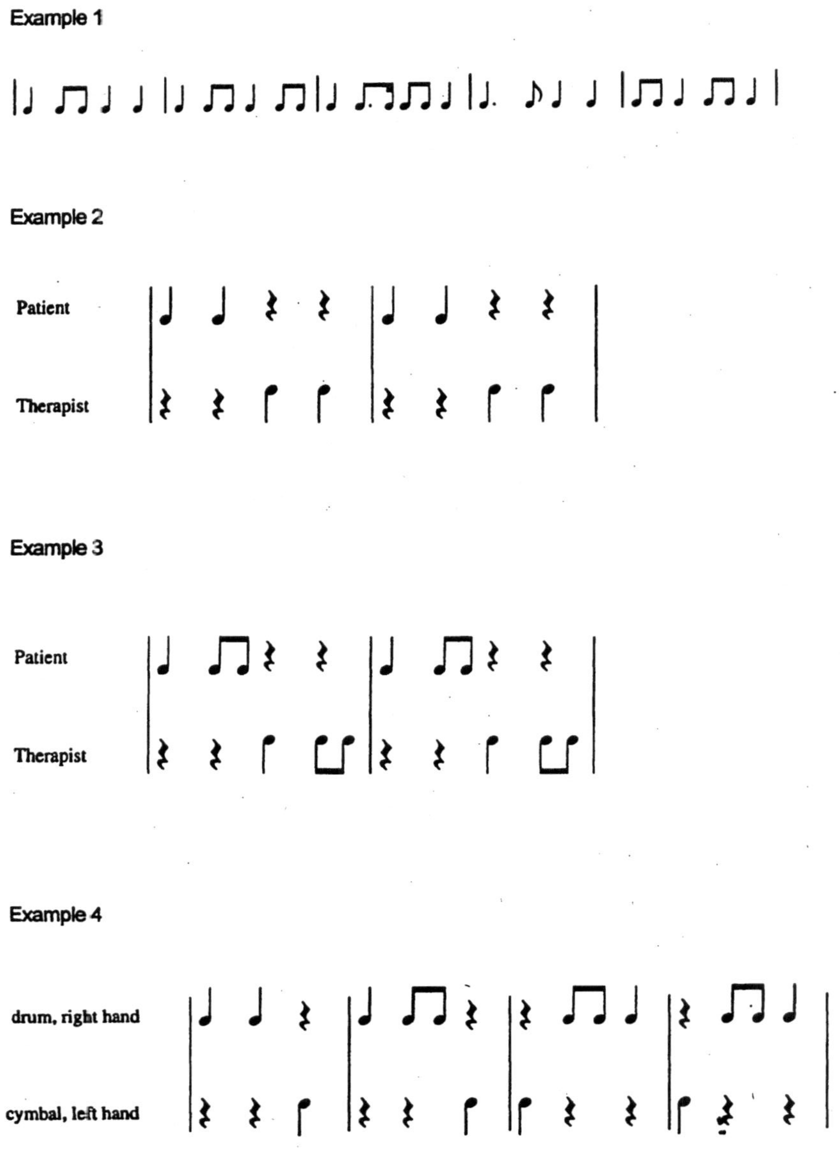

Example 1

Example 2

Patient

Therapist

Example 3

Patient

Therapist

Example 4

drum, right hand

cymbal, left hand

Figure 9.1 Examples of musical playing

playing on a single instrument, although she played mostly with a quick tempo (120 beats per minute). However, the introduction of two instruments brought a major difficulty for the patient, who stood disorientated before the instruments, unable to integrate them both in the playing. It was only with instructions and direction from the therapist that the patient was able to co-ordinate right–left playing on two instruments; changes in the pattern of the playing were also difficult to realize (see Figure 9.1, Examples 2 and 3).

Throughout the improvisations the inherent musical ability of the patient, in terms of tempo (ritardando, accelerando, rubato) and dynamic (loud and soft), was expressed whenever she had the opportunity to.

MELODIC PLAYING

Melody is an expression of motion which arises and decays from moment to moment. In this motion the size of the intervals provides a melodic tension which itself has a dynamic power. The experience of melody is itself an experience of form. As a melody begins there is the possibility of grasping a sense of the immediacy of the whole form, and preparing for the aesthetic pleasure of deviations from what is expected. This element of tension between the expected and the unpredictable has been at the heart of musical composition for the last two hundred years. In addition, it is melody that leads the music from the rhythmical world of feeling into the cognitive world of imagination.

When Edith played her melodies were always lively. She knew many folk songs from earlier times and was able to sing them alone. After only a few notes played by the therapist on the piano she could associate those notes with a well known tune. However, when she tried to play a complete melody on the piano or other melody instrument, it proved impossible. Although beginning spontaneously and fluently she had difficulty in completing a known melody.

Melody instruments like the metallophone and the xylophone, which were previously unknown to the patient, remained forever strange. At the introduction of a new melody she would often seek a previously known melody rather than face the insecurity of an unknown improvised melody. When the therapist sat opposite her and showed her which notes to play she was able to follow the therapist's finger movements. When presented with a limited range of tones she also had difficulty in playing them, which may have been compounded by visuo-spatial difficulties, in that it is easier to strike the surface of a drum than the limited precise surfaces of adjacent chime bars.

At the beginning of the very first session after entering the therapy room, Edith set her eyes on the piano and began spontaneously to play 'Happy is the Gypsy Life'. She easily accompanied this song harmonically with triads and thirds. The second song which she attempted to play proved more difficult as she failed to find the subdominant, whereupon she broke off from the playing and remarked '…that always catches me out'. This pattern of spontaneously striking up a melody and then breaking off when the harmony failed was to be repeated whenever she tried other songs like 'Happy Birthday' and 'Horch was kommt von draußen rein'. She showed a fine musical sensitivity for the appropriate harmony, which was not always at her disposal to be played. In the playing of the drum her musical sensitivity in her reactions to the contrasting sound qualities of major and minor was reduced, but overall she had a pronounced perception of this harmonic realm of music. We see here, as in tests of language functioning, that the production, in this case of music, is impaired while perception remains.

Changes in the musical playing of the patient

In the rhythmical playing on drum and cymbal the therapist attempted to develop the patient's attention span through the use of short repeated musical patterns and changes in key, volume and tempo. She hoped to through changes in the sound to steer the patient to maintaining a stable musical form. This technique helped the patient to maintain a rhythmical pattern and brought her to the stage in which she could express her self, more strongly, musically. Beyond the emphasis on the basic beat in the music, the therapist searched for other ways to respond to, and develop a variety in, rhythmical pattern by moving away from the repetitive pattern played by the patient. In a quick tempo the patient was able to maintain a basic beat for a certain time. As soon as the tempo changed and became slower, or the music varied with the introduction of a semiquaver, the stable element of the music was disturbed and took on a superficial character.

A further change in the improvising was shown when the patient recognized, and could repeat rhythmical patterns which were frequently realized as a musical dialogue and brought into a musical context. In the last session of therapy the patient was able to change her playing in this way such that she could express herself more strongly by bringing her thoughtful and expressive playing into line (see Figure 9.1, Example 4).

A crucial point in the music came when she chose to play for a bar on the cymbal. Although after a while she trusted herself to play without help on two instruments, she could not get to grips with a new personal initiative on these instruments. This was also reflected in her continuing difficulty what were initially strange instruments, like the temple blocks. She also expressed her insecurity as to how to proceed, and needed instructions about what to do next.

She displayed few changes in her dynamic playing. She reacted to dynamic contrasts and transitions, but powerful *forte* playing was only achieved in the last session. At times her playing had a uniform quality of attack which gave it a mechanistic and immovable character. For this patient it was not possible to build a freely improvised melody from a selection of fixed songs; therefore she chose the free form of improvising on rhythm instruments. It was as if she was a prisoner of the search for melodies of known tones.

INTENTIONAL PLAYING

From the first session of therapy the patient made quite clear her intent to sit at the piano, and play whatever melodies she chose and find the appropriate accompaniments. This wish and the corresponding will-power to achieve this end were shown in all the sessions. It was possible to use this impetus to play as a source for improvisation. In the sixth session Edith improvised a rhythmical piece in 4/4 time, which the therapist then transformed with a melodic phrase. At the end of the phrase the patient laughed with joy at the success of her playing and asked to play it again. The original lapses and slips in the form of the rhythmical playing could be carried by the intent and expression with which she played. While her overall intention to play was preserved, her attention to that playing, the concentration necessary for musical production and the perseverance required for completing a sequence of phrases progressively failed, and were dependent on the overall musical structure offered by the therapist.

Clinical changes

At the end of the treatment period, which also used homeopathic medicine, she was able to cook for herself and could find her own things about the house. The psychiatrist responsible for her therapeutic management reported an overall improvement in her interest in what was going on around her, and in particular that she maintained attention to visitors and conversations. The patient regained the ability to write her signature, although she could only write slowly. While wanting to speak, she still experienced difficulty in finding words.

It appears that music therapy has a beneficial effect on the quality of life of this patient, and that some of the therapeutic effect may have been brought about by treating the depression. While the patient came to the sessions with the intention of playing her ability to take initiatives was impaired, mirroring the state of her home life, where she wanted to look after herself yet was unable to take initiatives. The stimulus to take initiatives was seen as an important feature of the music therapy by the therapist, and appears to have a correlate in the way in which the patient began to take initiatives in her daily life. Active music making also promotes interaction between the persons involved, thereby promoting initiatives in communication which the patient also enjoyed, particularly when she accomplished a complete improvisation. Furthermore, the implications for the maintenance of memory by actively making music is significant. As Crystal *et al.* (1989) found in an 82-year-old musician with Alzheimer's disease, the ability to play previously learned piano compositions from memory was preserved, although the man was unable to identify the composer or titles of each work; and the ability to learn the new skill of mirror reading was also preserved while the man was unable to recall or recognize new information.

A contra-indication for music therapy with such patients, who are aware of their problems, is that the awareness of further deterioration in cognitive abilities (as this patient experienced in her piano playing) may exacerbate any underlying depression and demotivate the patient to continue. For Edith, not being able to find the appropriate harmonies to well-known tunes, that she could play when she was younger was yet another sign of her deteriorating status.

Music Therapy as a Sensitive Tool for Assessment

If we are unsure as to the normal process of cognitive loss in aging, we are even more in the dark as to the normal musical playing abilities of adults. The literature suggests that musical activities are preserved while other cognitive functions fail. Alzheimers patients, despite aphasia and memory loss, continue to sing old songs and to dance to past tunes when given the chance. Indeed, fun and entertainment are all part and parcel of daily living for the elderly living in special accommodation (Glassman 1983; Jonas 1991; Kartman 1990; Smith 1992). Quality of life expectations become paramount in any management strategy, and music therapy appears to play an important role in enhancing the ability to take part actively in daily life (Lipe 1991; Rosling and Kitchen 1992). However, the production and improvisation of music appear to fail in the same way in which language fails. Unfortunately no established guidelines as to the normal range of improvised music playing of adults is available.

Improvised music therapy appears to offer the opportunity to supplement mental state examinations in areas where those examinations are lacking (see

Tables 9.4 and 9.5). First, it is possible to ascertain the fluency of musical production. Second, intentionality, attention to, concentration on and perseverance with the task in hand are important features of producing musical improvisations and susceptible to being heard in the musical playing. Third, episodic memory can be tested in the ability to repeat short rhythmic and melodic phrases. The inability to build such phrases may be attributed to problems with memory or to an as yet unknown factor. This unknown factor is possibly involved with the organization of time structures. If rhythmic structure is an overall context for musical production, and the ground structure for perception, it can be hypothesized that it is this overarching structure which begins to fail in Alzheimer's patients. A loss of rhythmical context would explain why patients are able to produce and persevere with rhythmic and melodic playing when offered an overall structure by the therapist. Such a hypothesis would tie in with the musical hierarchy proposed by Swartz (Swartz et al. 1989, p.154), and would suggest a global failing in cognition while localized lower abilities are retained. However, the hierarchy of musical perceptual levels proposed by Swartz may need to be further sub-divided into classifications of music reception and music production.

Table 9.5 Musical elements of assessment and examples of improvised playing

Musical elements of assessment	Examples of improvised playing
testing of musical skills; rhythm, melody, harmony, dynamic, phrasing, articulation	improvisation using rhythmic instruments (drum and cymbal) singly or in combination
	improvisation using melodic instruments
	singing and playing folk songs with harmonic accompaniment
cortical disorder testing: visuo-spatial skills	playing tuned percussion (metallophone, xylophone, chime bars) demanding precise movements
cortical disorder testing: ability to perform complex motor tasks (including grip and right–left co-ordination	alternate playing of cymbal and drum using a beater in each hand
	co-ordinated playing of cymbal and drum using a beater in each hand
testing for progressive memory disintegration	the playing of short rhythmic and melodic phrases within the session, and in successive sessions
	the playing of a rhythmic pattern deteriorates when unaccompanied by the therapist as does the ability to complete a known melody, although tempo remains
motivation to sustain playing improvised music, to achieve musical goals and preserve in maintaining musical form	the patient exhibits the intention to play the piano from the onset of therapy and maintains this intent throughout the course of treatment
'intention' a feature of improvised musical playing	
concentration on the improvised playing and attention to the instruments	the patient loses concentration when playing, with qualitative loss in the musical playing and lack of precision in the beating of rhythmical instruments
flexibility in musical (including instrumental) changes	initially the musical playing is limited to a tempo of 120 Bp and a characteristic pattern but this is responsive to change
ability to play improvised music influenced by previous musical training	although the patient has a musical background this is only of help when she perceives the musical playing; it is little influence in the improvised playing
sensitive to small changes	musical changes in tempo, dynamic, timbre and articulation which at first are missing are gradually developed
ability to interpret musical context and relationship	the patient develops the ability to play in a musical dialogue with the therapist demanding both a refined musical perception and the ability of musical production

Music therapy appears to offer a sensitive assessment tool (see Table 9.5). It tests those prosodic elements of speech production which are not lexically dependent. Furthermore, it can be used to assess those areas of functioning, both receptive and productive, not covered adequately by other test instruments; i.e. fluency, perseverance in context, attention, concentration and intentionality. In addition it provides a form of therapy which may stimulate cognitive activities such that areas subject to progressive failure are maintained. Certainly the anecdotal evidence suggests that quality of life of Alzheimer's patients is significantly improved with music therapy (McCloskey 1985, 1990; Tyson 1989) accompanied by the overall social benefits of acceptance and sense of belonging gained by communicating with others (Morris 1986; Segal 1990).

Prinsley recommends music therapy for geriatric care as it reduces the individual prescription of tranquilizing medication, reduces the use of hypnotics on the hospital ward, and helps overall rehabilitation. He recommends that music therapy be based on treatment objectives: the social goals of interaction co-operation; psychological goals of mood improvement and self-expression; intellectual goals of the stimulation of speech and organization of mental processes; and the physical goals of sensory stimulation and motor integration (Prinsley 1986). Such goals as stimulation of the individual, promoting involvement in social activity, identifying specific individualized behavioural targets, and emphasizing the maintenance of specific memory functions are repeated throughout the music therapy literature (Prange 1990; Smith 1990; Summer 1981). Similarly, Smith (1990a) recommends behavioural interventions targeted at the more common behavioural problems (e.g., disorientation, age-related changes in social activity, sleep disturbances) of institutionalized elderly persons. In a matched control study of music therapy, or no music therapy, in two nursing homes, life satisfaction and self-esteem were significantly improved in the home where the residents participated in the musical activities (VanderArk, Newman and Bell 1983).

In terms of research, single-case within-subject designs with Alzheimer's appear to be a feasible way forward to assess individual responses to musical interventions in the clinical realm. Such studies would depend upon careful clinical examinations, mental state examinations and musical assessments. Unfortunately most of the literature concerning cognition and musical perception is based upon audition and not musical production. Like other authors we suggest that the production of music, as is the production of language, is a complex global phenomenon as yet poorly understood. The understanding of musical production may well offer a clue to the ground structure of language and communication in general. It is research in this realm of perception which is urgent not only for the understanding of Alzheimer's patients but in the general context of cognitive deficit and brain behaviour. It may be, as Berman (1981) suggests, that the non-dominant hemisphere is a reserve of functions in case of regional failure and this functionality can be stimulated to delay the progression of degenerative disease. Furthermore, it is important to point out that when the overall rhythmic pattern failed, the patient was able to maintain her beating in tempo. A similar situation applies in coma patients who cannot co-ordinate basic life pulses within a rhythmic context and thereby regain consciousness (Aldridge 1991b; Aldridge, Gustorff and Hannich 1990). We may need to address in future research the co-ordinating role of rhythm in human cognition and consciousness, whether it be in persons who are losing cognitive abilities, or in persons who are attempting to gain cognitive abilities.

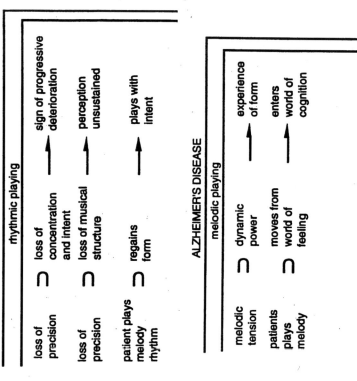

Figure 9.2 Constitutive rules relating to the rhythmic and melodic improvised playing of Alzheimer's patients

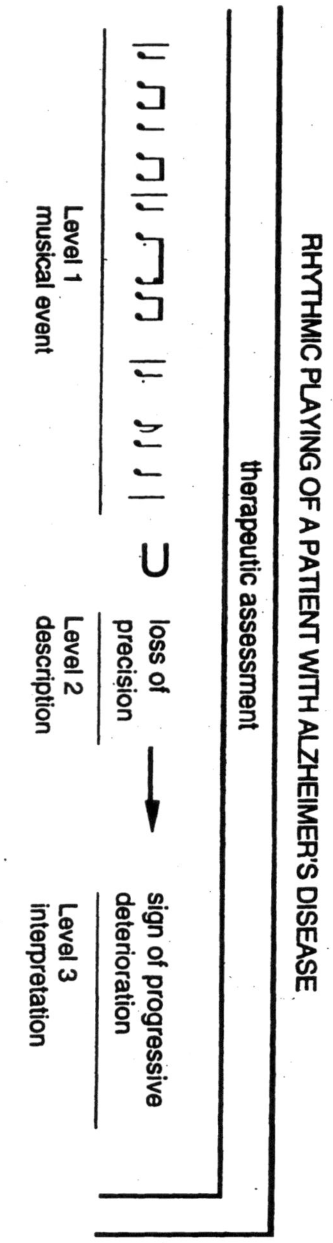

As a research point we can see how the use of texts relating to clinical practice can be used to build up a picture of clinical reasoning, as we also saw at the end of the last chapter. In this case we have constitutive rules (see Figure 9.2) relating to the rhythmical playing, where rhythmical precision is seen as a sign of progressive deterioration and evidence of a loss of concentration or loss of intent. Conversely, the maintenance of rhythm is construed as regaining form and evidence of playing with intent.

It is not only texts themselves that can be used to elicit meanings. We can see graphically in Figure 9.3 how a 'musical text' can be used as the basis for therapeutic assessment using a constitutive rules perspective. This assessment is based upon the same musical material as seen in Figure 9.1, Example 1 and the constitutive rule seen in Figure 9.2. By presenting material in this way we have a flexible means by which musical understandings can be constructed and demonstrated. That musical texts can be used is an important bridge between the experiences of the musician as therapist and the musician as researcher. This is a vertical understanding where level 1 is the musical experience itself, that is then 'neutrally' described at level 2, and interpreted at level 3.

Using these elements of rhythmical playing we can construct regulative, horizontal rules as they refer to the therapy process in time. In Figure 9.4 we see how when a repetitive pattern, which is interpreted as an inability on the part of the patient to express herself, is played, the therapist varies her own rhythmical pattern. If the patient recognizes such a change in rhythmical pattern, she is able to express herself communicatively and maintain the therapeutic dialogue. Having both a vertical form of analysis and a horizontal form of analysis allows us in some ways to display the element of performance that we have in a musical score. Vertically we have harmony and horizontally we have a substrate of time. In my method we have a vertical complexity of elicited understandings that are constructed horizontally as descriptions of therapeutic development. The benefit of this approach is that we can be clear about the material we are using as a basis for our description, and elucidate the stages of interpretation as they move away from the experience itself.

RHYTHMIC PLAYING OF A PATIENT WITH ALZHEIMER'S DISEASE

therapeutic assessment

Level 1 musical event	Level 2 description	Level 3 interpretation
♩ ♫ ♩ ♫ ♩ ♬ ♫ ♩. ♪♩ ♩	⊃ loss of precision	→ sign of progressive deterioration

Figure 9.3 Textual understandings of a musical phenomenon in therapeutic assessment

context of close friendship

| patient plays a repetitive pattern | ⊃ | { invalid: loses musical contact } | inability to express herself | ⊃ | vary rhythmical pattern |
| patient recognises rhythmical pattern | ⊃ | { valid: plays dialogue } | able to express herself communicatively | ⊃ | maintain dialogue |

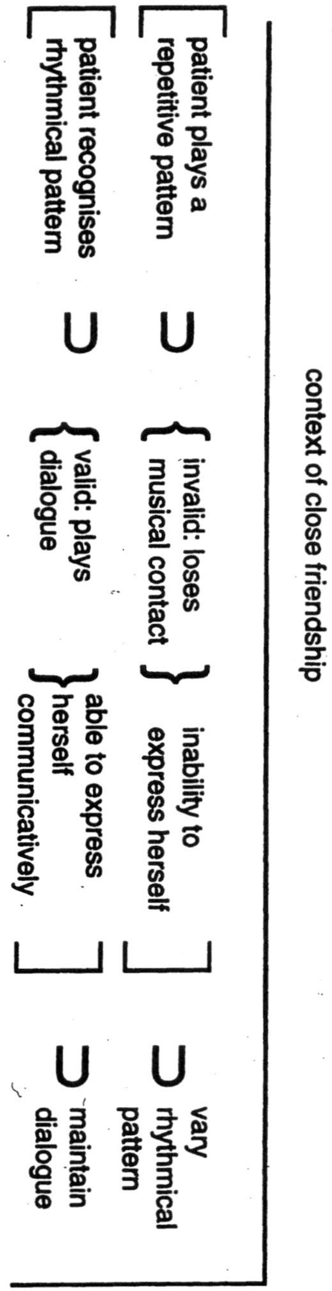

Figure 9.4 Regulative rules relating to the rhythmic improvised playing of Alzheimer's patients and its meaning for dialogue in therapy

CASE ELEVEN

Preverbal Communication Through Music To Overcome A Child's Language Disorder

AMELIA OLDFIELD, M.Phil., R.M.Th.
Music Therapist
Child Development Centre
Addenbrookes Hospital
Cambridge, Great Britain

Abstract. This case describes two years of group and individual music therapy for a five-year old boy with a language disorder. A wide variety of music therapy techniques are used, all aimed at motivating Jamie to communicate, either nonverbally or verbally.

BACKGROUND INFORMATION

Jamie is the only child of very caring and capable parents. As a young child, he appeared somewhat smaller and slower than other children in his age group, and eye contact was often difficult. His mother reports that, as a baby, he did not babble at all, and used very few other non verbal means of communication, such as pointing. He was always a very quiet child, and only occasionally and inconsistently used words.

At two and a half, Jamie found mixing with other children very difficult, and would often appear to be in a world of his own. However, he did not present any major behaviour problems and was able to play by himself. At this stage, the pediatrician reassured his parents that Jamie's development was not necessarily abnormal. Nevertheless, both his parents and other professionals involved continued to be concerned. Jamie's health visitor wrote a report at this time describing him as: "rather worrying in a not altogether definable way."

When Jamie was three, he was assessed by a clinical psychologist who suggested that, although his overall intelligence was within the normal range, there were great discrepancies in his skills. He had high scores for manipulative skills, such as putting puzzles together, and marked problems with both comprehension and expressive language. Jamie's hearing was also tested at this stage as he seemed both oversensitive to some sounds and oblivious to others. It was found to be within the normal range.

Jamie was then referred to the Child Development Centre where he began having regular sessions with the speech therapist. He also started attending a small play therapy group of four children. This is a structured group run by a clinical psychologist where the emphasis is on encouraging social integration. She reports that, over a period of a year, Jamie took part in more group activities and managed to overcome some of his fears and obsessions. He became more able to tolerate the screaming of another child in the group, for example, which he had been terrified of at first.

When Jamie was four, he was assessed by the local specialist consultant in child psychiatry. He suggested that, although Jamie's language was very restricted, he was showing signs of imagination. In spite of his difficulties, Jamie seemed to be developing an understanding of the meaning of words; therefore, there seemed to be potential for the development of abstract thought. The psychiatrist felt that Jamie's social problems and occasional disturbed behaviour were the result of his great difficulties in understanding social practices. Thus, he diagnosed Jamie as having a specific language disorder. In his opinion, there was no evidence of autism or an autistic like disorder.

The term "language disorder" generally describes an atypical pattern of language acquisition and development. Unlike children whose language may be with language disorders have both a delayed and deviant pattern of development (Webster & McConnell, 1987). Deviancy or disruption may occur in any or all aspects of speech and language: context, form or use; or as a result of a distorted interaction between them (Bloom & Lahey, 1978). Jamie had difficulties in all these aspects of language development, and particularly in the area of language use. This affected his ability to establish social relationships and to relate to the world around him.

A speech therapy report written a couple of months later agreed with this diagnosis. The speech therapist explained that Jamie had difficulties processing sentences in order to comply with a task. Although he responded to everyday instructions, he was reacting more to the context and the routine than to the actual meaning of the instruction. Jamie could say quite long sentences, but had difficulties learning when to use these sentences appropriately. He was mainly silent and only made occasional, spontaneous, self-generated comments.

From the age of four to the present, Jamie has been attending a small language unit for eight children with language disorders. The children in this class receive very specialised schooling, and the main focus of the work is on improving their language difficulties. The class is based in an ordinary school, and the children are integrated into other "normal" classes at times, as well as working together as a group at other times. Both the teacher from the unit and Jamie's parents are still unsure about Jamie's diagnosis, and suspect that he might have some autistic tendencies.

At five, Jamie was referred to me at the Child Development Centre by his language unit teacher. She had noticed that Jamie seemed to respond to words in songs more easily than spoken words. She hoped that I might devise some exercises for both her and Jamie's parents to use with him to improve his speech.

MUSIC THERAPY ASSESSMENT

I saw Jamie for three consecutive weekly, half hour music therapy assessment sessions. The purpose of these sessions was: (1) to determine whether music therapy would be a useful way of helping Jamie, and if so to roughly outline what kind of direction this treatment might take; (2) to see whether he responded to me in a different way through music and thus to shed new light on some of his difficulties; and (3) to suggest ways in which both his teacher and his parents could use music with him.

Jamie presented as a small, attractive looking boy with a serious and often puzzled expression. He had no difficulties separating from his mother, and showed no anxiety about coming into the music therapy room with me. He seemed to understand simple requests or comments such as: "Here is a chair for you, Jamie" or "Shall we finish this now?" He was able to point to me and to choose an instrument for me on request. He could listen to my playing and also play himself and was good at taking turns with me. He made very few verbal contributions or vocalisations, but at one point suddenly and surprisingly, made an appropriate comment about an instrument, saying in a very clear voice, "There's a ball inside."

Jamie particularly enjoyed activities where we teased one another, or where he could "control" me by, for example, making me jump when he played the drum. At these times, he would look straight at me and have a beautiful mischievous smile.

Jamie seemed pleased to listen to the music and the songs I improvised on the piano and the clarinet. He anticipated the ends of harmonic phrases by looking up at the appropriate moment, and showed that he knew and recognised a number of songs by occasionally filling in words when I left a gap. For example, I would sing: "London bridge is falling....," and Jamie would say: "Down!" Sometimes he would sing the words at the correct pitch to fit in with the song.

Jamie enjoyed playing the instruments, and would spontaneously explore various ways of playing them in a creative way. For example: he seemed to experiment with the different sounds the drumstick made on various parts of the drum, and played the cabasa in a number of ways, stroking and rattling the beads as well as shaking the whole instrument.

Jamie generally seemed to prefer the quieter instruments. He did not appear particularly frightened of loud sounds, but would blink slightly anxiously when they occurred. With a little encouragement, he could join in and enjoy both quiet and loud improvisations. He was able to follow dynamic changes when we improvised together, but had more difficulty following rhythmic changes. He appeared to be able to play in a regular pulse for short periods, but the pulse was hesitant and gave his playing a slightly tentative feeling.

Jamie found it difficult to move freely or spontaneously to music. His physical reactions were slow, and he needed encouragement to do things such as march or jump to the music.

Jamie seemed to be developing a positive relationship with me. He was at ease playing the musical instruments, and was able to both listen to and contribute musical ideas during our improvisations. I felt he would benefit from a situation where he could communicate with an adult without having either to understand spoken language or use words himself. The areas I thought we could work on were: increasing his motivation to communicate with another person; providing an opportunity for Jamie to vocalise freely and spontaneously; increasing Jamie's confidence and enabling him to speed up his reactions so they were more spontaneous. I therefore recommended that he should have weekly individual music therapy treatment for at least six months.

Jamie appeared to be more spontaneous in his communication with me during our sessions than he was with other adults. This was probably because far less speech was necessary in my sessions than in other situations. The fact that he was more at ease in this non verbal situation seemed to confirm the diagnosis of language disorder. After reading Jamie's notes, I had expected him to be more sensitive to loud sounds and was surprised when he did not seem to mind hitting the drum very loudly. On reflection, however, it became clear that it was unexpected and unexplained loud noises that particularly troubled Jamie, and not loud sounds that he knew were about to occur or sounds which he himself produced or controlled.

I did not think that it would be beneficial to give Jamie's parents or his teacher structured musical exercises to improve his speech. I felt the priority was to help Jamie feel at ease with a non verbal means of communication, so that he would eventually become more spontaneous in his efforts to communicate. I also thought that Jamie should be encouraged to enjoy making sounds and vocalising without the pressure of using the correct word or structure. Jamie had never babbled or experimented with sounds as a baby, and I thought that he needed to discover the fun of producing sounds. I therefore suggested that both his parents and his teacher should encourage Jamie to vocalise in any way, and that they should try to engage him in playful vocal dialogues. I also suggested they do "toddler" like rhymes such as "Incy Wincy Spider" or "Round and Round the Garden" with him, so that Jamie could laugh at them with an adult, and learn to enjoy communicating in a simple way.

TREATMENT PROCESS

Phase One: Introductory Group Work

Unfortunately, I did not have any spaces available to see Jamie for individual music therapy sessions immediately, and he was therefore put on a waiting list. As it happened, however, I had already arranged to see the group of children in the language unit that Jamie attended for a a twelve week period, starting four weeks after I had finished the assessment on Jamie. I was, therefore, able to observe and work with Jamie in a group setting before I started to work with him individually.

The group sessions occurred once a week, lasted approximately forty minutes and went on for one school term (twelve weeks). Both the teacher and the welfare assistant took part, and I reviewed our work with the teacher every week, directly after the session.

All eight children in the group were diagnosed as having language disorders. Jamie, however, was shyer and more withdrawn than the other children. The group sessions had two or three specific aims for each child. These were determined jointly by the teaching staff and myself after a couple of "exploratory" sessions. Generally, the goals were: to provide a

and difficulties, and to give the teaching staff ideas of musical activities to use in the classroom. Given my large case load, this is one of the only ways I can provide some input to a large number of children.

The musical material and the activities used in the group would vary from week to week, and was largely determined by the aims for individual children. Although suggestions for activities for the following week's session might be made when we reviewed our sessions, I would always remain flexible and would usually choose activities on the spur of the moment, based on the children's reactions and moods on any particular day. Nevertheless, I would always start off with a familiar greeting song and end with a "good bye" activity. Throughout the group I would often alternate between activities which involved the group as a whole and activities which involved one or two children playing on their own. An example of a general group activity would be: the whole group plays together on various percussion instruments led by improvised music I play on the piano. When the piano stops the children all move around and exchange instruments. Playing starts again when the piano begins. An example of an activity involving two children would be: two children sit back to back in the middle of the circle, each with a different instrument, and are asked to have a musical conversation. The rest of the group is encouraged to listen. I would also try to alternate between activities where the children were actively involved in playing instruments, singing or dancing, and activities which required concentrated listening without so much active involvement.

After observing Jamie within the group for two sessions it became clear that he was much more withdrawn in this setting than he had been with me or a one to one basis. We therefore decided that individual aims for Jamie would be: to help him concentrate and listen to instructions; to encourage him to communicate in any way with either adults or children; and to encourage him to make eye contact and to make any vocal sounds.

During the first five sessions, Jamie seemed to understand some but by no means all the instructions, and was able to take part in a few activities only. He seemed to enjoy choosing and playing instruments, but was unable to pass an instrument to another child. He did not understand the games involving drama where we pretended to put a tambourine to sleep, for example, and he needed help whenever any of the activities involved moving around the room. He made little eye contact, and only used a few sporadic single words. He often appeared to be in a world of his own, and made no efforts to communicate with either the children or the adults in the group.

During the sixth session, there was a marked change in Jamie. He suddenly appeared more at ease, smiling happily and looking straight at me when I played the clarinet. He was able to contribute some vocal noises to a song where all the children were suggesting different sounds, and even gave his instrument to another child when this was suggested by him. From this "conduct" by pointing to other children and adults. He would listen to instructions better, and he began to take part in even quite complicated activities. He started using more words, both on request and spontaneously. Both Jamie's teacher and I were pleased with Jamie's progress within the group, however we felt that he would benefit even more from individual sessions.

Phase Two: Individual Sessions

Two weeks after the group finished, a space became available, and I started to see Jamie for regular weekly individual music therapy sessions. Although he had made some progress during the group sessions, the aims remained the same: to increase communication, eye contact, vocalization, and spontaneity. As Jamie's use of words had improved, I continued to keep a record of both spontaneous speech and the speech he used to answer direct questions. Nevertheless, I still did not want Jamie to feel that this was the focus of our sessions, or that I was putting pressure on him to talk.

The individual sessions lasted half an hour, and were held at the same time and in the same room every week. After each session, I would briefly discuss with Jamie's mother how he was progressing.

Like the group sessions I would start and end each session with familiar "hello" and "good bye" activities. In between, sessions would vary from week to week depending on Jamie's mood, on what had happened the previous week, and in what particular areas I felt I should be helping Jamie. In general, I would spend some time encouraging him to choose instruments or activities, and then attempt to follow and support his playing; at other times, I would make suggestions myself. For example, I might suggest that we take turns playing the glockenspiel, and pass each other the stick when our turn was finished; or I might encourage Jamie to play three different instruments that would make me jump, wave my arms or shake my head depending on which instrument he played; or I might suggest that we have a "noise" dialogue on the kazoos. I would always try to give each of our activities a structure with a clear ending. I would prepare Jamie for each ending by saying "One more turn each," or "Try to find a way to finish this off."

Jamie was at ease with me straight away, and was delighted with the familiar "hello" song on the guitar. This led to a sung "noise" dialogue accompanied by shared guitar strumming. Jamie initiated vocal sounds such as "Hey" with great delight, and would then laugh happily. He gradually added "funny" faces to these noises, particularly when I encouraged him by mirroring and extending his contributions. Jamie was clearly excited and pleased with these humorous exchanges, and I was able to keep them mischievous and creative rather than just silly. These vocal dialogues immediately followed my greeting to him, and became a regular part of our sessions. Sometimes Jamie would respond immediately, and at other times it

seemed to take him a little time to relax and allow himself to enjoy this basic form of communication.

Over the first six months of treatment, Jamie continued to become more spontaneous in any familiar activities that we shared. However, he would revert to a blank, puzzled expression whenever I introduced anything new. I, therefore, made a conscious effort not to allow the sessions to become too stereotyped and, while always keeping some familiarity, tried to vary the way we played together, always introducing at least one new idea every week.

As Jamie became more able to make his own choices and contributions, he started to use more single words or two word phrases, both spontaneously and in answer to direct questions. In a conducting game, Jamie gradually managed to give me more and more complicated instructions, such as "Play the drum and the cymbal loudly." Nevertheless, his speech was still far from normal, and at times he would be unable to say something as simple as "Goodbye, Amelia" or tell me which day of the week he came for music therapy.

Jamie still found it difficult to move quickly or spontaneously. However, he started to enjoy and understand imaginative games where I pretended to fall asleep on the piano, or I hid from him in the room. At these times he could react quite fast to "Wake me up!" or "Find me!"

Jamie continued to enjoy experimenting with various ways of playing the instruments, and seemed to become more sensitive to various tone colours. He began to listen much more carefully to the sounds he produced. His sense of rhythm also improved. He would enjoy improvising on the piano and quickly became able to pick out tunes such as "Ba-Ba Black Sheep," "Happy Birthday To You" and "Puff the Magic Dragon." As he apparently wanted to learn more tunes, and enjoyed playing the piano, I arranged for him to start piano lessons with a teacher who had an interest in children with special needs. This also meant that there could be a clear separation between my work and more formal piano teaching.

As Jamie gradually became more spontaneous in his contributions, he also developed some slightly obsessive behaviours, such as repeating a tune fragment again and again, or insisting on holding the drumstick in a certain way. Nevertheless, he could be distracted from these obsessions relatively easily. As time went on, these rituals seemed to die away, and were replaced by ordinary "toddler like" naughtiness and rebelliousness. The only slightly strange behaviour that did occasionally creep back was that of Jamie "telling off" his right hand for misbehaving.

By the end of six months of individual music therapy sessions, Jamie had made great progress, and the aims set out at the beginning of our work together had been achieved. Progress had also been noticed at school, and at home Jamie's parents were delighted with his greater willingness and ability to communicate. However, they were also finding him a great deal naughtier and less easy to manage.

I therefore decided that, as I had developed such a good rapport with Jamie, I would continue to see him for another four months with a view to helping both Jamie and his parents to cope with these new "naughty" behaviours. I also thought that his communication skills could be further improved.

Phase Three: A Slightly New Direction

Aims for the last four months of treatment were: to diminish silly behaviours such as screaming or deliberately throwing objects; to encourage longer spontaneous and creative dialogues with me (nonverbal and verbal); and to help Jamie to answer questions appropriately (and not let him divert me from this).

When dealing with Jamie's "naughty" behaviours, I felt it was important to explain what I thought about these behaviours, and why I was responding in a particular way. I told him that we would work out ways of stopping his naughty behaviours together. At times, I would smile at him, and tell him in a "teasing" way that I thought he was trying to be naughty. At other times, I would suggest to him that it was easier to opt out of an activity and be naughty, than to continue our work. When he threw an object, I would take his hand and physically help him to pick it up again, saying that it was important for us both to make the naughty behaviour "better."

Occasionally he would get "stuck" when asked to do something and say "I can't." In this case I would either help him physically (and comment that I was giving him a "helping hand"), or I would say that perhaps what I had asked Jamie to do was too difficult. This approach seemed to work well. He remained mischievous but became more accepting of direction, and would allow himself to be diverted from whatever was causing a problem more easily.

During the last few sessions, Jamie sometimes became "moody," and on one occasion, he cried when he did not have time to play an instrument he had wanted to play. He seemed relieved to be told that there was nothing wrong with being sad and crying.

During the last four months, Jamie continued to make progress in his communication skills. By the end of my time with him he was able to hold ordinary conversations with me. He would initiate a conversation and ask appropriate questions. However, he would still sometimes need encouragement to answer questions.

Overall, the progress he made during that year was remarkable. From a quiet often mouse-like child, he had become a vocal, boisterous child, often full of mischief and fun.

DISCUSSION AND CONCLUSIONS

In the first instance, the musical instruments and our music-making interested Jamie, and motivated him to be actively involved with me. This enabled me to start building up a relationship with him which was initially based on shared enjoyment of the music and the musical activities. Jamie was able to maintain this positive relationship with me because I used very little speech in our assessment sessions. He could, therefore, relax and simply enjoy being with me. We were playing music together and communicating through sound, but very few specific words needed to be said or understood. It was the use of music as a means of communication which was essential at this point, and this could only have been achieved through music therapy.

For the first few group sessions, Jamie again became very shy and withdrawn. This was probably because far more speech was necessary in this situation to understand what was going on and what was expected of him. However, he was able to maintain an interest in the group because of his fascination for music. The familiar structure of the sessions gradually reassured him, and gave him the confidence he needed to take part with the other children and make his own contributions.

When I started working with Jamie individually, the familiar framework of a "hello" and "good bye" activity reassured him, and allowed him to start work with me straight away. In fact, it became clear that Jamie relied too heavily on familiar and predictable activities, and I had to start introducing "surprises" so that he did not become entirely dependent on this familiarity.

One of the most important things that we worked on throughout Jamie's individual sessions was vocalisation. As Jamie had never babbled as a baby, I felt that he needed to discover what fun it could be producing sounds and experimenting with different vocal noises. It is interesting to note that it was during these vocal exchanges that Jamie first started using his face in an expressive way, wrinkling his nose and making "funny" faces. This ability to encourage a child to have vocal sung dialogues which can be varied and made interesting through musical improvisation is unique to the music therapist.

Another important aspect of our work was the fact that I was able to put Jamie "in control" by encouraging him, for example, to conduct my playing. I think this was helpful in building up Jamie's confidence, as his language difficulties often made him feel confused and "out of control."

Slowly, and almost in spite of himself, Jamie discovered that it was not only easy to communicate with an adult, but that it could be fun and therefore worth the effort. This was my main aim with Jamie but it happened so gradually that I only realised how much progress he had made when I looked back at how little he had initially contributed.

Finally, it is interesting to note that as Jamie's abilities to communicate improved, he developed new "naughty" behaviours. The approach that I used to help him with these behaviours was based on explaining my actions very carefully, and making use of his new found language and comprehension skills. At this stage, I was also able to put more pressure on Jamie and be more

Group Music Therapy With a Classroom of 6-8 Year-Old Hyperactive-Learning Disabled Children

JULIE HIBBEN, M.Ed., CMT-BC
Director: Programs for Special Needs
Powers Music School

Music Therapy Faculty
Lesley Graduate School
Cambridge, Massachusetts

Abstract: *In this case, the author recounts the progress toward group cohesion of an early elementary special education classroom. Most of the children are described as Attention-deficit Hyperactivity Disordered. In the twice-weekly sessions during the year, the therapist uses active music making and movement to engage the children in interactive play, and to develop intimacy and cohesion in the group. The instruments, props, and songs serve as objects which encourage and contain the children's action and feelings. Developmental stage theory provides a framework for anticipating and planning group interactions, and for evaluating individual progress. Group activities are described in terms of five dimensions: interaction, leadership, movement, rules, and competency.*

---

demanding, something I would have avoided doing in the earlier stages. I think it was my relationship with Jamie which was crucial at this point, rather than the special skills that I have as a music therapist. Nevertheless, I had developed this relationship through our music-making, so it was important for me to continue and complete our work together.

When I recently telephoned Jamie's family one evening to find out whether they would be happy for me to write this case study, I heard a familiar voice in the background: "I don't want to go to bed!" Certainly, this is a well-known and unwelcome communication for any parent to receive from a child, but in this instance, I could not help feeling moved. I was reminded of the amount of progress Jamie had made since I first saw him two years previously, when he had hardly been able to use speech to communicate in any way at all.

Although I generally enjoy my work as a music therapist, I do sometimes wonder whether I am really achieving results, and whether the children could equally well be helped through means such as special teaching or play therapy. Cases like Jamie make up for the times when progress seems to be very slow or nonexistent, and help to maintain my belief that music therapy is a truly unique and invaluable form of treatment.

REFERENCES

Bloom, L., & Lahey, M. (1978). <u>Language Development and Language Disorders</u>. New York: John Wiley and Sons.

Webster, A., & McConnell, C. (1987). <u>Children With Speech and Language Disorders</u>. London: Cassel.

BACKGROUND INFORMATION

The eight children in this self-contained classroom had chronological ages of 6-8 but in most cases they were academically at pre-first grade level. Many of the children had disruptive behavior disorders associated with *Attention-Deficit Hyperactivity Disorder (ADHD)* as well as *Learning Disabilities*. In some cases the children were at risk because of the severity of their anti-social behaviors and/or the lack of support from their family systems. Some of the children were on psychostimulant drugs such as Ritalin which controlled their hyperactivity to some extent. The children lacked developmental experiences such as nurturing play and spontaneous game playing with peers, either because of environmental deprivation or because of their learning or behavioral disorders. Their behaviors ran the gamut from excessive activity, interruptive talking, and physical aggression to negativism, lethargy, and introversion.

The brief description of the children below points up the diversity of their needs and behaviors:

Paul came from a special needs preschool, and at age 6.5, had just entered the classroom. He had no reading skills and had expressive and receptive language disabilities so severe that *auditory aphasia* was being considered as a diagnosis. Paul learned visually. Perceptual motor disabilities were apparent in his awkward maneuvers around the classroom. His relationship to his father was close and active.

Arnie had a history of depression and low self-esteem. His interaction during the music therapy assessment showed him to have ability (fluency, memory, originality) and confidence in expressing himself musically.

Al was moody and sulked a lot. Because of his lack of boundaries, he felt threatened by others in the group, even when the threat was not warranted. His voice was often raised in complaint.

Nathaniel had a history of passive aggressive behavior. He used his intelligence and verbal skills to manipulate those around him. Nathaniel, 8 years old, left the class after the first month.

Ken was dependent and passive, encouraged in this by his doting parents. He was medicated with Phenobarbital which slowed him down motorically. His thinking was very concrete. Ken was not able to verbalize his feelings, which often led to violent outbursts. His body was overweight and flaccid, and he showed signs of perceptual-motor disabilities.

Michael was anxious, hyperactive, and intelligent. During the middle of the year his cousin was taken to court for continually sexually abusing him.

Jose was humorous and friendly at times, and at other times was negative and depressed. During initial music therapy assessment, Jose was in control of the interaction, though he interacted only with expressive mime and eye contact. Jose left the classroom at mid-year.

Hattie (the only girl) was 6 years old. She was defiant, and deliberately

CHAPTER 5

Individuals with Autism and Autism Spectrum Disorders (ASD)

Mary S. Adamek
Michael H. Thaut
Amelia Greenwald Furman

CHAPTER OUTLINE
> DEFINITION AND DIAGNOSIS
> ETIOLOGY
> CHARACTERISTICS
>> Communication
>> Social Interactions
>> Sensory Processing
>> Behavioral Issues
> MUSIC THERAPY GOALS AND INTERVENTIONS
>> Music Therapy to Improve Communication Skills
>> Music Therapy to Improve Social and Emotional Skills
>> Music Therapy to Improve Behavior
>> Music Therapy to Improve Academic, Physical/Motor, and Leisure Skills

Autism is a **pervasive developmental disability** that affects a person's ability to communicate and interact with others. The term *autism spectrum disorder* (ASD) refers to the fact that this condition affects individuals in different ways and to varying degrees (Autism Society of America, 2008). ASD affects approximately 1 in 150 people in the United States (Rice, 2007), which means that approximately 1.5 million Americans today have some form of autism. It is four times more prevalent in boys than in girls, and the rate of children diagnosed with autism is increasing by 10–17% each year. At this rate, the number of people with autism could reach 4 million within the next decade (Autism Society of America, 2008).

Many music therapists work with children and adults with autism in schools, residential settings, and community agencies. According to the U.S. Department of

Education (2007), over 92,000 students ages 6–17 with autism received some form of special services under IDEA during the 2001–2002 school year. (See Chapter 14 for more information about IDEA.) The majority of music therapy services with individuals with autism are provided to children, primarily in school and community settings. Adults with severe autism may receive music therapy services in residential facilities for people with developmental disabilities, or they may receive services in community settings with other adults who have developmental disabilities. This chapter will focus on the characteristics and needs of children with autism and music therapy interventions for children with autism. For more information on music therapy with adults who have developmental disabilities, refer to Chapter 4.

DEFINITION AND DIAGNOSIS

Leo Kanner (1943), a psychiatrist at Johns Hopkins University, was the first person to identify autism as a distinct developmental disorder. He described a group of children who were relatively normal in physical appearance but who exhibited severely disturbed behavior patterns that included the following: extreme social aloofness or aloneness; lack of emotional responsiveness; avoidance of eye contact; failure to respond to auditory or visual stimulation; lack of language development or failure to use language adequately for communication; excessive attachment to objects; and preoccupation with ritualistic, repetitive, and obsessive behaviors. Because the symptoms were presented in early infancy, Kanner coined the term *infantile autism*.

Since those early years, the definition and diagnostic criteria of autism have been changed and refined, mostly in terms of broadening the definition. Autism is described as a spectrum disorder, meaning that there are a variety of possible disorders and characteristics having differing levels of developmental delay ranging from mild to severe. Thus, generalizations are difficult to make since individuals with autism can be very different from one another, and there is a wide range of abilities and deficits.

Autism Spectrum Disorder (ASD) falls under the umbrella category of **Pervasive Developmental Disorders (PDD)**, listed in the *Diagnostic and Statistical Manual of Mental Disorders* (American Psychiatric Association, 2000). This category includes neurological disorders such as autism, **Rett's Syndrome,** and **Asperger's Syndrome**, which are characterized by severe and pervasive impairments in many areas of development (American Psychiatric Association, 2000; Autism Society of America, 2008). Autism and ASD affect children of all social classes, financial levels, educational levels, cultures, and races throughout the world (Autism Society of America, 2008; Scott, Clark, & Brady, 2000).

CHAPTER 5: INDIVIDUALS WITH AUTISM AND AUTISM SPECTRUM DISORDERS (ASD) — 119

Persons with autism have serious deficits in communication and social skills, and they may display behaviors that are unusual compared to their typically developing peers. Symptoms of autism begin before the age of 3 and continue throughout a person's life. All of the following diagnostic criteria must be present from early childhood in order to make a diagnosis of autism:

- *Qualitative impairment in reciprocal social interaction,* based on what is typical for developmental level. This may manifest in poor eye gaze, disinterest in personal relationships, and limited use of gestures.
- *Qualitative impairment in verbal and nonverbal communication,* based on what is typical for developmental level. This may manifest in language acquisition delay, limited or lack of speech, lack of spontaneous and varied make-believe play.
- *Restricted repertoire of interests and activities,* based on developmental level. This may manifest in stereotypical or repetitive movements such as rocking, hand flapping, or spinning as well as limited or abnormally intense interest areas. (Frith, 2003)

As a spectrum disorder, the range of abilities and degree of developmental delay result in unique profiles among persons with ASD; however, all children with autism have some sort of difficulty with communication, social skills, and behavior (Frith, 2003; Johnson, 2004; Mastropieri & Scruggs, 2000; Scott et al., 2000). Those who have difficulty with verbal communication and expressing needs may point, use gestures, or use other nonverbal forms of communication such as pictures or icons. Many, but not all, children with ASD also have cognitive impairments; however, children with Asperger's Syndrome have high cognitive abilities combined with severe impairment in reciprocal social interaction and restricted interests. A person with autism may have a combination of the characteristics listed in Table 1 on the following page (Centers for Disease Control and Prevention, 2008), which will be discussed more extensively later in this chapter.

Table 1
Continuum of Abilities and Limitations for Persons with Autism

AREA OF FUNCTIONING	VARIABILITY LEVELS
Measured Intelligence	Severely impaired ----------------Gifted
Social Interaction	Aloof ------Passive -----Active but odd
Communication	Nonverbal ------------------------Verbal
Behaviors	Intense -------------------------------Mild
Sensory	Hyposensitive ----------Hypersensitive
Motor	Uncoordinated -------------Coordinated

Individuals with autism or ASD may display some of the following specific traits or characteristics. It is important to note that not all people with this diagnosis have all of these traits, and the severity of the disorder varies by individual (Autism Society of America, 2008).

- Repeating words or phrases, **echolalic** language
- Unresponsive to verbal cues or directions; may appear to be deaf due to unresponsiveness
- Difficulty interacting with peers; minimal spontaneous socialization
- Oversensitivity or undersensitivity to stimuli or to pain
- Resistance to change; insistence on routine
- Minimal direct eye contact
- Odd or unusual play, particularly sustained play or attachment to objects

Contrary to common beliefs, children with ASD may make eye contact, develop good functional language and communication skills, socialize with peers, and show affection. Their skills in these areas might be different or less sophisticated than typically developing peers, but it is very likely that with appropriate educational and social interventions, children with ASD may develop functional and appropriate skills in all of these areas. Other behavioral or emotional disorders may co-occur with ASD as a secondary diagnosis, including obsessive/compulsive disorder, anxiety disorder, depression, and attention-deficit/hyperactivity disorder. (See Chapter 8 for a review of behavioral-emotional disorders.)

ETIOLOGY

When autism was first recognized as a distinct disorder, psychiatrists attributed it to an early emotional trauma or to faulty parenting. The unusual array of symptoms (i.e., relatively normal physical appearance and isolated skills coupled with the emotional unresponsiveness, social aloofness, and difficulty with language) led many researchers to believe that autism was the result of an emotional trauma in very early childhood. However, because no consistent patterns of social or emotional history emerged in these children, other etiological considerations emerged.

Since the 1960s, accumulated research evidence strongly suggests that autism is a developmental disorder of brain function that is manifested in a variety of perceptual, cognitive, and motor disturbances. To date, there is no single known cause of autism; however, there is general agreement that autism is related to abnormalities in the brain structure and function. Researchers have found differences in brain scans between brains of individuals with autism and individuals with typical development (Frith, 2003). Research is underway to test several theories related to the causes of autism. Some theories link the disorder to genetics and heredity, while others cite environmental risks as causal factors related to the development of autism. Currently, many national organizations are funding and conducting research to determine the causes of autism and best practices for intervention (Autism Society of America, 2008; Autism Speaks, 2008; Centers for Disease Control and Prevention, 2008).

The following sections describe three functional domains in which children with autism often have difficulties. Typical educational approaches to support learning will be described.

CHARACTERISTICS

Communication

As noted previously, a child with autism has qualitative impairment in language and communication skills. Some children may have no ability or interest in communicating verbally or nonverbally with others. Some have **echolalic** language, in which previously heard words or phrases are repeated without any intent to convey meaning. Children with autism have a marked difference in language skills compared to children who are typically developing. Impairments may be characterized by:

- lack of spontaneous social imitation (e.g., waving and saying "goodbye")
- failure to use language correctly (e.g., syntactic problems, not using verbs)
- limited vocabulary and semantic concepts, poor intonation patterns
- pronoun reversal (e.g., saying "you" instead of "I")
- lack of gesture or mime when trying to make needs known
- difficulty understanding spoken language

- failure to develop joint attention skills in preverbal children (e.g., pointing to a toy to share one's pleasure with another person). (Heflin & Alaimo, 2007; Mundy & Stella, 2000)

Children who have severe levels of autism may have little or no receptive or expressive language, while students with mild levels of autism may have developed language skills that allow them to communicate with others. Because communication is a primary deficit for individuals with ASD, the development of communication skills is often a key focus for therapy. This may include the development of verbal communication or effective use of alternative or augmentative communication systems.

There are many **alternative and augmentative communication (AAC) systems** available, which may enhance a child's verbal communication skills or become a child's primary means of communication. These alternative systems help a child express wants and needs, initiate and maintain conversations, and receive and understand information from others. AAC systems can be simple systems of pointing to pictures, words, or letter boards, or more sophisticated methods, such as use of sign language, voice output computers, or visual tracking devices (National Research Council, 2001; Scott et al., 2000). These communication systems can provide a means for students to communicate with others in a meaningful way and can facilitate two-way, interactive communication between the student with autism and others.

The **Picture Exchange Communication System (PECS)** is a good example of an AAC system that is used in many homes and classrooms. PECS is system that teaches children to use pictures and symbols in order to ask for wants and needs, respond to others, and initiate conversations. Using PECS, a child learns the meaning of a set of pictures or symbols by exchanging those symbols for something he or she wants or needs. Using a sentence strip that says "I want _____," the child learns to fill in the blank with a picture (attached to the sentence strip with Velcro) that stands for whatever he or she wants; then the child hands the sentence strip back to the teacher, therapist, or other conversational partner in exchange for the desired object (Bondy & Frost, 1994; Frost & Bondy, 1994; Kravits, Kamps, Kemmerer, & Potucek, 2002). Other AAC systems might be a simple picture/symbol book, board, or wallet used for making requests or responding to questions. Some children may use basic signs to communicate with others. More sophisticated technology such as computers with voice output systems can also provide an effective means of communication. Music therapy implications for the use of ACCs will be discussed later in this chapter.

Social Interactions

Social skills play a major role in child development and support a child's ability to function in integrated classrooms or community settings. Appropriate social skills are necessary for successful interactions with peers without disabilities and for participation in normalized activities. Individuals with ASD have core deficits in social interaction and social perception, which manifest in difficulty initiating interaction, difficulty maintaining social relationships, and difficulty understanding the perceptions of others (Scott et al., 2000). Social deficits can range from mild (such as difficulty making and maintaining eye contact), to severe (such as the inability to share experiences and interests with others). Some individuals with less severe deficits may interact spontaneously with others, while those with severe social deficits may seem oblivious to others and the environment. Even individuals with higher functioning skills may have problems understanding the perspective of others, and understanding that the thoughts, beliefs, and intentions of others may be different from their own. Some children have difficulty with physical touch or in maintaining socially acceptable personal space. For example, some children stiffen and avoid physical contact, while others may be clingy and have inappropriate boundaries (such as always wanting to sit on the therapist's lap or in uncomfortably close proximity to others). Social behaviors can also vary over time.

Because social deficits are a key feature of autism, these children need direct training to improve social skills in a variety of settings. While children with autism can develop more socially appropriate behaviors through social skills training, it is important to note that communication skills provide the foundation for developing and maintaining social relationships; consequently, children with autism need to develop functional communication *along with* social skills in order to enhance interactive skills, make friends, and be included in classroom and social activities.

A variety of techniques can be used to teach social skills to children with these deficits. When choosing social skill interventions, teachers and therapists must keep in mind the age, language skills, developmental level, and interests of the child in order to develop effective approaches. Some current educational approaches used to teach social skills include:

- **Direct instruction**—teaching children directly to interact with peers with the support of prompts, modeling, or physical assistance during the interaction
- **Social communication training**—teaching children to ask questions and seek out information in a social setting
- **Use of social stories**—stories developed to teach social skill concepts and strategies (Gray & Garand, 1993); these stories can also be set to music to create social story songs

- **Leisure-related social skill development**—teaching social interaction and rules of play through leisure skills. (Scott et al., 2000)

Sensory Processing

Children who are typically developing have intact sensory systems that help them perceive the world around them. Their senses of vision, hearing, touch, taste, and smell work in an integrated fashion to help them make sense of their environment. Many children with autism have sensory processing problems. To a child with sensory processing problems, the environment may be confusing, painful, or even frightening. Some children with autism have sensory processing problems that can cause oversensitivity or undersensitivity to certain stimuli. For instance, some children with autism are particularly sensitive to high or loud sounds; when presented with this type of sound, they will shriek, hold their ears, or become aggressive in some way. Because they may process and respond to information in different ways, children with autism may exhibit atypical, inappropriate, unusual, or **stereotypical behaviors.** They may exhibit aggressive or self-injurious behaviors when they are unable to understand or unable to communicate their confusion. Keep in mind, however, that not all children with autism exhibit these types of behaviors.

Because musical sounds are such an integral part of music therapy, the processing of and response to musical sounds by children with autism is of particular interest. A number of research studies with this population document unusual sensitivity and attention to music. In fact, in 1964, a prominent researcher, Bernard Rimland, even listed unusual musical capabilities as a diagnostic criterion for autism (Rimland, 1964). Sherwin (1953), in a case study of boys with autism, noted strong melodic memory; recognition of classical music selections; and strong interest in playing the piano, singing, and listening to music. Observations of 12 children with autism over a two-year time period indicated heightened response and interest in musical sounds as compared with other environmental stimuli (Pronovost, 1961). Studies by Frith (1972), O'Connell (1974), Blackstock (1978), and Thaut (1987) showed improved task performance or attention on tasks involving music compared with those using other modalities.

Studies by Applebaum, Egel, Koegel, and Imhoff (1979) and Thaut (1987) indicated that children with autism could perform similarly to age-matched children with typical development on musical tasks involving imitation or improvisation. Koegel, Rincover, and Egel (1982) described music as an efficient motivator and modality for enabling autistic children to learn nonmusical material and emphasized its use as positive sensory reinforcement in decreasing self-stimulation behaviors.

Recent studies provide evidence that a high level of musical responsiveness can co-exist with low functioning in other cognitive areas in autistic children (e.g., Heaton, 2003; Heaton, Hermelin, & Pring, 1998; Heaton, Pring, & Hermelin, 2001; Hermelin, O'Conner, & Lee, 1997; Mottron, Peretz, & Menard, 2000). In addition, research examining the unique auditory perception of children with autism indicates higher performance in perceptual tasks involving music compared with other acoustic stimuli (e.g., verbal language [Foxton et al., 2003; Heaton, 2003, 2005; Heaton & Wallace, 2004; Mottron, Peretz, Belleville, & Rouleau, 1999; Nieto del Rincon, 2008; Young & Nettelbeck, 1995]). It is important to note, however, that some children with autism may show unusual and negative sensitivity to some musical sounds, or some combinations of music and movement.

It is, as of yet, unclear why many children with autism show heightened interest in and more typical responses to music than to other types of stimuli. However, the fact that music can be engaging and can support optimal functioning in children with autism explains in part why music therapy can be an excellent therapeutic choice for this population.

Behavioral Issues

Some children with autism have behaviors that are difficult to manage in a variety of settings such as the classroom, the home, or the community. Maladaptive behaviors include poor attention, aggression, stereotypic or self-stimulating behaviors, oversensitivity to sensory input, and difficulty with generalization of skills (National Research Council, 2001; Simpson & Miles, 1998). These behaviors can be among the most challenging and stressful factors for professionals and can interfere with learning and development in communication and socialization. Problem behaviors may be triggered or exacerbated by an inability to understand the expectations of the environment (including consequences of their behavior), inability to communicate wants and needs, or difficulty in initiating and maintaining positive social relationships. Aggression towards others, self-injurious behaviors, noncompliance, and disruption of session routines may create difficult and frustrating situations for everyone involved. Table 2 provides examples of the characteristic features of autism and how they might cause difficult behaviors (Adamek & Darrow, 2005, pp. 190–191).

Table 2
Characteristic Features and Examples of Difficult Behaviors

Characteristic Feature	Specific Difficulties	Possible Behavior
Language and communication impairment	Difficulty understanding directions and expressing self	Not following through with directions, aggression to others or self
Social interaction difficulty	Difficulty reading social cues from others, difficulty understanding the perspective of others	Difficulty interacting with others, sharing classroom materials, inflexible in social situations; isolation from peers, minimal spontaneous interaction with peers
Focus of attention problems	Difficulty processing information, focusing on the main feature of instruction; difficulty filtering out auditory/visual distracters	Not following through with directions, tasks, or assignments; engaging in off-task or self-stimulating behaviors; inability to follow multi-step directions
Aggressive, stereotypic or self-stimulating behaviors	Difficulty communicating needs or understanding expectations; frustrations	Acting out towards others; rocking or hand flapping to provide sensory stimulation; visually focusing on lights, fan blades, or shiny objects
Oversensitivity to sensory input	Processing problems that impair tolerance for tactile, visual, or auditory stimuli	Acting out or isolation; holding ears with hands; rejecting touch from others; refusal to play instruments that provide tactile stimulation
Difficulty generalizing behaviors	Difficulty applying skills learned in one situation to another situation	Difficulty with transitions; may act out physically, vocally, or refuse participation; difficulty transferring skills from one setting to another without additional instruction

Fortunately, problematic behaviors can be reduced by setting up a structured environment and through the use of behavioral strategies (providing examples and cues to clarify expectations, reinforcing positive behavior, etc.). Environmental structure (such as a well organized room with consistent work spaces and limited clutter) can help the child organize and focus attention appropriately. Some children derive structure and support by being close to others for structure and support, while others may need more space due to issues such as tactile defensiveness or hyperactivity. Providing instruction in close proximity is important for some children. Close proximity makes it possible for the music therapist to provide physical and gestural prompts when needed and gives the child a clear idea of where he or she should be looking for instruction.

In addition to setting up a structured environment, it is important to understand causes of inappropriate behavior so that strategies for developing appropriate behavior can be devised. For example, some children are more likely to misbehave if they sit next to one another—they either irritate one another or egg each other on. The mere fact of sitting by one another can trigger negative behaviors. A seating chart that places these children away from each other can prevent problems from beginning. For some children, sitting near the therapist may foster calm and focused behavior. It is important to recognize antecedents (what happens before the target behavior) and consequences (what happens as a result of the behavior) in order to determine some possible causes and reinforcing events.

While no single intervention will deal effectively with all problem behaviors, most professionals recommend using a preventative approach to decrease problem behaviors and increase positive behaviors. A proactive approach, such as utilizing **positive behavioral supports** (assessing what maintains the behavior and developing strategies to replace the behavior), can create an environment for success. This approach builds on the strengths of the child and focuses on changing the environment, instructional strategies, and consequences to promote positive behaviors.

MUSIC THERAPY GOALS AND INTERVENTIONS

Music therapy is an effective approach for addressing language and communication skills, social skills, cognitive skills, and behavioral skills for children with autism (Bettison, 1996; Davis, 1990; Edgerton, 1994; Goldstein, 1964; Hairston, 1990; Hermelín, O'Connor, & Lee, 1989; Hollander & Juhrs, 1974; Humpal, 1990; Kostka, 1993; Lim, 2007; Litchman, 1976; Ma, Nagler, & Lee, 2001; Mahlberg, 1973; Nelson, Anderson, & Gonzales, 1984; Reitman, 2006; Saperston, 1973; Schmidt & Edwards, 1976; Staum & Flowers, 1984; Stevens & Clark, 1969; Thaut, 1984, 1988; Umbarger, 2007; Walworth, 2007; Warwick 1995; Whipple, 2004; Wimpory, Chadwick, & Nash, 1995). Music therapy goals for children with autism focus primarily on improving communication, social interactions, and behavior. Secondary areas of focus include improvement of academic skills, physical skills, and leisure skills.

As noted earlier, some children with autism are more attentive and responsive to musical stimuli; thus, music therapy can be a highly motivating medium for addressing these goals. In addition, music is a flexible medium (see Chapter 3); therefore, it can be used for a variety of goals and readily adapted to suit the diverse strengths and limitations found within this population. Music therapy interventions involve the child in listening, singing, playing, moving, or responding verbally and nonverbally. Through goal-directed music therapy interventions, a child can also work on several skills at once. For instance, an intervention that involved participation in a percussion ensemble could focus on communication (nonverbal communication and self-expression through drumming, making choices about what instrument to play), social skills (interacting appropriately with peers, taking turns playing, listening to others, taking leadership) and appropriate behavior (following directions, listening to the leader, following through with tasks).

Music Therapy to Improve Communication Skills

As noted previously, children with autism have deficits in expressive and receptive communication skills. Music therapy provides a rich opportunity for language experiences through age-appropriate and interesting music interventions. Several studies indicate that music therapy can improve communication and language skills (Edgerton, 1994; Litchman, 1976; Mahlberg, 1973; Saperston, 1973). Music therapists use the elements of music (melody, rhythm, pitch, dynamics, form) to develop basic listening skills such as **auditory awareness** (sound vs. no sound), **auditory discrimination** (are two sounds same or different?), **sound identification** (recognition of the sound, such as a flute or a piano), and **localization** (locating the source of the sound). Music therapy interventions can encourage **expressive** (speaking, signing) and **receptive** (listening, understanding signs and gestures) **language**.

Because music is interesting and motivating, it can promote attention, active participation, and verbal and nonverbal response. For instance, action songs, chants, and instrument playing can elicit vocal/verbal and physical responses that promote receptive communication skills. Rhythm paired with speech can encourage verbalizations and appropriate pacing. Call-and-response rhythmic chants can increase imitation skills, first on instruments, then in speech. Songs with repetitive lyrics and melodies can facilitate memory for vocabulary and other information. Pairing songs with visual cues and movement can enhance comprehension of vocabulary and concepts. For instance, a song about winter could be used to introduce and reinforce concepts such as temperature, seasonal changes, appropriate attire (winter coats and mittens), and directions. Music can be a highly motivating tool to encourage imitative and spontaneous language (see Figure 1).

> **EXAMPLES OF MUSIC THERAPY INTERVENTIONS FOR COMMUNICATION**
> (Thaut, 1999)
>
> 1. **Music interaction to establish communicative intent (facilitate desire or necessity to communicate)**
>   - Offer musical interactions (e.g., question-and-answer, imitative) on drum, metallophone, or other instruments.
>   - Accompany the child's movements or habitual sounds (crying, laughing) on the piano.
>   - Sing an action song to the child and cue the proper physical responses.
>
> 2. **Action songs to promote interaction (after communicative intent is established)**
>   - Introduce chants or songs that integrate rhythm, body percussion, and vocalization that present instructions for active physical and vocal response.
>
> 3. **Oral motor exercises to strengthen awareness and functional use of lips, tongue, jaws, teeth**
>   - Play wind instruments.
>   - Performing oral motor imitation exercises of the articulators.
>
> 4. **Sequence imitation of gross motor, oral motor, and oral vocal motor skills (after perceptual and imitative skills are established)**
>   - First, introduce the name of a body part (e.g., "arm") while moving that part.
>   - Second, have the child practice oral motor positions of the articulators for that word (e.g., "a" and "m").
>   - Third, while the child moves the body part in an imitation exercise, ask him to sound out the parts of that body part (e.g., saying "arm" while moving, or parts of the word as is possible).
>
> 5. **Shaping vocal inflection of children who have some speech sounds**
>   - Vocal improvisation on vowel and consonant combinations.
>   - Sustaining sounds on wind instruments.
>   - Producing vocal sounds combined with graphic notations to represent speech inflection.
>   - Breathing exercises to improve vocal strength, exercise laryngeal function, and refine oral motor function.

Figure 1. Examples of Music Therapy Interventions for Communication Skills

If a child is using an **alternative and augmentative communication (AAC) system**, the music therapist can collaborate with the speech language pathologist to create responses for use in music. Examples include:

- Icons to represent music, or a picture of the music room
- Pictures or names of teachers, therapists, or peer buddies in music
- Pictures or drawings of instruments or props used in music
- Names of favorite songs sung in music

- Iconic representations of note values, such as whole notes, half notes, quarter notes, eighth notes
- Pictures related to the schedule or order of events in music, such as a "hello song" or opening song," "movement time," "play instruments," or "sing songs"
- Functional signs used for directions such as "stop," "play," "dance"

Because communicative deficits are a key problem area for children with autism, it is important to promote receptive and expressive communication in all aspects of instruction. Many children are more successful when presented with visual cues along with verbal instructions. Visual cues (**icons, photos, functional signs**) can be used for giving directions, offering choices, teaching new skills, or providing structure for an activity. Visual enhancements should be simple and consistent throughout the child's day to encourage generalization of skills and to support comprehension (Scott et al., 2000). Suggested uses for visual cues include:

- Describing rules (listen, hands to self)
- Presenting schedule of interventions, which creates predictability for children
- Modeling movement
- Pairing pictures with songs to allow choice (a picture of a sun for "Mr. Sun")
- Presenting a calming routine for coping with change or anxiety (e.g., take two breaths, squeezing/releasing hands). (Adamek & Darrow, 2005)

> *Abdi faces several challenges in his education. Not only does he have autism, but his native language spoken at home is not English. Abdi frequently becomes upset and aggressive in the classroom because he is unable to communicate his choices. Music therapy provides a consistent structure and the opportunity for repeated practice of words he needs to communicate choices. A calming song, written by his music therapist, lists six of Abdi's favorite things to do (e.g., rest, read a book). His classroom teacher keeps a copy of Abdi's special song (along with visual cues) in the classroom for use during choice time, or to help calm him when he becomes upset. The songs learned in music therapy are integrated into other instructional times to help hold Abdi's attention, increase his comprehension, and increase his time on task in the group. His ability to communicate choices about songs, instruments, and feelings has also contributed to his improved behaviors in school.*

CHAPTER 5: INDIVIDUALS WITH AUTISM AND AUTISM SPECTRUM DISORDERS (ASD) — 131

Music Therapy to Improve Social and Emotional Skills

> *Evan, a student with Asperger's Syndrome, entered the school as a 2nd grader. Although he was academically above grade level, he was having difficulty during lunch and recess. Some students found his loud voice and unusually deliberate speech patterns irritating and his social skills awkward. However, Evan was able to shine in a special classroom project, a musical written and produced by the students, about how blood circulates in the human body. A number of students auditioned for the "scientist narrator" position, but most could not be easily understood through the microphone and speakers. Evan, an excellent and precise reader, was perfect for the part. As a lead part in the musical, he was able to utilize his strengths and be seen as an essential member of the group, especially by the students writing the script. The friendships and tolerance that developed during the musical carried over to the creation of a small music group in which social skills training became a part of Friday Fun Time. Evan realized that during music, he understood the rules and could be successful with peers. He later joined band and excelled in that structured experience right up through high school graduation.*

Children with autism and ASD have deficits in social skills, social interaction, and emotional expression. Because autistic children often reject or ignore others' attempts at social interaction, music can function as an attractive mediating object. Music provides a point of mutual interaction between therapist and child. Studies by Goldstein (1964), Stevens and Clark (1969), Hollander and Juhrs (1974), Schmidt and Edwards (1976), and Warwick (1995) have shown improved social behavior and interpersonal relationships as a result of music therapy treatment. In addition, music is an effective medium for eliciting and shaping emotional responses. Different types of music can be associated with different moods and emotions, which can in turn be paired with body language and verbal labeling of moods (Thaut, 1999).

Music making (singing, movement, instrument playing) with the therapist or with peers lends itself to interaction and the use of social skills. In one-to-one sessions with the child, the therapist can make musical contact and set up musical interactions that require social interaction (such as imitation or call and response) (Thaut, 1999). In group music experiences, children can practice responding to others, taking turns, listening, sharing ideas, greeting others, and sharing equipment. Simple skills such as holding hands with a peer, listening to others, or starting and stopping with the group can be difficult but important skills to develop. Below is an example of a social story song about *waiting your turn* (to the tune of ABC song) (Adamek & Darrow, 2005, p. 187):

Wait your turn, wait today, Then you'll have a chance to play.
First it's her, then it's him, Round the circle back to you.
Wait your turn, wait today, Then you'll have a chance to play.

Music therapists can promote meaningful social relationships with peers by providing structured and motivating opportunities for social interaction in the music setting (Adamek & Darrow, 2005; Brown et al., 1979; Jellison, Brooks, & Huck, 1984). Music groups including movement can also provide opportunities to practice appropriate personal space (how close one stands or sits next to others while still feeling comfortable), and socially appropriate touch.

Jamilia, who has autism, is a very musical child. She is able to learn new lyrics and melodies quickly and follows directions sung in lyrics well. Jamilia really wanted to be a part of the group, but her initiations were often rebuffed by other children because she had no sense of space or boundaries. She would squeeze herself into a classroom line, typically next to students wearing the prettiest dresses. Sometimes, out of the blue, she would lean over and touch or sniff other children's hair and talk about what they were wearing or doing. In music therapy, Jamilia learned songs that taught interactive skills, such as "find a friend and look them in the eye, find a friend and now say Hi."

For movement activities, the teacher marked the classroom floor with round Velcro pieces that were called "bubbles." These bubbles provided an easy visual reminder of where to stand in relation to others. In an intervention similar to the game Musical Chairs, the children would move as long as the music was playing. Whenever the music stopped, students jumped on to one of the bubbles. Students were praised for "good bubble space." As the children internalized this sense of appropriate social space, the Velcro spots were gradually removed so students needed to "think the space." The concept of bubble space (socially appropriate personal distance) was then integrated into other favorite activities, such as singing a favorite train song, which required the children to keep their social distance while moving. These skills were then successfully generalized to other classroom and social settings.

Music Therapy to Improve Behavior

Abdi, like many children with autism, does not like change. Sometimes, he has verbal outbursts or becomes physically aggressive when his teachers change the classroom routine. Fortunately, his interest in music and music activities helps him to tolerate change. For example, Abdi has become accustomed to and enjoys playing drums with mallets; but because the music is so motivating, he is willing to try a different type of drum played only by his hands as requested.

Behavioral difficulties are another key feature of ASD. Just as with all other characteristics of autism, behavior skills vary in severity from one individual to the next. As noted earlier, behavior problems may be related to difficulty communicating or limited comprehension of the expectations and consequences of their behavior.

Music therapy can be structured to provide predictable experiences in which children can practice appropriate behavior. The rules for appropriate participation in a music group (such as following directions, starting and stopping at the correct place) can be practiced step by step, even as the group members engage in attractive musical arrangements. Those students with more advanced musical skills can practice these basic behavioral expectations within the context of more complex and interesting music. For instance, a small group percussion ensemble can learn basic steady beat patterns that can be extended to include more complicated rhythms on a variety of instruments. Children who follow directions, meet expectations, and participate with others may be asked to perform for others. In this way, music can be used to improve self-esteem and leadership skills. Music can also be used as reinforcement for appropriate behavior, offered as a reward for following through with expectations. Extra time playing instruments, listening to music, or making music with others may be highly reinforcing and motivating for some students.

Music therapists can utilize various methods to promote positive behaviors, including the following (Adamek & Darrow, 2005, pp. 188–189):

- Creating a sense of predictability and routine in the session, such as using a visually prominent schedule board, having a predictable room set-up, or using familiar materials.

Mrs. Hawkins' music therapy space is a model of predictability. When the children enter the room, they know exactly where they will find the rhythm instruments, the chairs, and the music board, which spells out the order of musical events for each day's session. Today, the board presents a sequence of pictures that represent (1) the opening song/warm-up, (2) a movement activity, (3) time for singing, (4) playing instruments, (5) surprise to allow for teaching flexibility and student choice, and (6) closing.

Everyone thought James would do well in regular music classes. However, his need for consistency and difficulty with change become clear on the first day. Mrs. Lin, the teacher, looked at the clock and said, "Let's sing

'Five Little Monkeys Jumping on the Bed.' We have just enough time for 2 little monkeys to jump on the bed today." James's response was a major tantrum with screams of "No!! There must be 5." That's because every time he sang this song, they started with the number, 5. Only 2 monkeys! That was just more change than he could handle.

Mrs. Nelson, the music therapist, was contacted to set up a series of sessions to work with James on coping with a change in routine. A "surprise" symbol, selected with the ASD classroom teacher and speech clinician, was introduced. Visuals with choices for changes in how the music was performed including fast/slow, loud/soft, or instrumentation were made and familiar songs were sung with changes. Next, dice were presented and James practiced rolling, saying the number and setting out a matching number of items. "It's a surprise!" was said frequently when the dice were rolled. James was ready to choose a song, roll the dice, and sing using the "surprise" number. A social story song about "No Turn Today—but it's OK" was sung to the numbers that were not chosen.

- Practicing flexibility or tolerance of change by varying a musical element within the song or activity.

    During instrument playing, Mrs. Hawkins integrates small but tolerable changes in the routine by having the children play a favorite well-known rhythm pattern, but then adding a rhythm instrument different from that originally taught.

- Providing positive reinforcement for appropriate behaviors.

    As Jamilia keeps her hands to herself in the "Little Red Caboose" song, Mrs. Hawkins praises her for good bubble behavior, and she asks her to choose which instrument she would like to play during instrument time.

- Providing a means of communication for the child, and making sure that communication system transfers to all environments, including music therapy.

    One of the children in Mrs. Hawkins' ASD group uses basic sign language, while another uses visuals to communicate. Mrs. Hawkins makes sure that she utilizes of these communication systems in song time and all other aspects of her session.

- Teaching peers how to interact in a positive way with the child.

    Before Jamilia started to attend the regular music class, Mrs. Hawkins sat down with the children to discuss practical ideas for getting along with their classmates, such as moving a little bit further away if a classmate moves within your bubble space.

Music Therapy to Improve Academic, Physical/Motor, and Leisure Skills

In addition to the aforementioned areas of difficulty for children with autism (communication skills, social skills, and behavior), other areas of deficit such as academic skills, physical/motor skills, and leisure skills can be addressed through music therapy. Studies indicate that music can be used to enhance memory, attention, executive function, and emotional reasoning (Bettison, 1996; Hermelin et al., 1989; Ma et al., 2001; Reitman, 2006; Thaut, 1988; Wimpory et al., 1995). Figure 2 shows examples of how music therapy can promote preacademic and academic development.

Music as a carrier of nonmusical information
- Songs with lyrics about world facts, math, vocabulary, body parts, and other academic content.

Music listening to promote a learning environment conducive to attention and focused learning (Holland & Juhrs, 1974; Litchman, 1976).

Music as reinforcement (reward) for compliance in academic tasks

Music to teach specific concepts
- Music interventions that require use of numbers
- Music interventions that require following multi-step directions
- Music interventions that present colors, shapes, forms, and other concepts
- Music interventions that require practice of auditory memory or auditory motor memory

Figure 2. Examples of Music Therapy for Preacademic and Academic Development (Thaut, 1999)

Songs, chants, and rhythm activities can be used to reinforce math skills such as counting, 1:1 correspondence, and ordering. Songs with repetitive lyrics, rhythmic patterns, and added movements can give children many opportunities to count, add, subtract, and place items in order in a fun and interesting way. Categorization by size, shape, color, and sound can all be practiced through simple music activities and musical instruments. Other concepts such as high and low, in and out, front and back, slow and fast can be taught and practiced through music therapy interventions combining music and movement. Incorporating movement along with songs and rhythm gives the children different options for understanding and remembering the concepts, making the concepts come to life through music and movement. Music

Voices: A World Forum for Music Therapy, Vol 11, No 1 (2011)

Performance in Music Therapy: Experiences in Five Dimensions

By Peter F. Jampel

Introduction

Building community through music therapy performance has been at the heart of the work that I have done with a band of musicians who have serious mental health issues over the past twenty years at the Baltic Street Clinic in Brooklyn, New York. The complexity of their personalities as expressed through performing music intrigued me and challenged me to try to understand how to best work with them. This examination led me to ponder not only what worked and what did not in terms of treatment strategies, but also how it worked and why, questions that are critical in addressing what is therapeutic about performing music when working with people who experience persistent mental illnesses. Eventually an approach of identifying and treating these issues developed. In this process, I have considered the thorny question of how to promote the health of the individual performer, work with the manifestations of their illnesses while also attempting to build community.

This paper will address performance from a music psychotherapy perspective something that in the current context of community music therapy literature, is controversial. Additionally, it discusses the process of performing music in terms of dimensions of experience. This approach allows the clinician to describe, assess, analyze and evaluate the components of what is happening both over time and in the moment. It is my intention to develop a language not only *between* therapists but *with* clients. It is an attempt to promote a consistent means of description. The five dimensions of performance in music therapy are not meant to exclude other possible dimensions that might exist but were found to be a concise, descriptive shorthand that covers the essential aspects of the performance experience (Jampel, 2007).

Theoretical Perspectives on Performance in Community Music Therapy

Communities unlike the one at Baltic Street that are formed through shared neighborhood, religion, hobbies or employment have the advantage of the cohesive effects of having things in common, of membership that reflects a willing intention to be part of community (Stige, Ansdell, Elefant & Pavlicevic, 2010). Bonds built on the basis of having joined a community because a mental or physical illness has seriously impaired one's lifestyle or level of functioning, do not necessarily reflect shared beliefs and interests. These membership conditions of necessity can contribute to a sense of alienation, of having been thrown together with other people because of the unfortunate circumstance of an illness that itself, can be hard to accept. In order to promote community connection and belonging that is heartfelt, people in this instance need to find some greater sense of meaning and purpose. How can music performance foster a sense of volitional identification, strengthen the bond of connection, and promote a feeling of purposeful action?

The community discussed in this article initially reflects the kind of thrown together quality that Gary Ansdell (Stige et al, 2010, p. 44) discussed as *circumstantial*. As the music therapy program expanded from its origins in individual and group music psychotherapy, an environment was created which provided increasingly frequent opportunities for clients to perform music at a monthly cabaret called *The After Hours Club*. This seemed to strengthen the bonds not only between individuals who played music but also collectively among those who came to listen. Ansdell explains this process as communities forged through *communication and practice*. They increasingly share music as a way of communicating. It serves "to actively construct, sustain and develop particular modes of community, and its accompanying experience of belonging" (p. 47). Music performance groups in my experience are more motivated to learn how to communicate in music because such skills improve the quality of performances. In this view, communities are created through the developing competencies and shared interests of its members. Practice and rehearsals consist of doing and learning something together repetitively, through the experience of sharing passions, interests and knowledge, of planning together while learning to negotiate differing musical needs and tastes. Through this process, individuals can experience meaning, identity, engagement and ultimately belonging. An essential characteristic of this type of community is the acceptance of the difference, strangeness or otherness of each member of the group. Stige (2002) call this "unity beyond uniformity" (p. 173). Music making provides equipoise between the individual's state of existence and those groups to which they belong.

The achievement of a balance between individual needs and the good of the group is no small feat. In my experience, considerable skills are needed to prepare the individual musician to be able to contain personal agendas and to come to see the larger rewards of sensitive listening and playing. Central to this process is preparation to perform. For some music therapists like Stuart Wood (2006), preparation for performance involves individual sessions and music therapy workshops in order to create a psychological foundation for building meaning and readiness. His work with people who have experienced neurological trauma addresses the differing demands made on clients in stepping from private music making to the public nature of performance. His matrix model of community music therapy customizes the design of music therapy services around the particular needs of the individual. Though we work with different populations, I have also found that services that are designed around the special needs of the individual tend to promote a better balance between those personal needs and the context of working within a community.

It is of utmost importance in my experience to design music therapy services that take into account individual complexity along with the psychological ramifications of performance in order to avoid possible undesirable outcomes. Inadequate preparation can result in feelings of stress, anxiety or even worse, a sense of failure. This perspective on performance preparation or the lack thereof is offered by Jon Hawkes, a well-known Australian cultural analyst, in an interview conducted by the music therapist Katrina McFerran (O'Grady, 2008). Music performed publically, he warns, risks one's health by the effects of the adrenaline surge that often accompanies it. This he believes accounts for the prevalence of performance anxiety. He encourages music to be made rather than witnessed and goes on to discuss the culture-bound aspects of performance as *music making* versus *music witnessing*. In Hawkes' view, performers who perform with and for one another learn to direct their energy (and satisfaction) in connecting to each other and not to their audiences. He believes that only when performance emerges as a genuine client interest should it be then pursued as a possible direction by the music therapist.

Another perspective on the balance between the experience of the group and that of the individual is offered by Ansdell (2005, 2010) as he addresses performance as both a *self and collaborative* effort. In his view, reparative work is done both within the individual and to their connection with others in both spheres simultaneously. Careful attention to musical listening and organization of material in rehearsals is needed as clients are assisted to work through pathological attitudes in their self-identity, social relationships and work lives. He maintains that the collaborative nature of performance and the public completion of this process act powerfully to contribute to the meaning derived. Ansdell does recognize the pressures that can exist on performers when the experience is ladened by attitudes of competition and judgment. This position resonates with my own observations about the mutuality of growth and development that can occur for individuals within the context of a maturing performance group.

Although Ansdell and Wood seem to appreciate the potential pitfalls of performance, what is absent in their discussion is some systematic way of assessing who their clients are as performers, what clinical issues they present for treatment and how performance can address them. Without such procedures, I have experienced the discussion around individual cases to lack clarity and specificity. In his work with his client Maria Logis, Alan Turry (2005) addresses these challenges. Finding meaning in performance, carefully working through the implications of this process for the client, and understanding its impact on the therapeutic relationship are all hallmarks of Turry's work. Through the process of song improvisation, she went on to become a songwriter, performer and inspirational speaker sharing with her audiences the power that music and performance had on her struggles to survive cancer. Carefully sifting through her transference and his own counter-transference, Turry explores the implications of bringing these improvised songs into the public domain. He develops a procedure to assess and ascertain information about her capacity to form trusting, intimate connections through performance while also listening for the possibility of substituting external recognition for authentic relationships.

These theoretical perspectives illuminate the essential challenges that I have experienced. The ensuing discussion will develop the historical context in which they came to life.

Background

The people I worked with are adults diagnosed with mental illnesses such as schizophrenia, bi-polar disorder, severe anxiety disorders and recurrent depression. They are people from a diverse, heterogeneous ethnic, cultural and racial background typical of clinical populations in New York City. This cultural context is critical when considering the attitudes I encountered about performance. This was reflected by the many styles of music that were made, the attitude toward solo versus ensemble performance, and the expectations that these musicians have with and from their audiences. These embedded cultural aspects of music performance are very particular and vary significantly from that of other cultures (Nzewi, 2006; Oosthuizen, Fouché, & Torrance, K., 2007; & Inoue, 2007). The individuals discussed here are those drawn deeply to making music. This is a subset of the general adult psychiatric music therapy population. Their love of music is far more critical than the extent to which they are gifted. Almost invariably they share a sense that making music is a core aspect of their selves.

It is not my intention to imply a hierarchy here where performing music is somehow viewed as the pinnacle of therapeutic music making. It is just one possible direction but one that seems more likely to occur when music therapy is conducted in a long-term community setting such as the one described in this paper. In this context, wanting to perform can be seen as a natural extension of the evolving interest that can take place in community music therapy settings (Aigen, 2004; Jampel, 2007).

Though there was interest in performing music from the inception of the music therapy program that began in 1975, there were also challenges to address. The performers who emerged in the community sing that ended each week's program had problems ranging from insecurity and musical inhibition to narcissistic exhibitionism. Singers, bass players, drummers and the occasional keyboard player or solo instrumentalist would emerge and gain recognition for their emergent talents. Even though these musicians solidified into a back up band, it was difficult to find a consistent time and place to work on the problems they experienced in performing music.

By 1991 with the addition of a monthly cabaret called the After Hours Club, they had coalesced into the in-house performance group that has become The Baltic Street Band, a group that continues to this day (Aigen, 2004). The members of the band wanted more time to play with each other. They were motivated to accept more discipline as their interests in music performance grew. This process became more gratifying as their labors produced music that gained increasing recognition from their peers. New members joined the band as their exposure grew. Jobs developed by playing for other communities and some of these were paid performances. Today the band continues to both perform and record its own music. Yet as it became bigger and more skilled, personality issues became increasing obstacles. Lack of preparation, lateness, missed practices and ongoing conflicts between certain band members became disruptive and divisive.

My perception was that persistent personality problems interfered with the working environment of band rehearsals. Patterns emerged in the clashes between performers that appeared to be repetitive and pathological. Patterns of disturbance became evident regarding certain performers' relationship to their own music making process. Sometimes these issues seemed to be complicated by the presence of an audience. Interventions designed to address these issues were made during rehearsals but often the resulting process took time away from preparation for performances. This led to resentment from some musicians that valuable rehearsal time was being consumed by extra musical difficulties. Not to address these recurrent problems seemed out of character with my intention of promoting healthier group dynamics and facilitating individual growth. I perceived that the flaw in this strategy was not in my therapeutic intention but in trying to do both a therapy group and a band rehearsal at the same time. Neither was being done as consistently nor as effectively as was needed.

The Music Therapy Performance Group (MTPG) was first designed in 2004 to both research and treat this dilemma. Meeting as it did on the morning of rehearsals, it was intended to siphon off the need to make therapeutic interventions during band rehearsals. The group focused on the needs of the individual performer. It did not take time away from performance preparation but was in addition to it. Attendance was encouraged but not required for band members. Later after the research study was completed, another treatment group was formed in 2006. This group was opened up to other musicians who did not as yet feel ready to perform. Rehearsals were now free to get down to the business of making music in the time frames needed in order to get ready for upcoming gigs. Persistent and distracting pathological behaviors such as chronic lateness, unexplained absences, lack of work preparedness, or seemingly intractable personality conflicts were addressed in the MTPG. It was here that we could consistently work on performing music and the personality of the performer.

Assessment, Treatment and Evaluation Considerations

Interviews were conducted with each participant prior to the group. The interviews were designed to ascertain past personal history in music including the level of musical training each participant had. As a staff member, I had access to medical records that contained other aspects of their past personal, medical and psychiatric histories but music history was not part of the medical record. Additionally, information elicited in staff meetings from other members of the interdisciplinary team augmented my working knowledge of each member of the group.

Past personal history in music provides an assessment perspective that crosses an array of contributing factors: it provides a different glimpse into parent-child relationships and sibling rivalries; it allows the clinician to assess self-directedness, perseverance, and task completion; it offers a view on assessing the relative health of the creative personality from a viewpoint where spontaneous expressiveness is on one end of the spectrum and pathological anxiety, rigidity and narcissism are on the other; it also provides a window into cultural/family attitudes towards music and the effect this has on an individual's attitude toward making music. The assessment process takes into account the dynamics of musical activities in families where this is an important aspect of family life. Often times the expectations, musical accomplishments or disappointments of the parents are visited upon the child. These attitudes can be extended, altered or exacerbated by subsequent musical history with teachers, producers, promoters, musical juries or with other musicians.

The therapist should be looking to assess various areas of functional capacity. Does the individual engage differently in group music making environments than they do in one to one situations? Does the individual possess flexibility in their musical interactions with others or are they limited or inhibited by this? Does music highlight alternative areas for expression and learning that taps previously unknown or under-utilized pockets of intactness? This is particularly important for individuals who due to the onset of mental illness often suffer cognitive losses. Identifying past trauma in music making with parents, teachers, or in front of critics sensitizes the music therapist to the possible occurrence of traumatic re-enactment.

With sufficient knowledge of the person's musical background, the earned trust of the therapist, and the evolving safety of the group, conditions can now be established where promoting a re-working of the performance experience can allow for a greater sense of meaning and satisfaction to occur. The resulting treatment implications of this process point to the making of music in front of others as a necessary reconstructive strategy. Verbal interventions help create the corrective performance conditions and are also used to evaluate how effectively progress is being made. The relationship between assessment, treatment and evaluation are all bound together in a procedure that examines and analyzes performance from the five experiential components that will comprise the main focus of this discussion.

The Music Performance Personality Profile

This profile incorporates elements of the person's self-image as a musician and how this is embedded into the individual's overall personality development. This required assessing parental/family attitudes about music. In all but one case in the group, music was seen as a significant dimension in family dynamics. Often parents, siblings, grandparents, uncles and aunts were either musicians, musical or cared deeply about music. In some cases, the attitudes cited represented consistent and supportive parental involvement. For others, it was only a small island of support in an otherwise strained or neglectful relationship. Then for others still, past history of music demonstrated patterns of harsh and abusive behavior. With parents who were either musical or musicians themselves, aspects of the parent's past musical experiences often promoted a vicarious experience as the parent relived their own musical experiences through their children's accomplishments or lack thereof. Three group members had parents who were both musicians and abusive parents. For these participants, performance was an opportunity to try to understand and work through their still unresolved feelings about these troubled parents (Borczon, Jampel & Langdon 2010). Sometimes the histories indicated pathologically competitive environments in which siblings were compared to or pitted against one another in terms of the degree of perceived talent that led to preferential behavior. This often set into motion patterns of interaction within the group that seemed to recapitulate past family dynamics (Yalom, 1970).

When the assessment was completed, an initial plan evolved that targeted goals to build upon existing healthy ego structures and to identify pathological features in need of reconstruction. Patterns of behavior as they emerged within the group, were then brought to the awareness of the individual. The intention was to promote more accurate observing ego and the capacity for self-reflection.

Setting and Participants

The Music Therapy Performance Group occurred in a setting in which a multiplicity of music therapy services were provided including other group and individual approaches. One of the participants was 78 years old at the time and had been an active recipient of services at this facility since 1972. Many of the group participants had long-standing connections to the music therapy program. The long-term nature of their connection to treatment at this facility is vital in understanding the impact that the MTPG had.

The work described herein occurred over a period of two and a half years from 2006 to 2008. The new clinical group provided services to a total of 15 adults ranging in age from 24 to 78 years old. Five participants completed their participation prior to the end of the group. This was due to various reasons: changes in schedule due to work or school, moving away or ending treatment at the clinic or in one case, the completion of short term goals. The ethnic and cultural backgrounds of the participants varied. There were three people of African background (two from Caribbean origins and one African-American), five Hispanics, and seven white participants of various ethnic backgrounds.

Group size in any given week varied from as few as three to as many as nine members. They met once a week for forty-five minutes. Most of the group members were also members of the Baltic Street Band consisting of about twenty mentally ill musicians. The group met in the auditorium space where weekly rehearsals and monthly performances took place. The meeting space was in front of a small spot lighted stage located nearby to an acoustic piano. We sat in a circle in front of the stage. My antique tenor banjo sat waiting in its brown alligator and green velvet-lined case. One client loved to play it and his instinctive musicality allowed this to happen almost immediately. Guitars both acoustic and amplified, a bass guitar, hand drums, floor drums and a full drum kit were all made available to participants in order to facilitate the use of instruments for accompanying singers or for instrumental work. The stage, the stage lights and the instruments were all used to create an environment that replicated being in a performance.

Group Structure and Process

"So what would you like to work on in today's Music Therapy Performance Group?" threw the initial direction of the session onto the participants. Their self-image as musicians came up, how they worked with and reacted to other performers, and how they felt about particular audiences. This sometimes led to past performance memories and how their current experiences often had their origins in the past.

Once a theme was centered upon, we might process a recent performance experience including how they felt about it, what it meant to them, and what their reactions were about. For example, one group member who felt anxious and distracted by audience inattentiveness in the After Hours Club the day before, discussed her fear that nobody was listening to her because they did not like her singing. She recounted how in the past, she would become petrified to sing before her parents who she felt were dismissive of her singing when she was a child. After much encouragement from other group members, she sang the Cole Porter (1932) song "Night and Day" accompanied on tenor banjo by the group leader. This time with a new arrangement, she was able to sing in a more intimate way and connect more deeply to the song. The group response was warm and appreciative. This promoted her sense that she could re-construct the performance experience thereby making her less vulnerable to worrying about how she sounded to others. She developed a clearer picture about how the distraction she feared in her audience was really her own projection. By redoing this particular song, connecting more fully to the message in the lyrics, trying a different tempo, accompaniment and arrangement, she was able to alter her relationship to the music, her accompanist, the audience and herself.

We often processed how they experienced the music, how connected they felt to the song, how connected they felt to the other musician(s), how they experienced being listened to. This often brought up aspects of their pasts when similar feelings occurred and what this might signify. Repeating a song invited the musician to try to connect more deeply, concentrate more fully or to realize how the images that sprang to mind while performing might offer them additional fuel to work with. Explorations included: memorable past performances both good and bad; what life was like in their past performing lives; life on the road, special audiences, amazing performers they had seen or with whom they had played. They talked about drugs, money, jealousy, competitiveness, anxieties, self-image, sexuality, hopes, dreams and nightmares. The culture among performing musicians was a favorite topic. They talked of the camaraderie that developed between performing musicians. Their common fears, inattentive audiences, anxieties and insecurities but also the closeness forged by pushing through these difficulties and learning how to cope with them. While they acknowledged their appreciation for each other's skills, they also were able to acknowledge their envy and jealousy of each other as well. They learned by watching and imitating each other. Fine points such as intonation, breathing, microphone technique, body language and movement, story telling through song, stage presence, dressing and costumes, shaping your appearance, the use of make-up, and the capacity to read audiences all were frequent content areas in the group.

Performances were taken apart by the group and analyzed. Rivalries, fears and insecurities were processed but so too were triumphs. Feelings about the leader emerged, sometimes spontaneously, sometimes elicited. Often group members had powerful needs for attention or approval. If these dynamics seemed to be repetitive, the leader offered them back for individual reflection and feedback and as opportunities for the identification of triggering mechanisms. As pathological patterns among members of the group diminished, trust and cohesion developed which then allowed for more risks to be taken both in the music and verbally.

The five dimensional evaluation model was explained and used in the group to foster a systematic representation of performance as a dynamic psychotherapy process. The dimensions formed a shorthand language that objectified each individual experience into something that could be shared and comprehended. By exploring the family music history and the performance background of each group member, people came to a better understanding of themselves and of each other. It provided a focused context for personal disclosure that promoted a sense of safety and trust.

Attendance, Individual Communications and Transference

People who missed a session were expected to call. Unexplained absences or excessive lateness were addressed in the group. If it became a pattern, I met with the individual in my office. One member left the group due to his inconsistent and erratic attendance. He did continue to participate in the band. Several members experienced medical and psychiatric problems that kept them from coming in but as long as they kept in touch, they were encouraged to return as soon as possible. Three people were hospitalized during the course of the group, two for psychiatric reasons and one for medical reasons. Only one did not return to the group after his psychiatric discharge.

Attendance in the group was offered to but not required for members of the band. Eight of the active members in the band attended. Six members of the performance group eventually joined the band. The only one who did not was a nightclub singer who came to group after experiencing severe performance anxiety following a vocal lesson from a teacher who she felt was severely critical of her. This criticism brought up pre-existing areas of sensitivity that made her feel vulnerable and self-conscious. These conflicts illuminated historical patterns of criticism in her family. She was encouraged to try to perform in the group when she felt ready. After she finally did so, she reported that the support she received had helped her to resume her nightclub career as well as prompting her to find a new vocal coach. With this, she left the group reporting that she had accomplished what she had set out to do.

A number of people sought me out to talk to me about a range of issues outside of the group. I would see them but not to discuss group issues. If however I felt that a member was being disruptive to the group either by repeated unexplained absences or chronic lateness, I would request a meeting. I did this in an effort to provide additional support or clarification of problems that were occurring for them. This happened most frequently with two particular people who both had fragile and abuse filled histories. One person eventually left the group and the other Trisha, will be the subject of the case study discussed later in this article.

The issues brought up in group were considered confidential and group participants were asked not to discuss them outside of group. When necessary, I discussed significant developments both with the director of the band and with other clinicians on the treatment team.

I also attended the last hour of band rehearsal each week. I was thus able to observe how each individual operated. This gave me first hand information that I found useful in my work in the next weeks's group. I was an occasional instrumentalist and back-up vocalist in the band as well as the Master of Ceremonies for the monthly cabaret. In both of these roles I was able to witness their performances.

I played other roles outside of the group: administrator, clinician, and internship supervisor. I was also the individual therapist to three members of the group. These multiple roles had evolved over the many years that I worked there and tended to complicate my relationships in the MTPG. They became topics for discussion in the group and added complexity to the transference process.

One of my individual clients saw me as too busy and at times less than available to him. He dropped out of group after he exhibited inconsistent attendance but continued in individual verbal psychotherapy. He focused on his relationship with his deceased, abusive musician father who when not constantly working on the road, got into drunken rages at home where he threatened and abused his wife and children. He reported feeling that in the group, I did not having enough time to see him and that he stopped coming because of this. Over time, he became more able to discuss his feelings about my perceived lack of availability to him and established a better capacity to process his feelings. As he worked through his anger, his attendance in band rehearsals and in performances improved. The relationship that he had with his father affected his ability to connect with other musicians. The dimensions of how this process works will now be explained.

The Five Dimensions of Performance

The experience of performing music involves a complex interplay of connections: between the musician and the music that is being played; between performing musicians in terms of how they feel together playing on stage; between the performer and the audience in terms of the connection that develops between them in both directions; and between the performer and the thoughts within his/her own mind while performing. The experiential totality of these four co-existing states or dimensions, represent the presence of a fifth dimension - the feeling state of the performer. If all four previous dimensions are in a relational state of maximum connection toward themselves and each other, a complementary process ensues. The performer and the music are one, players riff off of each other and move more deeply into sync together, the audience gets drawn in by the action on stage which is felt by the musicians who then play off of the audience's energy, and the performers inner thoughts and feelings act to provide emotional connection which heightens the act of music making by adding depth and meaning. When all of this is synergistic, the effect can be riveting, transforming the moment into a *peak experience* (Maslow, 1971) or as Ansdell (2005) describes it *performance as epiphany*. Such reports described by the performers in the 2004 research group (Jampel, 2007) used the word "spiritual" most often to try to capture this electrifying sensation. But when one or more of these dimensions becomes disturbed, the result is a lessened sense of satisfaction. This can take the look of a musician who does not feel connected to the music, or performers who feel out of sync with each other, or an audience that by being noisy and distracted either affects or were affected by the performers on stage, or the inner thoughts and feelings of the performer (inner audience) becoming a source of negativity and loss of focus. All of this affects the fifth dimension. When looked at from this perspective, the goal of the music therapist is to identify areas of conflict within the four previous dimensions that may be inhibiting the performer's optimal sense of satisfaction and meaning.

These phenomenal states may be all operating simultaneously or in different combinations with each other. A performer can be so absorbed in the music that they might not be fully aware that they are performing before an audience. On the other hand, internal thoughts of doubt, insecurity or negativity may overwhelm the performer and promote a sense of isolation or alienation between the player and fellow performers or from the audience. Because it is a shifting and interactive process, evaluating the performance experience in this multi-dimensional model adds descriptive and causal flexibility. These five states can be best understood as a fluid experience with each dimension containing shifting phenomenological aspects. Repetitive patterns of disconnection in any one or more of the dimensions can be seen as performance psychopathology. Bad performances happen and the dimensional disturbances may be merely transient or reactive to recent stressors. But persistent patterns whose roots extend deep into personality formation tend to be more durable and difficult to work through. On top of this, one must account for the abnormal psychopathology states of psychosis, mania, or severe anxiety and depression that exist within this population. This often complicated the treatment process.

The evaluation process revolves around perceiving changes in any one or more of the dimensions and then adding to or modifying long term or short-term goals accordingly. This process entailed highlighting dimensional strengths and identifying and working through dimensional pathology. Self-reports and first hand observational data were the means by which this clinician was able to understand the impact that this approach had on each of the five dimensions. In the ensuing discussion, clinical vignettes will illustrate each dimension to be followed by a case study that will integrate all five.

The First Dimension: Connecting Within to the Music

Since the end of the MTPG in 2008, I continue to observe performers having difficulty connecting to their music. Whether it is a student, a client or a professional, one can at times detect through body language, facial expression or a perceived lack of conviction in the music that something is missing. Yet only so much can be known through observation.

Choosing the right material is a critical and necessary step. Some performers are clear about what they want to do, what feels right to them. They know themselves musically and when the time is right they may rediscover some old chestnut or to try something new or different. These individuals seem adept at interpreting their material and finding some deeper meaning that promotes connection to the lyrics or to the music. For others however, connecting on the first dimension brings up difficulties in making appropriate musical choices that seem to reflect on the larger problems they have in making appropriate life choices. They are unsure of themselves and of what may be expressive of their present mood. They lack conviction or passion about decisions, or are over determined to try something, or constantly change their mind or just give up too easily. Addressing this situation is tantamount to addressing issues such as why they cannot seem to find themselves, or not know what feels right for them, or how they continue to have persistent feelings of uncertainty about the direction they find themselves going in. Deeply connecting to one's own music can be seen as a statement about how well a person has learned to regulate life, of understanding what works best, of learning how to choose among the myriad options that life and music can offer and learning how to make the best decisions. Inside of this process, there is considerable room for making adjustments, finding new meanings and interpretations, looking and listening with fresh ideas and perspectives. If one cannot consistently regulate how to choose music satisfactorily, broader problems with life regulation often persist.

"What made you choose that song?" is a question that begins exploring the experience of internal connection to song choice. "How did that feel?" allows for the identification of associated affect after the song is performed. The crucial intervention is "Did that song seem right for you?" This question promotes an understanding about whether both song and affect were mood congruent. In other words, if the song evokes an unwanted mood or association even if the song had felt right at other moments, the song will start off as ill-suited for that person in this moment. Sometimes it may just be a matter of changing tempo, key, instrumental accompaniment or arrangement. These adjustments may allow the musician to feel the song differently and permit them to find an alternative path to get into it. But some pieces of music are just not right and if this is the case, the music therapist must facilitate that awareness in the client.

If left unresolved, the first dimension (D1) can spill over into dimension two (D2) and to three (D3). If the music does not feel right, playing it with others gets off track. At times, musical interaction may experienced as a beacon promoting one to come back. But if the music within is not sufficiently connected, the second dimension of connecting to other performers is often negatively impacted. This is I believe discernable to the audience. When disconnected to their own music and consequently to other performers, connecting to an audience is ever so much more difficult. The little voice in one's head experienced in dimension four (D4), can intrude into the performer's thoughts and wreck havoc with concentration and effort. Wrong notes, forgotten parts, overplaying can all result. This will all register in the performer's fifth dimension (D5) report of satisfaction and meaning. It is therefore most critical to find music that promotes the experience of inner connection. This process might be different with professional musicians who are required to play certain kinds of music whether they want to or not but in a music psychotherapy group such as this, this first element is vital. Knowing that you don't feel it but having to play the music anyway is one thing. Not knowing how to get that feeling is quite another.

A discerning performer may change or modify their play list depending on how they feel that day, or how they read the mood of the audience, or how illness or injury can affect song choice. An experienced musician uses these factors in calculating when to make certain adjustments. However, when these choices grow out of fear or anxiety about the music chosen, the result can reflect internal disturbances that can project unresolved D1 states onto the music. The question then becomes one of how to promote more accurate self-perception through greater connection to song choice.

Sometimes evaluating these factors is easier to do in a post performance process. After the dust has settled, an individual can often better assess how well they adjusted to the performance environment. Such discussions were frequent in the Music Therapy Performance Group. As trust developed, group feedback was more seen as supportive, non-judgmental and not as intended to be critical. Group members shared their observations with each other much like a Monday morning quarterbacking session where the team might look at the videotape (which sometimes happened) and discuss the performance from a detailed technical analysis viewpoint. Risk taking was promoted as performers encouraged each other to try out new ideas. However when this experience was perceived as criticism, the therapist had to carefully monitor this process and point out if old transferences were being kicked up. When things got to this point, often it was an indication that some pathological D2 aspects were emerging that required further exploration and understanding.

Though he no longer enjoyed playing music as a drummer, he was an enthusiastic singer and was also the one who loved to strum the tenor banjo. When given permission to sing, he was able to concentrate completely on his voice and enjoy himself again. This led to his performance in the After Hours Club several months later singing a duet of the song "Strangers in the Night" (Singleton & Snyder, 1966). He reported in the group the next day that he had felt relaxed and comfortable. To this observer, he looked and sounded fully connected to the music.

Dimension Two: Performers Connecting with Each Other

The conversation between musicians on stage is at its best a healthy, balanced and reciprocal relationship. There is a sensitivity in listening, selflessness, being together yet maintaining individuality, lifting and holding each other, a lightness, passion, a sharing of beauty and discovery. But when the musical conversation is a struggle, maturity is needed in order to resolve the inevitable conflicts that are normal even necessary in the creative relationship between adult musicians. Managing this phenomenon successfully promotes authenticity and healthy collaboration. But when patterns of conflict repeatedly emerge between particular performers, there is a likelihood of deeper disturbances dwelling within or between them.

According to the musicologist Christopher Small (1998) the meaning to be found in *musicking* is in the creation of relationships formed through the act of playing together not in the sound they produce. These relationships promote and nurture communication and listening skills and represent an ideal of how people work with one another. "Performance does not exist to present musical works, but rather, musical works exist to give performers something to perform" (p. 8).

Such was not the case initially for two members of the who fought incessantly with each other and who often but less frequently, battled with other group members. Performances for them were often highly mercurial events filled with behind the scenes drama that at times, spilled over into tantrums and sudden withdrawals. During performances these individuals often tugged in different directions from the other musicians on stage in terms of tempi, dynamics, pitch accuracy, feel and interpretation. Conflict always seemed to swirl around them. They collaborated with other musicians but could not work together. They did not seem to listen well and isolated themselves. They were easy to anger and to suffer emotional injury. Performance day reflected a high drama of uncertainty about whether they would appear at all or if they did, what they would perform and with whom. Trisha (our case study subject) would inevitably show up but late, unprepared and disorganized. She would often appear visibly upset during performances, grimacing and shaking her head while hurtling ahead of the instrumentalists ignoring cues and cadences. Another group member who was her primary antagonist in the band, would just not show up on performance day leaving fellow performers to scramble without his keyboard, drum accompaniments and vocals. These precipitous actions left the band shaken and mistrustful of both of them. Each had been in the original research group and both were encouraged to enter the new Music Therapy Performance Group.

Not surprisingly, these two individuals, one a 53 year old, white male, who I worked with in individual psychotherapy, and the other Trisha, a 62 year old white female, each had histories of being in abusive relationships. Both were diagnosed with Post Traumatic Stress Disorder. Both were the victims of abusive parents, both had abusive sibling relationships, and both had been involved in adult partnerships where patterns of abuse emerged. They also perceived each other as abusive.

The work for them in D2 involved uncovering the reasons for their tendency to be distrustful of others. Through a gradual process of disclosure of their family histories in music in the group, a context was developed between them in which they became better able to understand how they triggered feelings of being abused in each other. In fact a bond started to develop between them as they came to realize that they had much in common. They began to experience an empathic connection. They felt encouraged to try and sing together in group and when they did, both expressed satisfaction about how it felt. Finding a way to join their voices instead of using them to fight with each other helped to form a bond. They later decided to perform as a duet in the After Hours Club.

What unfolded for Trisha was a tendency to feel a sense of rivalry with others. She reported that positive attention in her family for her artistic achievements was hard to come by but for her pretty younger sister, it seemed to simply rain down for just being attractive. Criticism on the other hand seemed to pour down on her. She experienced this as ridiculing her efforts to sing or play an instrument. Her mother's critical voice often sounded within her head that she was just worthless, untalented and unattractive. For him, praise was just not available from his alcoholic and violent father. No matter how hard he tried, he and his efforts were belittled. Along with several of his eight siblings, music was a central

A MTPG member who had not performed for years reported he no longer did so because he did not like to play the drums. They brought up memories for him of playing in bands past where he felt too responsible to keep the beat.

aspect of family life. He performed with three brothers in a Rock 'n Roll band. This disintegrated into constant disputes, violent confrontations and episodes of alcohol and drug abuse although he reported that he never drank, smoked or abused drugs. Feuds persisted for years in this family. Music was the only means by which members of the family could come together though this was only a faint connection amid a sea of emotional family turmoil.

They fell into a relationship with each other where she thought that he was getting all the attention and he felt that her outbursts and tantrums were emotionally abusive to him. The group leader sought to bring their historical patterns of social interaction to their attention and by so doing, promote self-reflection and observing ego in terms of the causes and triggers for their behavior. Though his erratic attendance eventually resulted in his leaving the MTPG, he did become more consistent in attending After Hours Club performances.

She integrated the feedback in the group, learned to recognize similarities in the present to past patterns of abuse and victimization, and eventually opened up to partnering musically with him. They still had their moments together but each developed a greater capacity for connecting musically and emotionally. Both seemed less prone to missing cues, singing too loudly, making errors or experiencing other musicians as insensitive to them. They were able to perceive how their personal tensions affected the way they made music together. This resulted in their acquisition of greater nuanced musical expressiveness.

The relationship that evolved between these performers displayed aspects of the kind of rapport that Small (1998) referred to. The interpersonal themes were extracted through the filter of their family histories in music. For the music therapist, making this process conscious opened up new possibilities for connection in D2 in terms of musical collaboration. From a group therapy viewpoint as Yalom (1971) observed, the group allowed them to experience a corrective recapitulation of their primary family group. It seemed to create a new kind of musical family, one in which each could be safely heard and listened to.

Dimension Three: Connecting to the Audience

The first two dimensions are present in most music therapy experiences. Connecting deeply to music is a desired outcome for therapists who work with music as an expressive modality. Optimizing the musical connection between members of a group playing music together is a highly desirable social and communication outcome. Though groups may also serve as audiences for each other on occasions, the presence of an audience whose role is distinct from that of the performing musicians, is a phenomenon unique to the performance environment and one that can alter the experience of being in the first two dimensions. Evaluating how an audience alters the experience in dimensions one and two offers additional information to the clinician. It can enhance or disrupt connections to the music within or between performing musicians. Self-consciousness, anxiety or exhibitionistic tendencies may psychically protrude resulting in feelings ranging from constant inhibition and distraction to feeling the need to show off. The mere presence of an audience alters the experience. From a clinical assessment standpoint, the phenomenon of playing music in front of others allows the therapist to understand the degree of health or psychopathology that may exist. What patterns of behavior does the performer exhibit and what do they mean?

The audience effect may vary for the same person from each audience to each performance. Such variability may be an accurate reflection of certain variables like the room acoustics, the quality of the other musicians, ambient noise, difficulty of the music and the degree of preparation, or the health of the performer that day. However, certain people display patterns of behavior in front of an audience that seem less dependent on the variability of the performance environment and more the result of the internal state of the performer. This has been discussed in the music therapy literature in terms of developing working strategies to deal with performance anxiety in musicians (Berger, 1999; Montello, 1989; Montello, Coons, & Kantor, 1990). What has not been discussed in the literature is the significance of this phenomenon for people who may have been too frightened to perform and who were not working musicians. The work described herein is designed to address performance psychopathology for all people. Some may have been interested in performing but for many reasons, may not have had a chance to do so. For others, the experience was brief and buried in their past. For others still, mental illness may have terminated their careers prematurely. In each instance, discerning what performing before an audience means to the individual is the critical link. For the music therapist the salient concern is to understand how that individual operates in front of an audience.

For example one performer in the 2004 research group did not want to see the audience because it made her feel self-conscious "She performed best when she felt enveloped by the music and darkened by house lights. 'I don't want the audience to be known to me. They're not hidden. I want them hidden, no lights and not there'" (Jampel, 2007, pp. 125-6). The significance of this experience may lie in her relationship to her mother who at that time suffered from

Alzheimer's disease. Both of them were professional singers but her abusive mother constantly derided her and her voice saying that both were worthless. She reported that she tried to freeze these thoughts out of her mind when performing before an audience. She also said that the songs that she sang were songs that her mother loved and in this way, she was trying to reconcile with her ailing mother by performing her songs (Borczon, Jampel & Langdon, 2010).

Creating reconstructive experiences for the performer in the presence of an audience was a major group strategy. People not only learned about the importance of thorough preparation but perhaps more importantly, discussed the reasons why they had a hard time being on time and consistent in their work habits. These behaviors were examined from a psychodynamic viewpoint in which avoidance and withdrawal were possible signs of internal distress.

Practical skills were shared such as cuing each other on stage during the music and learning to look at and feed off each other's energy during concerts. In this way the group members were able to incorporate ideas for warding off distractions, improving focusing and concentration and building confidence through repetition. The power of the third dimension was huge. The group learned how to become each other's best audience. The feeling of reciprocal interplay going from performer to audience and back again was palpable. When that feedback loop did not happen during live performances, the performers attempted to compensate for that by sitting together in the audience and shouting vocal support. They would hush the crowd by standing up and rotating 180 degrees while putting a finger to their lips in an attempt to hush the crowd when the ambient noise became too much. Often they would hunch forward in their seats, applaud instrumental solos, and stand up and cheer wildly for each other. Handshakes, high fives and hugs would greet the performer as they returned from the stage.

Applause was the single most telling evidence of success for each performer. As one performer commented, she felt devastated when she received only "pity claps" after one particular performance (Jampel, 2007, p. 132). The quality of the applause seemed to trigger memories of her need for approval from her family. "I never had approval. If I wasn't good nobody said I was good... What I learned from that is I can't judge by my feelings. I never had approval" (p. 140). The issue of being applauded and what it meant to each person was a frequent topic of conversation in the group. The idea of how popular culture focused on audience approval came up when one member discussed her fascination with how contestants were judged and treated on the TV show *American Idol*. She commented in particular about the "spectacle" made by the daughter of another member of the band whose appearance on the show seemed to play up her obvious symptoms of mental illness. By appearing confused and rambling in response to not being chosen to advance to the next round, the group saw this segment as a shameless effort to humiliate a mentally ill performer. Several members of the group felt this episode was scary and depressing. What was even worse was the seemingly insatiable appetite of the audience to revel in the degradation of the performers who did not make it. It was thought by some that this reflected negatively on the larger cultural attitude of ridiculing vulnerable or less talented performers.

Some performers were more susceptible to patterns of self-doubt and lack of focus. For them a pre-disposition to anxiety states seemed rooted in historic patterns of harsh parental criticism and abuse. The treatment process involved working with them to gain insight into understanding the reasons for these patterns, developing the capacity to self-reflect when they began to emerge, and in promoting a stronger sense of self-worth in order to be able to withstand the emergence of these feelings in the group and on stage. The goal was to establish more stable emotional conditions within the performer so as to promote more musical consistency in each performance. This involved the working through of ingrained patterns of self-doubt, diminished self-worth and self-inflicted failures.

The audience in the After Hours Club was comprised of community members and friends and family of consumers. This gathering was mostly a familiar and friendly crowd. It was the kind of atmosphere that encouraged people and often inspired members of the audience to want to perform themselves. Many times over the years, someone would spontaneously get up and want come on stage to sing or play. An open microphone segment in the After Hours Club promoted this phenomenon that frequently led to the recruitment of new members for the band. However, when the performers went on the road, the audience experience was quite different. The room, the sound and the audience presented new challenges. The more experienced performers offered tips to the less experienced ones on how to read the audience, feel out the house and alter your play list accordingly. After having played a particularly tough house in the Bronx in 2004, one member of the performance group remarked, "You know what that proves? When you want to do something, you can do it. I don't think any of us in this group can say, no I can't." (Jampel, 2007, p. 151).

Dimension Four: The Audience Within

Performers carry their own audiences around inside of them. These are our music teachers and mentors, as well as our critics, juries and doubting parents. This audience is unseen to others but present in the mind of the performer. They may be heard intoning words of admonishment, advice, warning or support. These internal presences can serve a deepening, connective function. A face from the past associated to a particular song can evoke an authentic emotional memory. When produced intentionally it can provide an emotional basis for the music much in the same way an actor does in preparing for a role. It may also happen without design as when in the musical moment an internal association occurs that transports the artist to a particular image, feeling or place.

Performance however can also manufacture the presence of ghosts who hover in the shadows of artistic insecurity. When feeling the need to be perfect in order to gain special recognition or by getting caught up in feelings of competition with other performers, inner voices may be stirring underneath. These stirrings may be exhibited as anxiety, feeling distracted or as the fretful anticipation of a certain musical passage. Without understanding the source or origin of these issues, the performer may experience others as potential critics or rivals. Performance failures can be seen as self-fulfilling: the fear of the noxious element ends up interrupting the moment of musical flow that then leads to the undesirable outcome that was feared all along.

The capacity to harness the inner audience effectively is an evaluative landmark of creative health. Musical personalities that successfully internalize the presence of one's formative influences tend to display the capacity to bring them forth and integrate them into new and original experiences. Even when disturbances emerge, these performers can rapidly identify the triggers, know the origins of what is happening to them and through accurate self-observation, move through this process. However, when the internal presences are pathological, one sees an increase in the frequency and severity of these disturbances. The internal presences feel like an inner audience sitting in continual judgment of the performer. At its most extreme point, the performer is either frozen in a state of dreaded terror, unable to function, or overcome by a feeling that the inner audience has crept out of its internal sanctum and now sits in place of the real one. In such instances, this process may not be a part of the performers conscious awareness. This often results in the occurrence of distortions and projections.

The reality is that many performers' lives are stressful. Harsh critics not only exist but they abound. The music education system of much of Western music promotes performance pathology through rigid and highly inflexible standards of perfection and stressful competition. For the mentally ill musician whose inner life has been torn by unusually high levels of psychological trauma and cognitive difficulties, the toll is even worse. For people who are psychotic, the inner audience is real and alive. Helping them to focus on performing for the outer audience is the goal. Seven out of the fifteen members experienced visual or auditory hallucinations at some point during the duration of the group. Remarkably, making and performing music seemed almost invariably to provide them with relief from their psychosis. They each had the capacity to draw upon when healthy, a range of past memories and feelings that provided meaning to the act of performing.

Messages must be deciphered from the members of the inner audience to the performer. Who are they and what are they saying? This requires restoring some balance to the person's self-image when these inner states become unduly punishing. The leverage of the group is especially important here. It is more persuasive when eight people tell you that your singing is lovely than it is when there is only one. The structuring of feedback loops can break the cycle of self-deprecation. Conversely, when narcissistic features emerge that overvalue or hoard the spot light, a balanced group perspective may be more powerful than an individual therapeutic framework. Overall however, the likelihood of success for the narcissistic personality in music performance psychotherapy is more problematic due to the pathological social defensive structure of this personality type.

Through the experience of leading the Music Therapy Performance Group for two and a half years, the concept of the fourth dimension went through a process of expansion and clarification. I have come to appreciate the significance of the inner audience for assessment, treatment and evaluation. It seemed clear even six years ago that the inner audiences were present. The process and significance of how they were internalized and then projected onto the music performance experience was not then fully articulated or understood. The dualistic nature of performance with its inner and outer audiences has also evolved. I now believe that pathology in the other dimensions is most often the result of D4 pathology. One can liken it to the process of forming healthy/pathological attachments through the connection that develops in the musical relationship. Disturbances can impair the performer's ability to connect within themselves to music (D1), between others (D2), with the audience (D3), and resulting in a diminished sense of satisfaction (D5).

Dimension Five: The Totality of Experience

The fifth dimension (D5) has also undergone revisions with the passage of time. In 2004 several participants reported their performance experiences in terms of peak, altered or spiritual states (Jampel, 2007, pp.151-3). This author speculated that the experience of exultation occurred when all four dimensions optimally came together. This produced a heightened state of consciousness. Yet the reports also indicated that each performance experience differed, sometimes radically so. Disappointment or frustration occurring in one or more of the dimensions resulted in a range of feeling outcomes. For example, one person felt that her two most recent performances (in 2004) were "like a flip-flop. The best audience and the best time, the best everything that I had was up in the Bronx and then I can flip it around and say it was the worst" (p.130). She described her second performance like an "elevator that never got off of the first floor" (p. 130).

It is only reasonable to expect that there will be a variety of reactions to a given performance. Although peak states in performance were reported with greater frequency than in other situations, the evaluation of this phenomenon should take into account all nuances of experience. What seemed like a great concert to one person might seem very different to another. Though the variations in reports of felt experience were clearly present in the original research study, the discussion of the fifth dimension did not sufficiently factor into it the richness and diversity of how the performer felt about the performance and how useful this is as an evaluative device.

As I now understand it, the experience of the fifth dimension represents the totality of the performer's reactions. This includes the feelings of inner connection to the music, how that individual felt about the way the musicians played together, how they experienced the audience, and the felt presence of the inner audience. Together this might or might not rise to the level of a spiritual or peak moment but more importantly, it describes the precise contours of the feelings, concerns and thoughts of the performer. Here is how one group member described her recent performance experience, "It's a high when everything hits with the audience and you're clicking with the musicians and you're true to yourself. I can't think of any better expression. It's the totality of who you are" (Personal Communication, May 2008).

This dimension is based on the report of the individual and it is entirely subjective. If it seems exaggerated, distorted or extreme in its account of what happened as compared to the reports of other participants, the clinician's evaluation should consider the possibility of dimensional pathology. For instance, other group members who were present experienced the devastation that was felt by the performer who received "pity claps" after one particular performance, very differently. She felt that she sang miserably while others who were there (including this clinician) did not perceive this. One might postulate that the inner audience had been shouting negative comments. Some skewing of felt experience in performance is to be expected. However when the D5 experience of one person tends to reflect more consistent negativity than that reported by others, the likelihood is that pathological features exist in the person's performance personality profile. The evaluation process should follow the trail to the affected dimension(s) and explore the underlying causes. In the group, the music therapist should facilitate awareness of these issues, encourage feedback from others, and try to promote a greater sense of accuracy in the person's capacity for healthy self-regulation. The MTPG provided a supportive environment where feedback from other musicians who also frequently experienced musical insecurities, helped to balance out and even to outweigh those negative self-images. The reports of the D5 experience over time, reflected more consistently satisfying performance experiences.

Case Study

In May 2008, I conducted interviews with fifteen people who had received music therapy services in performance. I hoped to find out why they performed, what it meant to them, and what drawbacks they experienced in doing it. The following case study was partially drawn from one of these interviews.

Trisha was 63 years old at the time of the interview, an Italian-American female, divorced without children who had come into treatment in 1995 complaining of having experienced episodes of panic that prohibited her from working as a mid-level executive in a large corporation. She had recently divorced an Egyptian man who she reported was violent and abusive toward her throughout their marriage of eight years. Her early history revealed multiple episodes of abuse starting with her mother and brother who were reported to have been physically and emotional abusive toward her throughout her childhood and adolescence. Trisha was a trained dancer who also had participated as a member of several choirs throughout her life. Her younger sister was musical and according to Trisha, received all the praise and attention not because of her talents but because of her beauty. Neither parent was trained musically but her father was an opera lover and was the more loving and understanding parent. Trisha experienced her mother's attitude toward her interest in music as negative and discouraging. Her psychiatric diagnoses were Panic Disorder and Post Traumatic Stress Disorder.

Trisha has been involved with the band as a singer since 1997. Her ongoing difficulty in working cooperatively with the other members of the band, led to the idea that she could benefit from individual music therapy where she could focus on her own music. It was there that she began to compose her own songs and since then, has composed more than twenty songs that she has both performed and recorded. Songwriting offered a structure, which as DeNora (2000) observed, helped her to find a container for traumatic memories. Her music became an outlet for putting the past behind her and finding a way of moving ahead with her life. Her voice was another focus in individual music therapy. It was the target for reducing stress, improving her focusing and concentration, and providing greater emotional expressivity through changes in her vocal breathing technique.

Despite progress in these areas, she continued to labor in the band with difficulties in working with other musicians. She often erupted into arguments that spilled over into personal disputes that left her feeling victimized and abused. In the music, she had a tendency to race in front of the melody, sing out of turn, and find difficulty in maintaining accurate pitch. These disturbances in the music were closely connected to the interpersonal problems that she experienced. What became apparent was that her pitch and rhythm issues grew out of her problems with other people. Interventions strategies developed in band rehearsals to address her pitch and timing issues focused on promoting movement while singing so that she could both feel the music as a singer and as a dancer. This helped to a degree but recurrent personality issues continued to interfere. Despite efforts to address the destructive dynamics between her and other band members in rehearsals and in individual meetings, it became evident that too much time was being taken away from the music and from other band members without sufficient resolution of her interactional dysfunction.

After her entrance into the Music Therapy Performance Research Group, her psychotherapy needs could be attended to without time being taken away from rehearsals. No longer were individuals pitted against each other in proportioning time based on the need to get ready for the next performance. Now rehearsal schedules could be more closely adhered to. Once this inherent conflict was resolved, the level of tension between Trisha and the rest of the band eased considerably.

Dimensional Evaluation of Trisha

Trisha's performance experience was characterized by her harsh self-criticism that she reported in the following manner "I'll believe the negative before I believe the positive. I'm very self-critical. I have my mother's voice in my head all the time" (Personal Communication, May, 2008). From a dimensional viewpoint, one can look at this as D4 pathology. The intrusive, self-critical nature of her introjected maternal voice developed into a punishing musical super-ego. She was her own worst critic who often revoked permission to herself to complete a performance when she felt that she did not meet up to her own punishing standards of perfection "My self-consciousness takes over... which is extremely painful and embarrassing." This anxiety spilled over when she sang in front of an audience. "I am self-conscious in front of an audience. I always have been. That's why I always sang in groups." The anxiety of performing before an audience can be likened to singing in front of a room full of critics. She projected her D4 self-expectations onto others. The D3 audience effect can be seen as a pathological projection of her self-criticism. When activated in this way, Trisha's projections extended to her experience of working with other musicians in D2. Her relationship to the 53 year-old group member was sibling-like as he was perceived as an abusive brother. Her relationship with other females was characterized by anger and jealousy as was the case with the 78 year-old member whose deep and husky female contralto voice received much praise from others. Trisha often felt that she was given preferential treatment in rehearsals and said this in reference to her "I have had a very hard time in the band. We had women who had powerful lower voices than I did. I was very high and lyrical. You know I was criticized for whatever." Ironically, the 78 year-old was an abuse survivor herself and had always been belittled by her musician father for her voice that he regarded as unfeminine. Praise was hardy something she assumed was forthcoming.

It took Trisha time to place me in her constellation of family characters. At first, she experienced me as favoring other people. She also said that I never had a complimentary word for her music. It was only later on that she experienced me as being more caring and appreciative of her. I would say that her transference could be described as similar to her relationship with her mother. I seemed unappreciative of her talents and often I was perceived as highly preferential to others. Eventually I defied easy description, as a more healthy D2 connection became her dominant perception of other performers, myself included. But first we had to work on her overtly critical D4 issues in order to restore her capacity for self-worth. Over time she was able to balance out how she saw herself and consequently, how she saw herself in relationship to others.

All of this pathology on D4, D3, and D2 took a tremendous toll on her D1 inner connection to the music. "I have been judged and have been criticized but no one is worse at criticizing me than myself. I have had to let go of that." As she did so, she began to experience music differently. It was like she could hear it better, reproduce pitch more accurately, feel the rhythm and tempo better, remember the words and connect more deeply. She stopped fighting in rehearsals, moved more fluidly and became more expressive. The reaction of audiences was telling. She experienced recognition even admiration for her performances and as compliments came her way, "finally one day I decided to believe it."

Her D1 pathology looked like never being sure which song was right for her. Often she felt the register was too low or too high for her voice, the key was wrong, it needed to be faster or slower and finally, she just wanted to move to another song. With the breakthrough in her D4 and D1 pathology, new channels were opened to her. She re-examined her experience of playing with other musicians in the MTPG and began using the group as an opportunity to become more comfortable with her D1 connection to the music. Her vocal duets solidified her D2 connection. The group became a new kind of supportive audience that encouraged a healthier D3 connection. One day she received a standing ovation in the After Hours Club "that put me over. I crossed over from timidity, if that is a word, over to the other side." When asked about the importance of playing in front of an audience she responded:

> Yes, I got a lot of confidence by trusting in myself and the feedback that I have gotten. I'm really appreciative. I have never taken it for granted. Each time I perform it's a new day, a new performance that I don't take for granted. I will achieve what I want to achieve.

No longer did she transfer sibling issues onto other performers but now she could take in what they had to offer without seeming to flinch or duck as she had before. "They have come to accept me. We don't have that friction anymore." The improved regulation of projections from D4 onto D2 and D3 allowed her to concentrate better and focus on D1, D2 and D3 without as many intrusions. The synergistic effect of all levels flowing together produced a sense of lift and well being in her. She was able to balance out her perceptions of herself with what others thought of her. "I just balanced myself because if I'm satisfied with a performance, it doesn't matter what someone else thinks."

As her self-critic eased up, Trisha's sense of accomplishment came through more often. "Sometimes I'll be very good and sometimes I won't (laughs) but that doesn't take away from my expressing myself." The experience of performing music on D5 portrayed a person who had a greater degree of personality integration and realistic observing ego. This was evident when she said, "I feel like a whole person. I feel very cleared to all negativity. I may not always think that I performed my best but that's just a performance. It's not taking my voice away and forgetting who I am."

The quality of being more fully in each moment reflected a person who had managed to free herself of her inner tormenter. "However I could express myself at that moment is the best that I could do at that moment and there always is another moment." This fluid state of being characterizes a healthier personality that has opened more her optimal creative *flow* (Csikszentnihalyi, 1990).

It was not surprising that her D5 experience summed up how performance offered her transcendence.

> The spontaneity of being in the moment and feeding from the audience and seeing their faces light up. I still could look up or down, close my eyes. I could look at the audience and feed from the audience and the other musicians. If they are playing well and if they are in sync with me and I am in sync with them and you're feeding off each other, it's a tremendous experience.

In this statement, Trisha summed up the essence of how it feels when all the dimensions are aligned for optimal *flow*. The "feeding" from the audience, the "in sync" feeling when you are locked in with other musicians, and of being 'true to yourself' in the sense of connecting with your inner music and to your inner audience.

For Trisha, performance brought out her playful side. It allowed her to dress up in costumes, put on make-up, and use her talents as a dancer and actor. She found new ways to interpret the emotions of the characters in her songs. She composed music that employed her talents for poetry and writing. And perhaps most significantly, she found a new family that recognized and appreciated her talents.

Conclusion: Brothers and Sisters in Performance

The connections established in the MTPG produced a strong bond. A feeling of shared experience occurred that promoted a culture of belonging to some bigger entity than oneself. The traditions of performers, their customs, common language, their encounters and experiences, the sense of being part of a larger community of artists, was all felt. The relationships that evolved in the group explored, affirmed, and celebrated the empowerment of the performer. The members came to embrace performance as the domain of the committed not just the gifted.

Ansdell (2004) describes the experience of *communitas* (first used by the anthropologist Victor Turner and discussed by Even Ruud) in referring to the feeling of membership promoted by performance. Aigen (2005) uses this term to denote the camaraderie that develops between members of a band through the ritual of playing music together. He discusses the "liminal" or timeless qualities of performing as "losing oneself in the experience, leaving behind symbols and practices of previous positions, ambiguities, perceived danger, the absence of roles and a transcending of previously defined borders" (pp. 91-92).

Despite the strong presence of camaraderie that developed, inevitably individuals continued to struggle. The liminal aspect of the performance process can be deceptive. It can overshadow the personal experience of one performer who may not feel the same glow that is shared by the rest of the group. A therapist should not assume that all moments even the peak ones, are being felt in the same way by each person. What often develops is a special understanding between performers. The experience comes to feel more like a band of performing brothers and sisters in the way that people come to feel about having gone through a lot together even if it was not always easy. One difference between this group and their own families of origin however was in the support and encouragement that they found that was often missing there.

References

Aigen, K. (2004). Conversations on creating community: Performance as music therapy in New York City. In M. Pavlicevic & G. Ansdell (Eds.), *Community music therapy* (pp. 186-213). Philadelphia: Jessica Kingsley Publishers.

Ansdell, G. (2005). Being who you aren't; doing what you can't: Community music therapy & the paradoxes of performance. *Voices: A World Forum for Music Therapy*, North America, 5, Nov. 2005. Retrieved January 5, 2011, from

Aigen, K. (2005). *Playin' in the Band: A qualitative study of popular music styles as clinical improvisation*. Gilsum, NH: Barcelona Publishers.

Ansdell, G. (2004). Rethinking music and community theoretical perspectives in support of community music therapy. In M. Pavlicevic & G. Ansdell (Eds.), *Community music therapy* (pp. 65-90). Philadelphia: Jessica Kingsley Publishers.

Berger, D. S. (1999). *Toward the Zen of performance: Music improvisation therapy for the development of self-confidence in the performer*. St. Louis: MMB Music, Inc.

Borczon, R. M., Jampel, P. & Langdon, G.S. (2010). Music therapy with adult survivors of trauma. In Stewart, K. (Ed.) *Music therapy & trauma: Bridging theory and clinical practice*, New York: Satchnote Press.

Csikszentnihalyi, M. (1990). *The psychology of optimal experience*. New York: Harper and Row.

DeNora, T. (2000). *Music in everyday life*. Cambridge: Cambridge University Press.

Inoue, S. (2007). A study of Japanese concepts of community. *Voices: A World Forum for Music Therapy*, North America, 7, Jul. 2007. Retrieved January 7, 2011, from:

Jampel, P. (2007). *Performance in music therapy with mentally ill adults*. Dissertations Abstracts International. (UMI, Order #3235696).

Maslow, A. (1971). *Farther reaches of human nature*. New York: The Viking Press.

Montello, L. (1989). *Utilizing music therapy as a mode of treatment for the performance stress of professional musicians*. Doctoral dissertation, New York University. (UMI Order No. 9004310).

Montello, L. Coons, E.E., & Kantor, J. (1990). The use of group therapy as a treatment for musical performance stress. *Medical Problems in Performance Art*, March (5), 49-57.

Nzewi, M.(2006). African music creativity and performance: The science of the sound. *Voices: A World Forum for Music Therapy*, North America, 6, Mar. 2006. Retrieved January 6, 2011, from:

O'Grady, L.(2008). The role of performance in music-making: An interview with Jon Hawkes. *Voices: A World Forum for Music Therapy*, North America, 8, Jul. 2008. Retrieved January 7, 2011, from:

Oosthuizen, H., Fouché, S., Torrance, K. (2007). Collaborative work: Negotiations between music therapists and community musicians in the development of a South African community music therapy project. *Voices: A World Forum for Music Therapy*, North America, 7, Nov. 2007. Retrieved January 7, 2011, from:

Small, C. (1998). *Musicking*. Hanover, New Hampshire: Wesleyan University Press.

Stige, B. (2002). The relentless roots of community music therapy. *Voices: A World Forum for Music Therapy*, North America, 2, Nov. 2002. Retrieved January 6, 2011, from:

Stige, B., Ansdell, G., Elefant, C., & Pavlicevic, M. (2010). *Where music helps: Community music therapy in action and reflection*. Ashgate Publishing Co.

Turry, A.(2005). Music psychotherapy and community music therapy: Questions and considerations. *Voices: A World Forum for Music Therapy*, North America, 5, Mar. 2005. Retrieved January 5, 2011, from:

Wood, S (2006).. "The matrix": A model of community music therapy processes. *Voices: A World Forum for Music Therapy*, North America, 6, Nov. 2006. Retrieved January 6, 2011, from:

Yalom, I. (1970). *The theory and practice of group psychotherapy*. New York: Basic Books.

©VOICES:A World Forum for Music Therapy.

CHAPTER 12

MUSIC THERAPY IN HOSPICE AND PALLIATIVE CARE

Joey Walker
Mary Adamek

CHAPTER OUTLINE

    HOSPICE AND PALLIATIVE CARE: WHAT ARE THEY?
    WHO BENEFITS FROM HOSPICE OR PALLIATIVE CARE?
    MUSIC THERAPIST AS PART OF THE HOSPICE TEAM
    ISSUES AT END-OF-LIFE, TYPICALLY ADDRESSED BY MUSIC THERAPISTS
        Physical Issues
        Psychosocial Issues
    MUSIC THERAPY GOALS AND INTERVENTIONS COMMONLY USED IN HOSPICE AND PALLIATIVE CARE
        Music Therapy to Alleviate Physical Symptoms
        Music Therapy for Psychosocial Support

> *Mike, a 60-year-old male, had recently moved into a long-term care facility because of complications with his cancer. He was no longer able to care for himself at home. The home health aide had reported that Mike did not want to bathe, get dressed, or do his other activities of daily living. When the music therapist visited late one morning, Mike was lying in bed, unshaven, and he had not put his false teeth in his mouth. He was unkempt and not dressed. He agreed to a music therapy session, and 45 minutes later he was energetic and reminiscing about good times when he and his significant other would dance together in numerous small towns around the area. He asked the music therapist to return the same time the next week. Upon returning the next week, Mike was clean, dressed, and lying on the top of his bed. Soon his significant other entered the room and slid onto the bed with Mike. They were able to share a songbook together, sing, talk about dancing, and express their love for each other.*

HOSPICE AND PALLIATIVE CARE: WHAT ARE THEY?

The terms *hospice* and *palliative care* refer to a philosophy of care for people at end-of-life. This **team-oriented approach** provides compassionate **end-of-life care** to enhance comfort and improve quality of life for individuals who have **terminal illness** and for their families. The goals are to prevent suffering, relieve pain, and optimize each person's functioning. The individual's decisions about care are central to the hospice and palliative care philosophy, and the team is guided by the wishes of the patient and family.

People are eligible for hospice treatment when their death is anticipated in six months or less. Palliative care can be provided for persons who are dealing with terminal illness whether or not they have a six-month prognosis. The terms *hospice* and *palliative care* are closely related. Both are concerned with providing relief but not cure, and in some parts of the world the terms are used interchangeably. The term *hospice* will be used throughout this chapter to indicate a model of care to improve quality of life for people with life-limiting illness and for their families.

WHO BENEFITS FROM HOSPICE OR PALLIATIVE CARE?

Adults and children with terminal illness can be admitted to hospice care. The largest number of patients have a cancer diagnosis, while others are admitted with heart, lung, or **neuromuscular disease; Alzheimer's/dementia;** organ failure; HIV/AIDS; or other disorders. Adults and children may have developmental delays concomitant with their medical diagnosis. Children have different physical and psychosocial needs than adults, based on their ages and developmental levels. The family is also a recipient of hospice care while the patient is dying and during **bereavement** after the family member's death. The interdisciplinary team addresses the unique needs of each family unit throughout the dying and bereavement process.

MUSIC THERAPIST AS PART OF THE HOSPICE TEAM

The goal of hospice is to care for each person in a holistic manner. This requires an interdisciplinary team to address patients' physical, psychological, spiritual, and social needs. The interdisciplinary team plans coordinated care, holds regular team meetings, and continues ongoing communication to ensure that goals are met and frequently reassessed. The team includes the primary physician, hospice physician, nurse, social worker, chaplain, home health aide, bereavement counselor, and volunteers. Additional team members may include a music, occupational, or physical therapist; psychologist; pharmacist; and nutritionist, among others. Patients and families are considered part of the team and are able to direct their desired care by

CHAPTER 12: MUSIC THERAPY IN HOSPICE — 345

communicating specific needs to the rest of the team (National Hospice & Palliative Care Organization, 2008).

Music therapists utilize comprehensive skills to observe, report, document, and provide effective interventions. A music therapist may provide treatment for physical, emotional, spiritual, cognitive, or social needs. Viewing the whole person as the interaction of mind, body, and spirit, the music therapist has a unique place among other professionals on the team. Other team members may concentrate their efforts mostly in one area of expertise, such as with physical or spiritual needs. The music therapist may be able to offer insight for team members concerning the multidimensional needs of each patient.

Hospices are becoming more aware of the benefits of providing music therapy services. Music therapists provide support in a noninvasive, cost-effective approach. Music therapy in hospice care is one of the fastest growing areas in the field of music therapy, with the creation of many new employment opportunities in the last few years (American Music Therapy Association, 2007).

ISSUES AT END-OF-LIFE, TYPICALLY ADDRESSED BY MUSIC THERAPISTS

The needs of hospice patients and families vary greatly, and these needs may rapidly change from day to day, hour to hour, and within a single session (Krout, 2000). Therefore, the music therapist will provide services that concentrate on physical, **psychosocial**, spiritual, and bereavement needs of the moment for each session. For example, the music therapist may have concentrated efforts on a spiritual issue during a past session, and in a present situation may focus on pain control. A session in the future could consist of using music to stimulate memories and life review, or perhaps any combination may take place within a single session. Ongoing assessment is critical to ensure that the patient and family are receiving the care that they desire.

Physical Issues

Pain management. Pain management is a primary focus for the hospice team. Although not every patient in hospice care has pain management needs, pain is still the most common symptom experienced by hospice patients (Kastenbaum, 2001). Patients sometimes improve in hospice care because the team is able to find effective ways of treating the **total pain** of each patient. Cicely Saunders, who is considered the modern founder of hospice, created this concept of "total pain" in order to ensure that psychological, emotional, social, spiritual, as well as physical pain of patients and their loved ones is included in treatment (Hilliard, 2005). This concentration on the whole person interfaces easily with music therapy, as the music therapist can simultaneously address several goal areas with specific interventions.

Hospice care takes into account the desired level of pain management for each patient and family. Because pain is subjective and complex, each person's experience differs from another. For a variety of reasons, people also have different levels of pain that they will tolerate at any given time. One patient may want to be alert and thinking clearly when making legal or financial decisions, while another patient may want to be able to be fully awake to visit with a long unseen family member. Some families do not want to use pain medications for their loved one due to fears of addiction or sedation, and other patients are unable to use medications because of certain symptoms, disease process, allergic reaction, or other undesirable side effects. Some patients may not receive pain medication in a timely fashion, if at all. For others, generational, spiritual, or cultural considerations or stoicism may contribute to reluctance in admitting that pain is actually present. If untreated, unrelieved pain may lead to the following:

- Fatigue
- Stress
- Nausea
- Loss of appetite
- Isolation
- Anxiety
- Difficulties with daily activities
- Disrupted sleep patterns
- Depression
- Relationship difficulties
- Anger
- Thoughts of suicide

(National Foundation for the Treatment of Pain, 2008)

In addition to the problems listed above, patients may use much of their energy to deal with unrelieved pain. They may have little energy remaining to take care of other essential end-of-life issues like emotional problems or spiritual pain. Conversely, Trauger-Querry and Haghighi (1999) discuss the fact that treatment for pain can be resistant if psychosocial, emotional, or spiritual issues are disregarded.

Pain assessment. It can be challenging for adults to admit, describe, and discuss issues of pain. Children's expression and understanding of pain is compounded by their level of development. Instead of verbalizing about pain, children may exhibit behavioral distress, which may involve changes in behavior, sleep, or eating patterns; becoming withdrawn; decreased physical activity; increased irritability; or an increased need to seek comfort (Barrickman, 1989). Preschool children may not be able to verbally describe their pain or anxiety and may act out behaviorally, for example, by screaming, hitting, or having a tantrum. Older children may withdraw and become quiet as a means of control and may not verbally express pain because of fear of receiving painful procedures or treatment. Adolescents may have difficulty communicating their needs in general, and admitting to pain may keep them from spending time with peers or may curb their independence. Within a normalized musical environment, children may demonstrate more congruence with feeling and verbalization and may also express themselves on an emotional level more easily with music as the stimulus (Ghetti & Walker, in press).

Chapter 10 described a number of **assessment tools** that may be useful in a hospice or palliative care setting. Because of the nature of hospice care, the choice of a suitable assessment tool should take into account a number of factors: the functional level of the patient, an assessment that is as nonintrusive as possible, and an assessment that can be completed quickly, given what is sometimes a rapid change in patient status.

Music therapists have access to a variety of formal assessment tools with regard to pain and discomfort. Pain assessment tools such as **Numeric Rating Scale (NRS)** and Faces are recommended for use by nonnursing team members (Mills-Groen, 2007). The patients rate their perceived pain by choosing a number from the scale (NRS) or a picture/line drawing (Faces) of a face of a person experiencing different levels of pain severity. These assessment tools are easy to use and take little time to determine the patient's pain intensity at the moment.

A music therapist must be able to continuously observe in a less formal manner these possible indicators of pain:

- Vocal and verbal complaints
- Rubbing, holding a body part
- Bracing
- Facial grimacing/winces
- Furrowed brow, frown
- Irritability
- Anxiety
- Restlessness
- Physical repetitive movements
- Repeating words or phrases
- Change in behavior from the norm

(Cohen-Mansfield & Creedon, 2002; Maue-Johnson & Tanguay, 2006; Warden, Hurley, & Volicer, 2003)

Lower functioning patients may be unable to verbally express their pain and its symptoms; therefore, music therapists carefully observe for the indications listed above and monitor changes in behavior. Often the anxious or restless behavior of a patient in a long-term care facility may appear to be related to a medical condition such as dementia; however, it may be caused by unresolved pain. Other indicators of unaddressed pain in lower functioning patients may include:

- Eyes tightly closed
- Tense muscles, clenched fists
- Increased pacing
- Changes in sleep patterns
- Wanting to exit home or facility
- Increased agitation
- Pulling away or hitting when touched
- Decreased appetite

(Warden et al., 2003)

Symptom management. Symptom management is an integral part of hospice care. Similar to pain management, symptoms may not be eliminated but managed at a level desired by the patient or family.

***Dyspnea.* Dyspnea** is shortness of breath that occurs in patients with a variety of life-limiting conditions, but commonly occurs in **chronic obstructive pulmonary disorder (COPD)** and with some cancers. This feeling of not being able to get enough breath or suffocating causes anxiety, which may lead to increased dyspnea which subsequently may lead to increased anxiety in an unlimited cycle (Hilliard, 2005).

Agitation. Agitation can be a significant problem for patients and families. While there are many causes of agitation such as pain or disease process, agitation can lead to safety issues and be distressing for staff or caregivers.

Sleep difficulties. Patients may have problems regulating their sleep cycles. They might sleep during the day, making it difficult to fall asleep at night. Sleep problems can contribute to increase in anxiety and agitation.

Restlessness. Near the end-of-life when multiple body systems are shutting down, some patients (even those who have previously been calm) may experience terminal restlessness. This may include anxiety, thrashing or agitation, palpitations, shortness of breath, insomnia, pain, moaning, yelling, involuntary muscle twitching or jerks, fidgeting, or tossing and turning (Hospice Patient Alliance, 2008). This can be upsetting for the patient, family, and staff who are also coping with other end-of-life issues.

Psychosocial Issues

In hospice care, patients also face end-of-life psychosocial and spiritual issues. As noted in Chapter 10, medical conditions greatly impact a person's psychological, social, and emotional functioning. This impact on quality of life, according to Krout (2000) and Hilliard (2003), can be improved through music therapy psychosocial support. When patients reach a desired or tolerable level of physical comfort, they may have the basic energy or need for emotional support and comfort. Due to the sizeable amount of end-of-life psychosocial needs, concentration will be given to coping with illness and loss through the following areas: (1) anxiety reduction, (2) emotional support, (3) autonomy and control, (4) reduction of isolation, and (5) family cohesion.

Anxiety. Anxiety related to dyspnea was previously discussed; however, anxiety can also be caused by psychological, social, or spiritual factors. A terminal prognosis can create fear of the unknown and manifest in tension and anxiety (Hilliard, 2005). Patients and families may want to know why or how someone will die, if it will be painful, and when it will occur, etc. Family members may not agree on the plan of care (e.g., withholding aggressive treatment or measures given for comfort only), where to spend the last part of life, or merely how to care for the patient. This may compound stress and tension in an already unstable situation and cause more anxiety for the patient as well. Family members may have additional anxiety thinking about and dealing with unknown issues.

Emotional needs related to losses and spirituality. People experience many losses throughout the dying process. Patients may have the role loss that may have helped define who they were. For example, a mother who was the constant caretaker of everyone in the family who can no longer fulfill that role, or a child who cannot attend school, may feel the loss of who he or she is. Patients may also physically appear different and may have lost home and family; they may need an outlet that helps them feel serene, one that can help them express who they are. Patients and families need a way to express their personal identity, search for meaning, understand their relationship to God or Higher Power, and complete unfinished business (Trauger-Querry & Haghighi, 1999).

Each patient guides the depth of emotional involvement for the team according to his or her own individual needs. Patients may need someone who will take time to listen and validate their feelings, and at times they may feel more comfortable expressing feelings to hospice staff instead of a family member. Patients may not want to upset someone in their family or may feel that they shouldn't be feeling a certain way, or that it is wrong to feel an emotion that might be considered negative. It is also possible that they may be unable to verbally express emotions or they may not know what they are feeling.

In general, people of all ages and levels of functioning need help when coping with illness or loss. At end-of-life the problems may be magnified and may feel overwhelming. At times patients may experience a series of losses that appear to never end. Patients may lose independence with the inability to physically or mentally do what they desire, may have chronic and acute pain, may have moved to a different environment and are mourning the loss of a familiar place, may have to adjust to new caregivers and the stress that accompanies loss of privacy or dignity, may have financial concerns or feel like they are a burden, or may be separated from friends or loved ones. In addition to adjusting to a medical condition and their own mortality,

350 - PART TWO — POPULATIONS SERVED BY MUSIC THERAPISTS

patients may have these and other losses that make coping more difficult and contribute to emotional and spiritual pain.

Many people find a need for spiritual comfort at end-of life. If a hospice is **Medicare-certified,** it is required to provide a chaplain for spiritual support. However, the music therapist also provides comfort and additional spiritual support.

Autonomy and control. In some patients, feelings of helplessness and low self-esteem surface with the loss of normalcy and independence. Motivation to attempt straightforward daily responsibilities may decrease and depression may become more likely when people are unable to accomplish simple tasks. Patients who have developed dependency and helplessness may have difficulty making even a simple forced choice.

Isolation. Isolation is a common problem for many patients in hospice care. People may live alone at home or in long-term care facilities, or are in hospitals where it is more difficult for various people to visit. Many may be of an age where most of their friends and family have died. Others do not want people around to witness their decline. Some people avoid visiting friends at end-of-life, while other visitors do not know how to interact with someone who is withdrawn or may not communicate in a familiar way.

Socialization is an important component of quality of life (Hilliard, 2005). People have a need to feel as if they are accepted and belong. Integrating acceptance and belonging into musical interventions is typical and inherent in the musical process (see Chapter 3). When feasible and appropriate, group interactions take place within families, with friends, or with other residents of facilities. Making music together helps develop a sense of belonging, whether in a group situation or simply with the music therapist.

Family cohesion. When people gather at the end-of-life, there may be family members who have not seen each other since they were young. They may disagree on issues, and old patterns and resentments may reoccur. It can be a stressful time, with family members missing time from work and their own family responsibilities. Disagreement can be distressing for the patient as well as the family.

MUSIC THERAPY GOALS AND INTERVENTIONS COMMONLY USED IN HOSPICE AND PALLIATIVE CARE

The most widely used intervention, listening to live or recorded music, can reduce pain perception and anxiety; provide relaxation, comfort, and spiritual support;

and offer a means for life review and emotional expression. The music serves as a stimulus for active listening, which can offer a means for reminiscence, verbal discussions, and emotional expression. Music can also provide for a more passive means while creating a positive sensory environment, for enhancing relaxation, or for reducing anxiety and agitation (Krout, 2000).

According to Krout (2000), hospice and palliative care music therapists often use a combined treatment strategy to address multiple patients' needs and goals. Many interventions may be used in the treatment course or within a single session in order to provide individualized care; however, the techniques most often used are the following:

- Music listening
- Improvisation
- Singing
- Songwriting
- Music playing
- Song choice
- Music/imagery for relaxation—with progressive muscle relaxation and deep breathing
- Lyric analysis—music assisted cognitive reframing

(Hilliard, 2003; Krout, 2000; Mills-Groen, 2007)

Instrument playing, singing and *improvisation* are effective techniques for facilitating expression of emotions and improving communication with terminally ill patients (Krout, 2000). Many different kinds of instruments and styles of music can be utilized according to the preference of the patient. People of all ages and functioning levels are able to participate with adaptations prepared by the music therapist. Patients may play with great expression and musicality within a successful experience designed to foster creativity, enhance self-concept, and provide a means to the unconscious. Emotions not easily verbalized such as anger, fear, and existential concerns may be expressed unconsciously through improvisation (Krout, 2000).

The universal appeal and novelty of live music is an effective tool for distraction. *Listening to live or recorded music* may help patients focus their attention on something other than pain, **perseverative behavior**, painful procedures, daily cares, worry, or anxious thoughts. Distraction can be used with people of all ages and functioning levels; however, it works particularly well with infants and young children. Providing distraction with instruments of a **vibrotactile** nature may be effective for older patients with cognitive impairments. Utilizing a variety of easily adaptable and colorful vibrotactile instruments, which are both aurally and visually appealing, in combination with the skills of the music therapist allows for successful distraction.

Songwriting is a valuable technique for assisting patients with creative and emotional expression or self-awareness, enhancing self-esteem, providing validation, and creating a lasting gift for a loved one (Krout, 2000). A variety of songwriting techniques can be adapted for differences in functioning levels as well as age. Music therapists can design the music so that it is applicable to the situation and considers the musical preference of the patient as well.

Music-based cognitive reframing and *lyric analysis* use music to stimulate discussion about thoughts and feelings. Music listening, singing, songwriting, and song choice can all be used as a means for discussing the lyrics as they relate to a patient. Cognitive reframing refers to changing the way a person would view a situation by changing the way he or she would think about it.

Music can provide the structure for slow, deep breathing, and imagery may be added after *autogenic* or *progressive muscle relaxation* has occurred. Autogenic relaxation uses self-directed visual imagery like the repetition of a word, phrase, or feeling combined with body awareness. Progressive muscle relaxation involves slowly tensing and then relaxing different muscle groups within the body (Mayo Foundation for Medical Education and Research, 2008). The use of imagery in order to reduce anxiety or provide relaxation can be used with music assisted relaxation (MAR). However, in order to use the approaches of Guided Imagery and Music (GIM) or the Bonny Method of Guided Imagery and Music, one needs advanced training and certification. These methods also use music, imagery, and relaxation, but the goals of the practice are creativity, self-exploration, insight, and reorganization (Krout, 2000).

Music Therapy to Alleviate Physical Symptoms

Manage pain. Music therapy offers a comprehensive **nonpharmacological approach** for pain management, and there are many ways that music therapy interventions can be utilized to reduce pain perception. Because of the fragile interactive dimensions and complexity of total pain, music therapy as a multifaceted treatment is an effective modality for pain management. Standley (2000) compiled music research in medical treatment and generalized that music is most effective when:

- a patient experiences mild to moderate pain. As pain becomes severe, music is less effective.
- live music (as opposed to recorded music) is provided by a music therapist.
- it is patient preferred.

See Chapter 10 for descriptions of the following music therapy interventions associated with pain management:
- as a stimulus for **active focus** or **distraction**
- to facilitate a **relaxation response**
- as a **masking agent**
- as an **information agent**
- as a **positive environmental stimulus**

Jean was an elderly woman with dementia and severe arthritis who lived in a long-term care facility. Her days consisted of sitting in a reclining wheelchair with her eyes closed or lying in her bed. She sometimes would answer a closed question with "mm-huh" (yes) or a shake of her head meaning "no."

Because of her arthritis, Jean's hands had contracted so tightly that her fingernails were causing open sores in the palm of one of her hands. A hospice home health aide would soak and gently massage her hands over a period of time to help open them. The area could then be cleaned, medicated, and dressed. Even with pre-medication, this was a painful process; therefore, the music therapist would provide distraction, relaxation, deep breathing, and imagery to assist with pain control.

Jean would cry out and moan in pain during this process, so the music therapist provided live, slow, arpeggiated guitar accompaniment that matched the pitch of her moaning. The music therapist hummed the pitch of her moan and began gradually dropping the pitch as if in a sigh. Intermittent breathing in an audible manner by the music therapist (inhaling and exhaling slowly with music as the guide) as well as giving Jean cues to "keep breathing" gave her both a focal point and distraction from her pain. Jean began to follow the music therapist's drop in pitch with her moans as well as breathing more evenly and slowly. The music therapist continued to hum and sing, improvising and weaving images about Jean's farm into the music. Jean's grimace and furrowed brow disappeared and her face relaxed. Jean stopped moaning and listened as the music therapist sang about the sights, smells, sounds, and general feel of her farm on a warm, humid summer day. The nurse and the home health aide both reported that Jean had significantly less pain and discomfort when music therapy was provided during her dressing change. In addition, these caregivers also stated that they felt "much less stressed" during the procedure with support from music therapy.

This situation involved music therapy procedural support for acute pain. Music therapy provided the multifaceted approach that Jean needed to reduce her pain. The music therapist used the **iso-principle** (matching the patient's mood with the music) to provide sensory input, as well as cognitive strategies, breathing techniques, distraction, and a focal point in order to reduce Jean's pain perception.

Promote relaxation.

> *Bud's health had been declining rapidly for the last year; he lay in bed and was unable to move his arms. He was recently diagnosed with **amyotrophic lateral sclerosis (ALS)**, was becoming weaker, and had increasing pain and difficulty swallowing foods and liquids. His anxiety was increasing due to dyspnea. He had played guitar in the past and still enjoyed watching movies and listening to music. The music therapist provided live vocal and guitar music as requested by Bud.*

With the knowledge and skills of the therapist, the music was able to serve multiple purposes:

- As a focal point—Bud did not think about his pain or dyspnea as he concentrated on the lyrics and guitar.
- As a way of reducing anxiety through music assisted relaxation—As time progressed and Bud became more anxious, music was found to be the most comforting and effective means for relaxation. The music therapist was able to provide live sessions, recordings, and cognitive strategies with MAR to help Bud reduce his dyspnea and anxiety.
- As a stimulus for reminiscence—Bud was able to recall many happy times when he played the guitar. He was able to remember specific performances and how he felt at the time. This was a way of life review and validation of his life.
- As a means for spiritual support—Bud was unable to attend the services of his faith tradition, and he felt close to his Higher Power when his favorite spiritual music was provided.
- As a stimulus to improve social interaction—Bud's friends and family sometimes felt uncomfortable interacting with him. The music provided a vehicle for socialization. His grandchildren as well as his friends could all participate together and interact in a normalized way.
- As a means for control—Bud was able to make choices (e.g., fast or slow music, type of music, specific song, etc.) within an environment where he was slowly losing more and more control everyday.
- As a stimulus for finding meaning and purpose—Bud was able to teach the music therapist some advanced concepts for guitar. This helped give him purpose

and improved his self-concept as he was still able to help someone else despite his compromised health.

Bud's case illustrates the point that many patients in hospice care have more than one need. Bud had physical needs with his chronic pain and shortness of breath, as well as many psychosocial and spiritual needs. When a patient has more than one need, the music therapist must be able to assess quickly what need is most important to focus on at the time. Flexibility and the ability to change, modify, or create new plans at any time are vital when working in hospice care.

Using MAR at end-of-life can be an effective and powerful tool to relieve pain, reduce anxiety, and provide relaxation and a calm, soothing environment. However, level of functioning of the patient and disease progression need to be considered. Patients in the later stages of illness may not be able to participate in long relaxation and imagery sessions; therefore, shorter sessions may be advisable (O'Callaghan, 1996). Lower functioning patients may not be appropriate candidates for imagery but may be able to concentrate on breathing techniques paired with music. Patients with a history of emotional problems, abuse, low mental energy, or problems with concentration or reality may be better served by more passive music relaxation. MAR can be used with children when consideration is given to developmental level, goal of the approach, and type of intervention—sedative music listening, music facilitated deep breathing, music and imagery, or progressive muscle relaxation (Ghetti & Walker, in press).

Music can be tailored to calm, soothe, and orient people according to their specific requirements and musical preferences. Some lower functioning patients or those who have dementia may have increased agitation with daily cares such as bathing, dressing changes or other activities. Music therapists can co-treat and provide distraction and relaxation during procedures or daily cares to reduce agitative behaviors. A patient who is restless may be easily distracted or soothed by carefully administered musical stimuli. If a patient is observed to be restless, the music therapist can often reduce the likelihood of the patient becoming agitated. The music provides the same result as medication, but without the negative side effects that may accompany medications often administered to reduce agitation or restlessness.

Adjust sleep cycles. The music therapist can provide live or recorded music for people who have sleep problems. If patients sleep during the day, they are less likely to fall asleep easily at night, or remain asleep for a period of time. Therefore, stimulating music may be needed to keep the person awake during the day. Conversely, sedative music can be provided in order to help patients fall asleep. This can be a positive nonpharmacological strategy to assist patients who often do not want more medication. Taking less medication is less stressful for the patient and a cost saver for families and facilities. Music can also help mask unwanted noise from a hallway, a roommate, or medical equipment, while providing comfort.

Music Therapy for Psychosocial Support

Patients may be referred for music therapy services for an extensive range of psychological, emotional, and social issues including anxiety, depression, isolation, confusion, grief, impaired communication, ineffective coping, normalization, self-esteem, control, relationship/family problems, diversion, lack of insight, life review and reminiscence, disorientation, and motivation (Dileo & Dneaster, 2004; Krout, 2000; Maue-Johnson & Tanguay, 2006; Mills-Groen, 2007).

> *The music therapist enters the room of Dan, a 55-year-old nonresponsive male patient on the palliative care unit located within a hospital. Many family members are present; however, they are not interacting with each other. The television is on and they are sitting quietly around the perimeter of the room. The music therapist stands by the bed, talks directly to the patient and family, and gradually family members gather around the bed and begin interacting with each other and Dan. They respond to the statements by the music therapist, and a teenage son who was looking through a songbook states, "Dad always turned up the radio in the pickup when he heard this one." The music therapist suggests singing this song, and the family does so. The family begins telling stories about Dan, touching his arms and legs as they stand near the bed while others hold his hands. The music therapist encourages family to speak directly to Dan, as the sense of hearing is the last sense remaining before end-of-life. Dan may not be able to respond, but he possibly can hear what his family is saying to him. Family expresses a variety of emotions, sings, and talks to Dan, who responds by a slight raising of his eyebrows and barely noticeable nods of his head.*

This situation is typical in hospice and palliative care when a patient is nearing end-of-life. Other patients in hospice care are active, fully functional, and continue to work, while most others fit somewhere between on the continuum of nonresponsive to fully functional. In the scenario above, the music therapist provided a focus for the family members to interact with each other, to express emotions, and to express themselves directly to their loved one. The variety of emotions expressed was directly related to the music and the skills of the therapist who helped normalize the environment. Family members were able to laugh and shed tears when telling stories. They were able to review life and help put things in perspective while working together in their grief. The music was a way for the family to feel as if they could do something for Dan; they at least had control within this one area. The music therapist helped create positive memories in a situation where the family felt helpless and distressed.

Music therapy can assist with providing the focal point for the family to work together, everyone at the same time, for the best quality of life for the patient. Family can be encouraged to sing or play tone chimes or other instruments, working together as a cohesive unit for the benefit of the patient and everyone involved.

Music therapy also provides psychosocial support through music assisted relaxation, through music-based discussions for expression of concerns and fears, and by offering a focus for living in the present moment while enjoying the simple pleasures in life. Patients often find that a familiar meaningful piece of music may offer a calming and soothing presence. Songwriting, lyric discussions, singing, and listening to music can all assist patients and families with identification and expression of concerns or fears. Live music facilitated by the therapist brings the focus on the here and now, enjoying the moment with loved ones instead of worrying about the uncertainty of the future.

Provide emotional support. The music therapist has the means to reach patients on an emotional level (see Chapter 3). Instead of talking on an intellectual level, patients may be able to express themselves on the feeling level with assistance from the musical stimulus. Salmon (1993) maintains that most people have experienced "being profoundly moved upon hearing a piece of music" (p. 49).

Low-functioning patients may be able to cry, smile, or respond motorically, or express other emotions that would be more difficult or impossible to do with only discussion involved. Patients can be reassured that is it socially acceptable to release feelings to music, which may help normalize the situation. Often patients will express a certain emotion in reaction to music and not realize that this is what they were feeling. The music therapist can help identify and encourage expression of this feeling through music listening, songwriting, singing, instrument playing, lyric discussion, song choice, relaxation and music imagery, or making a recording as a lasting gift.

Music may be used to help someone visualize different ways of thinking or become self-aware, either through lyrics, music-based counseling, or self-growth within musical experiences. Patients may not need or desire extensive reframing or interpretation by the music therapist. Offering support and comfort through music-assisted supportive counseling and active listening when applicable may be most effective in providing the best quality of life for each individual.

As a stimulus for reminiscence/life review. Looking back at one's life and putting things in perspective helps a person discover a sense of meaning (Salmon, 1993). Music can effectively stimulate the long-term memory of patients, making it possible to recall in great detail long-forgotten past events and emotions (Bonny, 2001). This is particularly effective with patients who have short-term memory problems but retain all or part of their long-term memory. Families are able to contribute to a life review, enjoy, express emotions, and reconnect with each other through shared memories and experiences. Varied musical interventions can help the life review process become more vivid, detailed, and effective (O'Callaghan, 1996).

A musical life review can contain a mixture of emotions with patients and families expressing sadness, joy, hope, meaning, and release through the verbal process as well as the music itself. The musical presence in a life review tends to bring the emotional content to the surface, possibly making it more meaningful to those involved. For patients who enjoy singing, the release of tension, emotion, and creativity can be cathartic.

Provide spiritual support and comfort. The music therapist may work with the patient and family to select religious music according to specific faith traditions or with other music that is deemed spiritual by the patient or family. Patients may be physically unable to attend their place of worship or enjoy nature in a direct manner, so the music therapist can create opportunities for spiritual expression. Although spiritual needs are considerable and diverse, music therapists often provide comfort, a stimulus for reminiscence/life review, and an outlet for creativity (Hilliard, 2005; Krout, 2003; Trauger-Querry & Haghighi, 1999).

Music may be most comforting for a patient at end-of-life, as the bond between music, emotions, and spirituality is strong (Walker, 1995). Music may bring a sense of familiarity, intimacy, connectedness, tenderness, and peace as it blocks or masks other undesirable noise in the environment. Listening to favorite music from the past may be soothing for the patient, caregivers, and families. One person may wish to listen to favorite hymns sung quietly at bedside, which also helps reduce agitation later in the day. Another person may choose to hear upbeat gospel music that lifts mood and provides structure for motor responses such as toe-tapping and clapping. Both interventions provide spiritual support and involve passive or active music listening.

Music also brings the added dimension of comfort for patients who are not affiliated with organized religious practices. Offering comfort through musical pieces that have specific function or ritual can be particularly meaningful for patients and families. Music provides a venue for worship (Bonny, 2001). It helps access the deeper inner nature of being, opens communication between people and the divine, and provides structure for comfort, peace, and release (Lipe, 2002). Music, prayer, and the beauty of nature are effective means to access the close connection to a Higher Power for some patients (Wein, 1987).

Opportunities for choice and decision making. Patients may have little independence or autonomy at end-of-life. Singing and song choice can add increased control and self-expression to music listening approaches. The familiarity of choosing and singing even parts of a song seems to help memories become more vivid. Music therapists can encourage autonomy with simple choice-making interventions. For example, the music therapist might ask, "Do you want to hear 'Home on the Range' or 'As Time Goes By'?" This begins the process of enhancing feelings of control in a small manner. Patients make a selection, and then the music therapist can continue to offer an additional choice, "Would you like a fast song or a slow song?" and so on. Some patients who feel helpless need to practice making small decisions, and as they become more comfortable, they can make choices more easily.

The music therapist might provide the patient with an age-appropriate instrument, adapted so it is easily played in a successful manner, to enhance self-esteem and feelings of accomplishment. Nonverbal patients can often express themselves through motoric responses on a drum or other instrument. Songwriting can be adapted to ensure that a positive experience occurs and that autonomy will be enhanced. For example, a patient may need to fill in only one word or part of a phrase in a song that the music therapist has created. Discussion of song lyrics can help people identify strategies to develop realistic ways of taking control of things that can be controlled. Conversely, serious discussions of what types of things are beyond control can help validate experience and motivate change. The music therapist can help patients adjust to limitations, gain a sense of control, and raise self-esteem through interventions including song choice, music listening, songwriting, playing instruments, singing, making a recording for others, or lyric discussion.

Lower functioning patients may also participate in song choice and singing approaches. Allowing extra time for response, providing a forced choice between two selections, or having a visual aid helps some patients with making choices. For example, a nonverbal patient may be able to make a selection by pointing or directing a gaze at a picture of a sun, choosing the song You Are My Sunshine. Lower functioning patients may frequently join singing when adaptations such as repetition, slower tempo, lower range, and close proximity are implemented. They may be able to mouth words to songs, hum, and sing parts or ends of phrases with pleasure and a feeling of achievement.

Emily was a 6-year-old female with an inoperable brain tumor, no longer active due to disease progression. Music therapy provided sessions for

> *Emily with her younger sibling and other family members. Emily preferred quiet voices and low stimulation due to her diagnosis, but wanted to sing and have everyone around her. She gained great comfort by singing her favorite song for others and from having her family repeatedly sing her favorite song to her. In addition to comfort, providing group sessions and a recording of Emily singing also helped create positive memories for Emily's younger sister and family.*

Singing, music listening, and song choice are adaptable to all ages as well as levels of functioning. In addition to their illness, children in hospice care may have the stress of missing school, events, friends, and the normal situations of everyday life. Adolescents in particular may listen to music for peer acceptance, to tune out adults, and for an emotional outlet. Music helps provide a normalized environment for children, offers distraction and a means for emotional expression, as well as providing comfort.

Outlet for creativity. Using music and creativity as a means of living fully and finding inner peace brings comfort at end-of-life (Krout, 2001). People who have life-limiting or chronic conditions are still able to express themselves creatively through music-based interventions in a variety of ways (Hilliard, 2001; O'Callaghan, 1996). Patients can sing, play instruments, write songs or poems that can be set to music, make recordings for lasting gifts, and make creative suggestions while participating in music therapy sessions.

Support during bereavement. Music therapy services can also be tailored to effectively support individuals in their own grief process (Krout, 2000). Each person has his or her own time frame for healing because there is no typical way to grieve. **Bereavement** begins for families, friends, and others of significance after the death of a loved one (Krout, 2005). Some music therapists terminate services upon death, others provide music and support at funerals or memorial services, and others continue to see family members for grief support for a length of time. Music therapists may also provide music for memorial services offered through the hospice organization for all patients who have died within a certain time period. It is common practice to offer bereavement sessions through the hospice organization for specific groups based on age or type of loss. For example, there are music therapy sessions for children who are bereaved, and grief groups for teens, parents, or spouses who have lost a partner.

Collaborative Work: Negotiations between Music Therapists and Community Musicians in the Development of a South African Community Music Therapy Project

By Helen Oosthuizen, Sunelle Fouché & Kerryn Torrance

Abstract

Music therapy in South Africa is slowly negotiating a practice that takes into account our continent's musical vibrancy, as well as contextual understandings of "health" and "illness." Although music therapy in the (so-called) developed world is situated within the paradigms of medicine, education, psychology and research - in the formal and often scientific sense - in South Africa, this practice needs to be re-defined to make it relevant to the contexts in which we work.

The Music Therapy Community Clinic (MTCC) is a non-profit organisation whose aim is to provide music therapy services to previously disadvantaged communities in Cape Town, South Africa. Socio-political problems such as poverty, unemployment, gang violence and HIV and Aids have lead to the fragmentation and disintegration of many of these communities.

The MTCC's *Music for Life* project emerged out of a need to provide after-school music activities and to reach a wider group of children than those seen for clinical music therapy sessions. As the project has developed and expanded, the music therapists have drawn in community musicians to offer an increasing range of musical activities to children. The collaboration between music therapists and community musicians has led to many questions about the roles and identities of each.

This article is based on a presentation given by the MTCC at a Symposium for South African Arts Therapists held in Cape Town in June 2007. The article discusses the merits and challenges of the *Music for Life* Project and offers reflections from both community musicians and music therapists pertaining to our negotiated and changing roles as we continue to develop the project together.

Introduction

Six adolescent boys sit in a circle with a drumming instructor, energetically tapping djembe drums held tightly between their knees, as they wait for their drumming session to begin. A music therapist joins the circle, sitting opposite the drumming instructor, who begins to introduce a beat to the group. The music therapist joins in with the drumming, looking around at the various boys in the group. At times she moves closer to one boy whose drumming rhythms are a little unsteady. She subtly sounds out the rhythms vocally, so that he can follow more easily without feeling embarrassed about needing special help. At one point the therapist motions to the drumming instructor to slow his beat down a little. He obliges, but as soon as the boys begin to master the rhythm, he increases the tempo again, pushing them musically to achieve a product that begins to take shape, so that the resulting rhythms sound interesting, complex, even professional...

This vignette introduces a drumming circle, with a difference. The group is facilitated jointly by a drumming instructor and a music therapist, each taking on different roles. What is happening here? Why is it necessary to include both a drumming instructor and music therapist in this group?

Community music therapy work in any context needs to be negotiated in collaboration with other role players within the context, in order to ensure that our work can optimally serve the needs of a particular community (Stige, 2004). Collaboration with multidisciplinary teams of professionals, parents or staff members is of fundamental importance within most music therapy practices. As community music therapists are exploring options within various contexts, however, some are beginning to entertain the idea of working in collaboration, not only with parents or multidisciplinary teams, but with musicians - others who can make music, who know that music is powerful, and want to offer their musical skills to enhance the health of others. Kildea (2007) describes a pilot project in an adolescent hospital ward, where musicians from a local orchestra were integrated into group music therapy sessions. Through the collaboration between music therapists and musicians, patients attending music therapy groups were able to experience their own musical creations being supported and enhanced by the skilled accompaniment of professional musicians. This collaboration, Kildea notes, encouraged the music therapist and musicians to explore and negotiate new meanings and ways of workings. The *Music for Life* (MFL) Project shares some similarities with this project, as it also involves collaboration between music therapists and musicians. Only, in the MFL Project, the musicians run music activities, whilst music therapists take on the role of co-facilitating and supporting groups.

This article describes a project that the Music Therapy Community Clinic (MTCC) has developed within the past two years in collaboration with "community musicians". The article then presents some possibilities, questions and challenges pertaining to the roles of community musicians and music therapists (particularly community music therapists working in South Africa) in such a collaborative project. These thoughts are based both on the experiences of the music therapists involved and those of some of the community musicians working alongside us, who were interviewed. Rather than a set of formulaic answers, this article offers an exploration into the possibilities of collaborative work.

The Music Therapy Community Clinic and Music for Life Project

The MTCC is a non-profit organization that was founded by Sunelle Fouché and Kerryn Torrance, two music therapists, in September 2003. The primary aim of the MTCC is to render professional Music Therapy services to underprivileged and previously disadvantaged communities within the Greater Cape Town area. The broader vision of the organisation is to use active music-making to have an impact on the psychosocial fabric of the communities in which it works. The MTCC currently employs four music therapists as well as four community musicians and runs 5 separate projects. The *Music for Life* Project that will be discussed further in this article offers after-school music activities for children at schools in Heideveld and Nyanga, two of the many informal settlements or townships situated in the Cape Flats.

Many of the people living in communities such as Heideveld can still remember being forcibly moved here in the 1960's from inner city Cape Town. The community of Heideveld is weighed down by high levels of unemployment, drug abuse, family fragmentation and gangsterism. The violence in this community has a profound effect on the children's emotional and psychological lives. Children are frequently witnesses to the ongoing violence and boys as young as 12 years become involved in gangsterism. The gangs provide the emotional support that their families often cannot provide and being a member of a gang gives them a sense of identity and belonging, a sense of power and purpose which these children so desperately need (Pinnock, n.d.).

The MTCC started a music therapy programme at one of the nine schools in Heideveld in 2003. Teachers from the nine schools in the area refer children for weekly group and individual music therapy sessions. Referrals focus on children who have been traumatised through exposure to gang violence, children who have been abused, have lost family members (often due to gang violence, HIV/AIDS, or substance abuse), or children whose parents are in jail. Soon after starting the music therapy programme, the MTCC realised that there was a need in the Heideveld community for an after-school programme that could offer a wider range of children a positive social group to belong to. The MTCC therefore considered the possibility of initiating a structured musical activity based programme and the *Music for Life* (MFL) Project was born.

In 2006, the MTCC initiated a music therapy project at Etafeni, a centre in Nyanga offering support and resources to women and children affected or infected by HIV and Aids. The informal settlement of Nyanga boasts statistics of the highest murder rate, highest mortality rate, and the highest incidence of reported rape cases in the Western Cape (Gie & Haskins, 2007, p. 8). Despite the high murder rate, the primary cause of deaths in the community is due to Aids (Scott et al., 2003), showing that the community suffers not only from violence and poverty, but also HIV and Aids. The majority of people living in Nyanga have travelled from the Eastern Cape, in search of work (Statistics South Africa, 2001). The Eastern Cape remains their home, and so Nyanga lacks a sense of stability. Many children in Nyanga have experienced multiple losses in their lives. Some have been moved from one family to another as caregivers pass away, or are unable to care for them due to the severity of their Aids illness.

Although the MTCC had initially aimed to offer music therapy groups or individual sessions for those referred for specific needs at Etafeni, we quickly discovered that isolating "needy" individuals in this community was only reinforcing stigmatisation of those already stigmatised due to their HIV status or that of family members. We had to negotiate carefully how best to work in this community, balancing group and individual music therapy sessions with after-school music activities. Thus, we decided to expand the MFL Project to Nyanga.

The broader aim of the MFL Project is to "keep the children off the street" by providing them with a socially healthy alternative, a social group that they could belong to and a safe environment where they could build healthy relationships with their peers. Criteria for joining the MFL project is not based on a child's "musical ability," but instead the MTCC offers a place in the groups for children who we feel would benefit most from belonging to this social/musical group. The focus of this project is not on the product (the quality of the musical performance or the musical skills that children may acquire) but rather on the process (the social skills and life skills that they learn along the way).

The MFL Project began in Heideveld with a choir facilitated by the two music therapists working for the MTCC at the time. We were soon faced with a large number of children who were interested in attending the choir or other afternoon music groups. At the same time, the MTCC had musicians offering to help with some of our projects (some from communities in which we worked) and we considered that these community musicians would be able to facilitate music activities. Thus, part of our work began to include sourcing more musicians from these communities and learning how to utilise the skills of these musicians and share our own, so that we could expand and develop this project.

In Heideveld the MFL Project currently includes a choir of approximately 80 members run by two music therapists; two drumming circles (facilitated by Zweli Noto, a drummer from the neighbouring township Gugulethu); a Marimba group (facilitated by Ross Johnson, from the Marimba group AmaAmbush); and a rap group (facilitated by Mr Fat (Ashley Titus), a rap artist from a well-known Cape Town rap group, "Brasse Van Die Kaap"). In Nyanga, the MFL Project consists of an African music group where musicians Zwai Mvimbi and Vuyo Katsha teach the children a range of traditional African musical styles and songs, including gum-boot dancing, drumming, singing and playing the marimba. All the MFL groups are co-facilitated or supervised by one of the MTCC's music therapists to offer support for musicians and children.

Exploring Roles

In a collaborative project such as MFL, it is necessary to constantly reflect on and critique the process, which can at times be confusing or frustrating, yet also rewarding. Why are we, the music therapists, working together with community musicians? Is this the best use of our time and theirs or should we run groups separately to reach more beneficiaries? What are the roles of the community musicians and what are ours as music therapists? In order to grapple with these questions, we conducted informal interviews with two of our community musicians (Zwai Mvimbi who facilitates the African music group at Etafeni in Nyanga and Zweli Noto, who facilitates drumming groups at Heideveld) and one music therapist (Mandana Ahmadi, a music therapist who co-facilitates one of Zweli's groups). These interviews (of which extracts are quoted) offered ideas about our roles, those of the community musicians, and how we can and do work together, as well as highlighting some difficulties and struggles in this work.

The Role of Community Musicians

Zwai arrives at Etafeni and greets the caretaker loudly in Xhosa - a home tongue that they share. He greets us in English and we chat briefly, focusing on one subject that we both relate to – music and the power music has as a vehicle for expression and communication. Zwai does not yet fully understand our work as therapists, just as we are still getting around the complexities of certain African rhythms and the concepts that underlie these. Yet, we are able to work together and learn from each other as music therapists and community musician, our different skills and thoughts adding value to our collaborative work at Etafeni. As "white" music therapists we lack a sharing of cultural musical resources with the community. Language barriers further prevent us from relating closely to those we work with, who speak Xhosa as a first language (although Xhosa lessons have become part of MTCC therapists' skills development, none of us can speak fluently, yet). Zwai moves between the Xhosa and English languages, between certain musical understandings he shares with us and cultural understandings he shares with others at Etafeni.

Cultural Knowledge

When questioned about his role as a music group facilitator in this context, Zwai responded:

> I think my role in the group is to teach them (the children in the African music group) what I have, and to be able to make them...create their own thing. That's what I'm focusing on. But at first I need to show them, this is how you play the drum, this is how you sing. Then at the end of the day...the person can be able to be creative and they can compose her or his own song.

When Zwai said, "I teach them what I have", he gestured by placing his hand on his heart, suggesting that he offers *his* music, and also his knowledge and identity, as a black Xhosa man. Zwai is clear that his role moves beyond merely teaching musical skills. One of the unfortunate consequences of urbanisation and loss of family members amongst young people in Nyanga is that they often lose touch with their cultural and family traditions and thus lack this important basis for the development of their own identity. As Zwai brings *his* cultural and musical knowledge to this group, he also offers the children in the African music group an opportunity to reconnect with their traditional Xhosa music, cultural knowledge and values.

In the MTCC newsletter (September 2007), Mandana Ahmadi portrays some of the challenges and opportunities of young people in Nyanga. She says:

> The townships form a melting pot of influences from different generations and cultures. Culture is not a static entity and therefore the children face the challenge of reconciling where their ancestors have come from and forging the way forward, creating a new culture that allows traditional values and more contemporary norms to live side by side.

Whilst Zwai teaches the group what cultural heritage and tradition he has to give, he intends that these adolescents should ultimately be able to create their own music. If "musicing can both reproduce the legacy of another and allow the performance of the self" (Ansdell, 2004, pp. 67-68), this implies that by learning traditional music that belongs to their cultural heritage, these adolescents can engage with and reproduce some of their past. By creating music of their own, they are able to fuse the traditional movements and sounds of gumboot dances with sounds from popular South African or African American hip-hop groups - and the meanings embodied in each musical form - and can generate and explore their changing culture and traditions. This empowers these adolescents, highlighting their role as active agents in the development of their culture and community.

Musical Skills

Part of Zwai's role is to teach the members of the African music group musical skills, such as drumming and singing, as these are the tools through which Zwai can pass on his musical and cultural knowledge, and through which the group members will be able to create their own music, and identities. The MTCC's community musicians are experts, trained informally in particular cultural musical styles. As music therapists, we too have prior musical training and are skilled in performing certain musical styles. We have also gone to some effort to learn traditional cultural songs and musical styles of the communities in which we work, in order to remain sensitive to these contexts. However, though we can probably render reasonable performances of some well known traditional songs, our ability to master this music remains limited. Our Western-trained musical ears struggle at times to catch some of the poly-rhythms and different harmonic structures of music that is different to what we are used to. Often we find ourselves learning rhythms and melodies together with the children in MFL groups (and at times, the children's own musical-cultural backgrounds allow them to master these styles before we do). Thus, we require the community musicians to take the lead in offering this music professionally to the MFL groups.

Male Role Models

Mandana commented on Zweli's role as a drumming facilitator in their group, saying:

> Well, ... I wouldn't be able to run this group on my own. On a very practical level I'm not a drummer and Zweli brings something special there, and rhythm just seems to be very much a part of these children's lives. You can hear it in the way they bang on walls and everything. And, he's got the energy and dynamics to be able to pull the group together.

Mandana again refers to the musical knowledge that Zweli can teach the children (she mentions that she is not a professional drummer). Drumming is a part of these children's cultural tradition, so Zweli brings something that they can relate to, affirming their identity through the musical skills they learn.

Mandana also mentions the "energy and dynamics" that Zweli utilises to "pull the group together." This possibly refers to Zweli's energy as a male, which Mandana noted at other points in her interview. Here, Mandana touches on another very important point about the role of the community musician. All the music therapists involved in the MFL Project are female (in fact, there are only two male music therapists in South Africa). Our experiences of working within communities such as Nyanga and Heideveld often highlight the paucity of helpful male role models that participate in children's development. Many children have lost their fathers due to Aids or violence, many have fathers who are absent – perhaps in jail, or having to work long shifts far away from home (such as those who work as fishermen and are required to be at sea for months at a time). Gangs and gang related violence predominantly involves men or boys, offering young people negative male role models. The daily upbringing and nurturing of children seems largely left to the responsibility of women – mothers, and quite often grandmothers.

In contrast to this picture, the MFL Project invites men such as Mr Fat (Ashley Titus) to work with young people in these communities. The children in Heideveld all know Mr Fat – he is admired and esteemed. At the same time, he is a coloured man (like most of the children in Heideveld). He grew up in a very similar community, not far from where these children live. Each week, Ashley takes the time out of his schedule to facilitate rap workshops. His presence at the school, the mentoring role he plays in these children's lives and the conversations they have about life as they compose their own raps offer the children a model, an example. Here is a man from a community like theirs who has chosen *not* to participate in gangs or drugs. Ashley offers the rap group the possibility that they can make something of their lives, they can choose to express their experiences – both positive and negative - through clever, thoughtful poetry rather than shootings or stabbings. Ashley encourages his group to use their rap songs not only to describe their lives, but also to offer hope to others, leading others towards a positive community and world. Choices such as whether to join a gang or not may seem simple to an outsider, but in these communities some children do not see alternatives. The community musicians thus serve as much needed positive role models for the children in MFL groups, whilst bringing male energy to the often boisterous groups that can "pull the group together."

Product and Performance

As music therapists, we often tend to focus on the value of the *process* of MFL groups rather than the *product* or performance. For community musicians, a natural part of any MFL group process includes performances. MFL groups regularly perform at community events, or may travel to other communities to perform. Community musicians are experienced performers themselves and value the event of a performance. It is often the community musicians who will "push" MFL groups to achieve skilled and polished products to be performed. One of the challenges of co-facilitating MFL groups has been trying to find a balance between focusing on producing products and allowing time for the group to reflect on their process. Zweli comments:

> It is a challenge because...sometimes you want to accomplish something, so that at the end of the day, to say this is what I have achieved... this must be ready now, this should have been there, this should have been this way... although I think that I am learning from that......in terms of the perspective of a "flexi" kind of a pace, and my expectations with the children, so I've been adjusting myself ...But still, I have to demand these things...Someday, I want to see some product here... or something like that...because it makes me feel good as a musician.

The emergence of the discourse of community music therapy has stimulated much debate around the value of performance as part of a therapy process (Ansdell, 2005). Whilst conventional music therapy practices might view a public performance as counter-productive or possibly unsafe for clients, community music therapists have found that performances can be valuable and acceptable aspects of a therapy process. Performing for others allows clients to explore relationships, to perform and thus affirm their identities within their community. As Zweli's drumming group performs for others, their loud, strong drumming becomes a channel to hold and express their aggression and anger. At the same time, as these group members drum together, keeping the beats they have practiced, leading or supporting as required, they present to others their capacity for commitment, motivation, for listening and working together with others. In communities enveloped in social problems such as Heideveld or Nyanga, parents often lose hope for the future of their children. Performances give parents and other community members the opportunity to witness the potential, vibrant energy and resilience of their children, whilst also allowing children to enjoy the communities' enthusiastic response to their accomplishments. Through performances, the MFL Project moves out into the community, and those who are members of MFL groups become leaders of their community as they become a voice offering parents and children alike a positive social experience, offering possibilities for what their community can be.

When community musicians prepare groups for performances, we are often surprised by what they achieve. The community musicians demand far more "professional" products than we would from these groups as music therapists. This enhances the value of each performance and allows both community musicians and group members to "feel good as musicians," and also to feel good about themselves, about who they are in the community.

Community musicians are thus not an optional extra when working with MFL groups, but are vital, allowing the MTCC not only to reach more beneficiaries, but to connect more appropriately with young people's identities - within and outside of the music. Community musicians can offer group members cultural knowledge and encourage them to create and explore their music and identity for themselves. Community musicians are role models for young people and empower those in their groups as they encourage them to create aesthetic products that offer a message of hope to their communities.

The above discussion of the roles of community musicians hints at the possibility that these community musicians themselves offer something that may seem similar what we offer as music therapists. Both Zweli and Zwai suggested in their interviews that they were doing more than teaching children musical skills. Through music, these community musicians are able to work to enhance the social development of the young people with whom they work and their communities. As music therapists, we may struggle at times to offer what we sense these communities need due to language and cultural barriers. Why can the MTCC then not leave these community musicians to facilitate groups on their own? Could we not focus on offering more intensive training courses to community musicians, if they require such training at all? What is the role of music therapists in the MFL groups?

The Role of Music Therapists

Some of the first rap groups initiated by the MTCC consisted of young people who had completed a process of short term music therapy, and their therapists felt they would benefit from being in a long-term music group. Although a community musician joined these groups to teach the boys the finer skills of rap and Hip-Hop, it seemed apt for the group's music therapist to continue to attend these sessions, to offer group members a sense of stability within a long-term relationship. As with these group members, who had been referred for therapy due to their aggressive behaviour or difficult home situations, group members referred by teachers for most of the MFL groups are those perceived as "difficult to handle" or "not motivated", or as "behaving inappropriately." Therefore, we felt that our skills as music therapists might be required in these groups to handle difficult situations that occurred, to manage behaviour and group dynamics and to support the community musicians as necessary.

Just as we need to adapt to find different ways of working as music therapists in every context, we often experience moments where we question our role as co-facilitators in the MFL groups. At times we may take on an important role in groups, but at other times we seem to do very little. What is different about this work, that it requires music therapists and musicians to work so closely together? We thought it would be helpful to discuss our role with the community musicians. Do they feel we offer something of value to these groups, or do they think we attend to check up on their skills? Do they notice any of the music therapy skills we feel that we utilise in sessions, and do they feel that these skills are different to what they could offer?

Relationship

The community musician, Zwai described the role of Kerryn Torrance (the music therapist) as a co-facilitator in his African music group, as follows:

> The role of Kerryn...since she already started with these kids before I came on board, is to facilitate in terms of ...the way we deal with the kids and giving us some advice, because she almost knows some of them... better than we do...

Zwai commented further on Kerryn's role saying:

> She has...experience in terms of doing...therapy and had this kind of a music background, ...so, what specifically I can mention is that when we do the workshops, we come across, certain....kids, in terms of the way they behave, their response, and she ...knows exactly... how to deal with them... - so that at least they don't feel offended. So she's guiding us so that ... we're able to deal with them in a proper way.

It is interesting that Zwai noted that Kerryn had been working with these children for longer than he had, and so knew them very well. In fact, Kerryn and Zwai met this group at the same time. This reflects Zwai's recognition of Kerryn's acute intuition about children within his group – she has a way of knowing each individual, of sensing their needs and responding on a musical or relationship level. Kerryn is able to sense the meaning behind the behaviour and music that group members make and can reflect these meanings back to Zwai, so that together, they can respond to group and individual needs appropriately. Zwai's reflections of Kerryn's role in the MFL groups directly reflect some recognition of the music therapy skills that she uses in this context.

Zwai's leading role in group sessions requires him to guide the group as a whole towards creating music together. By taking a more supportive role in the MFL groups, Kerryn is able to come alongside individual group members, particularly those who may be on the margins of the group, who may not fit in, who cannot keep up with others musically, or those who display behaviour that is difficult to manage within the context of a group. She may simply sit next to a group member and play her drum loudly so that he or she can hear a rhythm more clearly, or may be able to take a group member who is distracting others aside and spend extra time with them. Her music therapy skills equip her to relate to these group members and to draw them back to the group's music, without "offending" them.

As co-facilitators of MFL groups, sometimes joining groups to learn musical skills together with group members, we are further enabled to build mutual relationships with both group members and community musicians. We ourselves may have to ask the community musician to slow down or help us, or may get a beat wrong. In this way, we can mediate between the group and community musician. We communicate to group members that it is OK to struggle with the music, whilst also notifying community musicians that they may need to adjust or simplify what they are teaching. Occasionally, group members will be able to help us to learn a rhythm, or may rehearse a performance piece for us to hear. In this way, we offer group members respect and dignity as we allow them to share their learning with us. This empowers the whole group – they are not simply young people learning from their "teachers," but can at times help to teach others.

Holding the Group Process

Mandana comments on her role as a co-facilitator for Zweli, saying:

> Part of our training as therapists means that we have to sometimes sacrifice the music a little bit just to keep the group strong and so it may mean making an intervention in a way that is not musically related, or simplifying something for the greater good.

Just as Zweli is primarily a musician and challenges the group members musically, Mandana is primarily a music therapist in this group and her therapy skills enable her to reflect on various group dynamics that are played out in the group's music through the process. Mandana needs to keep a check on both the long-term and immediate process of the group and decide whether to intervene and how, even if this means "sacrificing the music...to keep the group strong." If Mandana does not hold the group process, certain group members might easily be neglected or undervalued, or group tensions may threaten to break up a group.

A group's process, does not only manifest during sessions, and can be impacted by other factors and people, just as their process can impact others. Thus, our role of reflecting on and holding the group's process extends beyond session times. As co-facilitators, we may be required to discuss the process of the group with group members themselves or community musicians, or with parents, caregivers or teachers of group members. Sometimes we as music therapists may be required to arrange an outing or camp for a group, to negotiate with community members, or arrange performances. Some of these tasks may seem like administration or management rather than therapy – but each is played out in response to our reflections about what the group needs, where the group needs to go. We need to ensure that this process holds value for group members, so that through their participation in music groups, members can learn skills that will serve them in their lives outside of the music group.

Mentoring

In further reflections about Kerryn's role in the African Music Group, Zwai commented:

> She's also guiding us, saying, "OK, this will be this kind of a kid", and reminding us of some of the things that we've learnt also through our workshops   that we had last time, so probably it's a matter of guiding us as facilitators during the process of the workshop (or music group rehearsals) as we're going along.

Zwai suggests that Kerryn serves as a guide or mentor to the community musicians. After working with the first community musician, the MTCC initiated a training course for these musicians. This short course equipped them with basic skills drawn from music therapy for working musically with groups, whilst remaining sensitive to the individual and social needs of group members and their communities. The aim of the training course was *not* to encourage these musicians to do the work of music therapists, but rather to offer them skills that would be useful for facilitating any music group. The training course also served to inform the community musicians of the principles of the MTCC, highlighting our emphasis on enhancing the social development of group members through music, and the importance of the process of a group rather than the musical products achieved.

Over time, some of the community musicians have begun to develop some of the skills they learnt at this course, and may reflect on the behaviour and gestures of group members, or slow down their music when they feel that the group can't keep up. However, it is often our role as music therapists to offer clinical insights and reflections to community musicians, guiding them towards helpful ways of working with their groups. This expands the way we utilize our therapeutic skills. In our own music therapy groups, we would most likely react and respond spontaneously to instances where a child is not keeping up or when we notice a group member offering a spontaneous musical idea. In this situation, each reflection needs to be held in mind and discussed with the community musician at an appropriate time.

In some instances, our roles as mentors to the community musicians have also included offering debriefing. Though community musicians are from similar communities to those in which we work, there are children in MFL groups whose life stories can shock or upset community musicians, or whose behaviour is particularly difficult and community musicians can find this taxing to deal with. As music therapists we may then need to offer support not only to group members but to the community musicians themselves.

As music therapists, we then bring to the MFL groups our music therapy skills – a way of listening intuitively to the meanings behind the behaviour and music of group members, reflecting and responding to our intuitions, holding a group through the process and building relationships with group members that serve to empower them. This work then requires the same skills we would use as when doing "proper" therapy sessions. Is our role within the MFL groups then any different to working as a music therapist in a therapy session? When asked whether Mandana reflected on her drumming group differently to how she would reflect on a therapy session, she responded: "I don't know if there is a huge difference to be honest - the way I think about it is probably not that different." Mandana suggests that in these groups, we continue to utilise the same skills, only these skills are applied in different ways. In describing her experiences of a rural community in South Africa, where community members made music together spontaneously and had little use for the conventional music therapy skills she had to offer, Mercédès Pavlicevic (2004) offers similar reflections. She stated that "conventional music therapy skills were useful, but in a new way that needed to be negotiated." (p. 46).

Conclusion

The collaboration between music therapists and community musicians can be difficult, and yet this work has immense value for the communities where we have begun to work together. As white, female music therapists who struggle to come to terms with the complexities of communities who share different languages, socio-economic circumstances and cultural nuances to our own, we cannot presume to offer optimal services to these communities alone. The male community musicians who work alongside us bring themselves, their musical skills, and cultural knowledge to the MFL groups. As music therapists, we can enhance the work of each group through our awareness of and responses to group dynamics and interpersonal relationships played out through the music.

In writing this article, it was interesting to discover how easily we could define the skills and roles of community musicians within the MFL Project, whilst we struggled to think about our own value and roles. Community musicians bring concrete, defined musical skills and cultural knowledge to the project. On the other hand, we often find ourselves as therapists taking on many roles – reflecting like therapists, sometimes facilitating, project managing, making suggestions to the musicians, learning from them, offering behaviour management advice, consulting – the list is endless...In fact, at times we may be required to do no more than taking roll call, connecting briefly with children in the group, and leaving the rest of the session to the community musicians! Our roles seem to shift with every new MFL group, and even at different points through a group process and have led to constant reflections around how we could offer most value in each specific context. As the discourse of community music therapy has grappled with questions such as "Is this music therapy?", "What is the value of performance?" or "What is our role here?", we have asked similar questions regarding this collaborative project.

Pavlicevic and Ansdell (2004) offer an alternative to these questions and musings, suggesting that we should be asking "not 'what is music therapy?' and 'what is a music therapist', but 'what do *I* need to do, *here, now*?'" (p. 30). Brynjulf Stige (2004) notes that community music therapy cannot be defined by procedures, but there is rather a set of values and assumptions that underly the work that takes place. Community music therapy work is defined by context. Whilst the main aim or goal of the work could be social change, the way this is carried out can take on many different forms. Stige (2004) states that "the way I look at community music therapy, the music therapist is a musicking community worker – a person whose job is to promote social welfare in and through a community." (p. 92). Perhaps this is a more helpful consideration of our role as music therapists, whether we achieve this through leading a group musically, or just listening to their performances, guiding group facilitators or letting a group go on without us. Further, it seems that it is sometimes others who need to take the forefront in our work - sometimes it is when we step back and merely offer quiet support, hints or guidelines as necessary rather than running the show...that, through music-making, the social welfare of communities can be enhanced.

Notes

Community Musicians are musicians that the MTCC (Music Therapy Community Clinic) has employed on a part time basis to facilitate music groups within some of the communities in which we work. Importantly, these community musicians are from the communities in which they work, or from neighbouring communities that share a common language, history, value system, and infrastructure.

For more information about the Music Therapy Community Clinic, visit our website at

The Cape Flats is the common name describing a flat plain of land stretching inland from the Western Cape's coastline, situated about 20km East of Cape Town's city centre. This area was demarcated for the housing of coloured and black people as part of the Apartheid Government's Group Areas Act.

As South Africans our identity is often influenced or determined by the colour of our skin, and we therefore find it necessary to refer to certain people as being black, coloured, or white.

This refers to a training course held for community musicians, facilitated by music therapists from the MTCC.

References

Ahmadi, M. (2007). Creating Cultures: Reconciling the Old with the New. *Music Therapy Community Clinic Newsletter.* 2 (2), 1.

Ansdell, G. (2005). Being Who You Aren't; Doing What You Can't: Community Music Therapy & the Paradoxes of Performance. *Voices: A World Forum for Music Therapy.* Retrieved July 15, 2007, from

Ansdell, G. (2004). Rethinking Music and Community: Theoretical Perspectives in Support of Community Music Therapy. In M. Pavlicevic & G. Ansdell (Eds). *Community Music Therapy* (pp. 65-90). London: Jessica Kingsley Publishers.

Gie, J. and Haskins, C. (2007). *Crime in Cape Town: 2001- 2006: A Brief Analysis of Reported Violent, Property and Drug-Related Crime in Cape Town*. Cape Town: City of Cape Town Strategic Development Information and GIS Department, Strategic Information Branch

Kildea, Clare (2007). In Your Own Time: A Collaboration Between Music Therapy In a Large Pediatric Hospital And a Metropolitan Symphony Orchestra. *Voices: A World Forum for Music Therapy.* Retrieved August 4, 2007, from

Pavlicevic, M. and Ansdell, G. (2004). Introduction: "The Ripple Effect." In M. Pavlicevic & G. Ansdell (Eds). *Community Music Therapy* (pp. 15-31). London: Jessica Kingsley.

Pavlicevic, M. (2004) Learning from Thembalethu:Towards Responsive and Responsible Practice in Community Music Therapy. In M. Pavlicevic & G. Ansdell (Eds). *Community Music Therapy* (pp. 35-47). London: Jessica Kingsley.

Pinnock, D. (n.d.) *Gangs. Fighting fire with fire.* Retrieved April 12, 2005, from

Scott V, Sanders D, Reagon G, Groenewald P, Bradshaw D, Nojilana B, Mahomed H, Daniels J. (2003). *Cape Town Mortality, 2001, Part II, An equity lens – lessons and challenges.* Cape Town: City of Cape Town, South African Medical Research Council, University of Cape Town, University of Western Cape.

Statistics South Africa (2001). *City of Cape Town - Census 2001 – 2006 Wards: Ward 037 - Nyanga, Nyanga East.* City of Cape Town: Strategic Development Information and GIS from 2001 Census data supplied by Statistics South Africa. Retrieved September 9, 2007, from

Stige, B. (2004). Community Music Therapy: Culture, Care and Welfare. In M. Pavlicevic & G. Ansdell (Eds). *Community Music Therapy* (pp. 91-113). London: Jessica Kingsley.

Review Article

Music Therapy in Parkinson's Disease

Natalia García-Casares MD, PhD [a,b,c,*], Julia Eva Martín-Colom MD [a], Juan Antonio García-Arnés MD, PhD [d]

[a] *Department of Medicine, Faculty of Medicine, University of Malaga, Malaga, Spain*
[b] *Centro de Investigaciones Médico-Sanitarias (CIMES), University of Malaga, Malaga, Spain*
[c] *Instituto de Investigación Biomédica de Málaga (IBIMA), Malaga, Malaga, Spain*
[d] *Department of Pharmacology, Faculty of Medicine, University of Malaga, Malaga, Spain*

ABSTRACT

Keywords:
Music therapy
Parkinson's disease
auditory cueing
nonmotor symptoms
motor symptoms
quality of life

Objectives: Parkinson's disease (PD) is a chronic progressive neurologic disorder involving degeneration of the dopaminergic system. Its clinical manifestations include motor and nonmotor symptoms. Several nonpharmacologic therapies, such as music therapy (MT), have recently been developed in order to improve the clinical manifestations of this disease. The aim of this narrative literature review is to analyze the scientific evidence for the therapeutic effects of music in PD.
Design: We undertook a search in the databases of PubMed, PsycINFO, Scopus, MEDLINE, and Science Direct.
Settingand Participants: Inclusion criteria were articles including persons with PD rehabilitated with an MT intervention.
Measures: Keywords used were *music therapy, Parkinson's disease, auditory cueing, non-motor symptoms, motor symptoms,* and *quality of life*.
Results: We detected a total of 27 articles, all of which analyzed the therapeutic effects of MT in PD. Of these, 20 studies analyzed the effects in motor symptoms (16 showed beneficial effects and 4, non-beneficial effects); 9 studies analyzed the effects in nonmotor symptoms, 7 of which demonstrated beneficial effects; and 8 studies analyzed the effects on quality of life, with 6 reporting benefits. None of the articles analyzing nonmotor symptoms and quality of life showed negative effects.
Conclusions/Implications: Most of the studies analyzed demonstrated that MT has beneficial effects for the nonpharmacologic treatment of motor and nonmotor symptoms and quality of life of persons with PD. The use of music as a therapeutic tool combined with conventional therapies should be taken into account.

© 2018 AMDA – The Society for Post-Acute and Long-Term Care Medicine.

Parkinson's disease (PD) is a chronic progressive disabling illness considered the second most common neurodegenerative disorder in the world after Alzheimer's disease, and the disease involving the most serious movement disorder.[1] The prevalence of PD in developed countries is estimated at 0.3% of the entire population and about 1% in persons older than 60 years.[2,3]

The pathogenesis of PD involves degenerative loss of midbrain dopamine neurons in the pars compacta of the substantia nigra and intraneuronal Lewy body inclusions.[4] These conditions lead to changes in the central nervous system and cause an impairment of neuronal networks, including basal ganglia and supplementary motor areas. The main clinical signs characterizing PD are resting tremor, rigidity, and bradykinesia. Nevertheless, many other motor and nonmotor symptoms are frequently associated with the disease, such as postural, gait, respiratory, osteomuscular, and cognitive and memory alterations, causing severe impairment and decreased quality of life.

Several scales have been designed to evaluate the severity of the disease, establishing different stages. The Hoehn and Yahr scale is the classic scale to measure the severity of the disease. In PD, this scale evaluates clinical function combining disability and impairment, with degrees of severity ranging from Stage 1 (unilateral disease) to Stage 5 (wheelchair or bedridden).[5] Another important evaluation scale is the Unified Parkinson's Disease Rating Scale. This, in fact, is the most used clinical rating scale in PD. It has 4 parts and evaluates motor and nonmotor features of PD using a questionnaire.[6]

The authors declare no conflicts of interests.
* Address correspondence to Natalia García-Casares, MD, PhD, Departamento de Medicina, Facultad de Medicina, Universidad de Málaga Boulevard Louis Pasteur 32, CP 29010, Malaga, Spain.
E-mail address: nagcasares@uma.es (N. García-Casares).

https://doi.org/10.1016/j.jamda.2018.09.025
1525-8610/© 2018 AMDA – The Society for Post-Acute and Long-Term Care Medicine.

Treatment of PD involves multiple drugs, such as levodopa, dopamine agonists, monoamine oxidase inhibitors, peripheral dopa-decarboxylase inhibitors, and catechol-*O*-methyltransferase inhibitors.[7] Nonetheless, the difficulty to control the worsening symptoms and impairment caused by PD has led to huge developments in drug therapies and technological devices,[8] as well as other alternative and nonpharmacologic therapies such as music therapy (MT).[9]

Music therapy is an alternative complementary intervention with different approaches. Music can engage and modulate different brain areas involved in the perception and regulation of aspects like mood, behavior, movement, and cognitive factors. Thus, MT has a proven benefit as a concomitant therapy in several neurologic disorders such as stroke and dementia.[10,11] MT can be used in an active mode, with the patient playing an instrument or singing, or in a passive mode, with the patient just listening.[9–12] In addition, recent studies have demonstrated different outcomes depending on the type of MT intervention administered,[11] with music being able to modify different manifestations of PD depending on the approach.

The networks implicated in normal movements are the basal ganglia-thalamo-motor cortices and the cerebellar-thalamo-motor cortices. These networks are also connected with the auditory cortex. The basal ganglia-thalamo-motor cortices are engaged in the attention-dependent evaluation of temporal intervals and self-generation of movements, and the cerebellar-thalamo-motor cortices are involved in the preattentive encoding of an event-based temporal structure and matching of movements to exogenous auditory cues.[13] Pacchetti et al suggested that improvement in motor symptoms may be associated with the emotional response of the patient to music. This was based on the circuit regulating motivational-reinforcement of general behavior, which involves the dopaminergic mesolimbic projections to the striatum-intraccumbens nuclei. Thus, an emotional response to MT also stimulates the cortical-basal ganglia network.[9]

Regarding motor symptoms in PD, the damage produced by dopamine depletion affects these networks, leading to motor disruptions in persons with PD. Some studies have shown that auditory stimuli can reinforce the remaining activity of the basal ganglia-thalamo-motor cortices and the cerebellar-thalamo-motor cortices networks, ameliorating motor deficits[13] (Figure 1). This explains why during an auditory cueing persons with PD can improve movements, thus enabling a certain degree of rehabilitation with music. Interventions with rhythm may enhance these connections between motor and auditory systems and compensate for the lack of dopaminergic stimulation.[14]

Concerning nonmotor symptoms in PD, MT focuses on listening to different types of music, singing techniques, and improvisation with music, which, emotionally, can all impact the limbic system and neurochemical circuits (the reward system).[15] These effects are slightly more difficult to assess objectively, but different scales and tests can give results. Features like previous music formation, the patient's will, and adherence to the different programs may affect the results. Thus, significant conclusions require a characterization of the effects of music on the progress of the disease. These will help determine the duration of the different programs in relation to the aims and types of intervention.

The above individual studies all suggest that MT could be a beneficial nonpharmacologic treatment, especially useful in people with PD as it may have beneficial effects on motor and nonmotor symptoms. Accordingly, the aim of this work is to examine these studies collectively to identify the scientific evidence in this field through a narrative review of the literature.

Materials and Methods

Database Search

We undertook a search in PubMed, PsycINFO, Dialnet, MEDLINE, and Science Direct databases. The Medical Subject Headings (MESH) and key words included in the search strategy were *music therapy*, *Parkinson's disease*, *auditory cueing*, *non-motor symptoms*, *motor symptoms*, and *quality of life*. The Boolean operators AND and OR were used to combine the key words. The search was restricted to Clinical trials and clinical studies. Studies from 1996 to 2017 were included.

Inclusion Criteria

The inclusion criteria to select the articles included persons with a clinical diagnosis of idiopathic PD in any stage (mild, moderate, or advanced) in accordance with the Hoehn and Yahr and UPDRS scales. Other parkinsonisms or neurodegenerative diseases were excluded.

The search strategy did not include any specific criteria concerning modality of the interventions: active or passive, duration, type of instrument, singing, and previous musical knowledge and/or experience. Articles that included a concomitant nonpharmacologic therapy with the MT intervention were excluded. Articles including a dance intervention were also excluded.

Those articles not written in English, reviews, case reports, and letters to the editor were excluded.

After the search, the first step was to analyze the abstracts of the articles found to extract those that met the inclusion criteria. The second step involved a full reading of the articles selected to obtain the principal information about the studies: design, participants, inclusion and exclusion criteria, methods, intervention therapy, and results. In addition, we classified the articles into 3 categories according to the main music element included in the MT intervention: music (melodic sound), singing, and rhythm (with no melodic sound).

Results

The search strategy detected a total of 136 articles. After reading the abstracts, 48 articles were selected for deep reading. After a thorough reading of these articles, 12 articles referring to other concomitant nonpharmacologic therapy, and another 9 articles that did not meet the inclusion and exclusion criteria described above were excluded. Thus, 27 articles were finally selected (Figure 2). The studies are summarized in Table 1.

Participants' Demographic and Clinical Characteristics

The participants in all the studies were persons with a clinical diagnosis of idiopathic PD previously diagnosed by a physician. The stages ranged from mild to moderate according to the Hoehn and Yahr

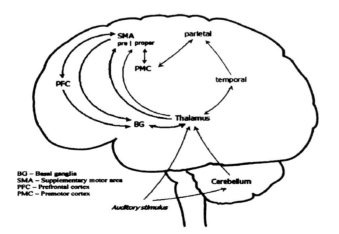

Fig. 1. Basal ganglia–thalamocortical and cerebellar-thalamocortical networks in Parkinson's disease during auditory cueing. Extracted from Dalla Bella et al.[13]

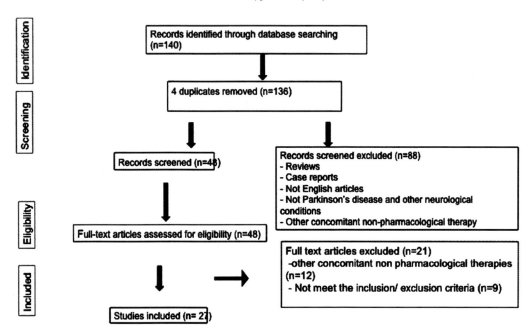

Fig. 2. Flowchart of the search strategy.

and UPDRS scales. All persons with PD were stable responders to medication, with no severe motor impairment (all could stand on their own 2 feet without help), and without dementia (Mini-Mental State Examination score >24). The studies that included a control group showed no significant differences between the groups, matched by age and/or gender. One study included only males[14] and another only females.[15] Weight was only specified in 1 study[14] and height only in 1.[32] Only right-handed participants were selected in 3 studies.[14,18,36]

Methods and Intervention Characteristics

Most of the studies had a longitudinal design[2,9,12–14,16–20,22–29,31,34] with some having a cross-sectional design.[3,21,28–30,33,36] Previous music experience or training was only specified in 5 studies.[3,27,30,36] The type of MT was divided into music,[3,9,12,17–22,29,35,36] singing,[24–28,35,36] and rhythm.[2,3,16,25,30–33,35] Most studies used only music as MT. Depending on the type of MT, studies focused on improving specific deficits or symptoms in PD (motor, nonmotor, and quality of life). No studies involved rhythm interventions and its effects on quality of life.

The response to MT in terms of motor capacity was assessed by a wide range of methods. These ranged from the application of a simple test, such as Romberg test, to more advanced tests, such as complex camera movement analysis systems, electromyograms, and computerized platforms.

Evaluation methods applied to nonmotor symptoms were specific in each trial. They included subjective evaluation tests, personal interviews, specific indexes, and more complex methods such as videostroboscopy or computer system voice analysis.

Those studies that analyzed the effects of MT on quality of life used scales and questionnaires, including the Beck Depression Inventory, visual analog scale, Parkinson's disease Quality of Life Questionnaire, and other depression and happiness rating scales.

To obtain statistically significant results, most of the studies used such tests as analysis of variance, Wilcoxon signed-rank test, Friedman test, or multivariate analysis.

Effects of Music Therapy on Motor Symptoms

Most trials focused on evaluating the effects of MT on motor symptoms (20 of 27 studies). Only 7 of the 20 trials were cross-sectional interventions.[3,21,30,32,33,35,36] The therapy was rhythm in 6 interventions,[16,30–34] music in 10,[9,12,13,17–22,29] and a mixture (of rhythm and music) in 4.[2,3,35,36]

Five studies found beneficial effects for propioception,[2] gait,[3,13,35] motor timing,[13] and eye movement latency.[18] And finally, 8 studies found significant improvement ($P < .05$) for coordination,[32] gait,[2,31,33,34] bradykinesia,[9,12,22,34] rigidity,[9] and mobility.[12] Five of these were cross-sectional interventions.[3,30,32,33,35] All those with a longitudinal design found statistically significant positive results with active MT if it lasted from 1 week to 6 months.

In contrast, 4 studies found that after the MT program, the participants either did not improve or presented a worse performance regarding gait (temporal stability when walking did not improve in the presence of an auditory cue),[31] decreased obstacle-crossing velocities with music,[19] decreased accuracy (in a motor timing task involving finger tapping along with an isochronous sequence),[13] or a decline in upper extremity functional task with an auditory stimuli.[21]

Effects of Music Therapy on Nonmotor Symptoms

Positive results were found in 7 trials analyzing the effects of MT on nonmotor symptoms, except for the study by Shih et al.[25] (voice), which presented no changes in the variables evaluated, probably because of the duration of the intervention.

A significant improvement ($P < .05$) was demonstrated in 7 nonmotor symptom studies with singing intervention on singing quality,[26] voice and vocal parameters,[24,26–28] respiratory and swallow parameters,[24,27] and dysarthria[28] with music intervention on cognition,[12,17] memory and attention,[17] and with rhythm intervention on dysarthria.[14] All the studies assessing nonmotor symptoms were longitudinal.

Effects of Music Therapy on Quality of Life and Mood

Of the 8 trials that analyzed the effects of MT on quality of life and mood, no negative effects were demonstrated; only 2 failed to show any improvement with music[36] or singing[26] intervention in a cross-sectional[36] and longitudinal[26] intervention, respectively. Beneficial effects were demonstrated with singing[28] interventions, and a

Table 1
Studies Performed in Parkinson's Disease and Music Therapy (1996-2017) Classified by Type of Intervention (Music, Singing, and Rhythm)

First Author and Year	Intervention	Type of Intervention: Longitudinal or Cross-sectional	Hoehn and Yahr Scale	Number of Participants	Controls: Parkinson's Disease or Non-Parkinson's	Variables Evaluated	Evaluation Methods	Results
Music intervention								
Chomiak et al. (2017)[16]	iPod Touch music vs podcast	Longitudinal; 4-week 10-20 min 3 times a week, in-home music-contingent SIP training	2-3	11	6 Parkinson's	Fear of falling, general cognitive functioning, self-reported freezing of gait, and dual-tasking step automaticity	FES-I, MoCA, FOG-Q, UPDRS	Significant training interaction in DT step automaticity (music vs podcast); no significant effect of training on FES-I, MoCA, or FOG-Q
Spina et al. (2016)[17]	MT	Longitudinal; 90 min once a week for 6 mo	Not specified	25	Not specified	QOL, motor symptoms and nonmotor symptoms	New freezing-of-gait questionnaire score, UPDRS, PDQ, Frontal assessment battery, Rey figure, Phonemic vocal fluency, Raven test, Fluency test, Stroop test, Clock drawing test, and Trail making test	SSI in cognition, memory, attention (frontal lobe function), and QOL
Dalla Bella et al. (2015)[13]	Musically cued gait training	Longitudinal; sessions of 30 min, 3 times a wk × 1 mo	2	35	20 Non-Parkinson's	Stride length and gait; Perceptual and motor timing	Vicon MX motion capture system, UPDRS; BAASTA, Multi Layer Perception Matlab toolbox and BAT	Beneficial effect of stride length and speed; Beneficial effect at motor timing; decreased accuracy in tapping along with isochronous sequence; in most cases, effects were manifested 1 mo after training
Pohl et al. (2013)[12]	Ronnie Gardiner Rhythm and Music Method	Longitudinal; 12 sessions of 1 h × 6 wk	2-3	18	6 Parkinson's	Mobility, cognitive function, and QOL	UPDRS, 2-dimension motion analysis system based on the Posturo-Locomotion-Manual method, Time Up and Go, PDQ, Cognitive Assessment Battery, Recall test, Symbol Digit Modalities Test, Clox and Cube, Naming 30 items, SCWT, PaSMO	SSI in posturo-locomotion-manual movement time and UPDRS motor score, 3 cognitive tests, and QOL
Sacrey et al. (2011)[18]	Familiar music on and off medication	Longitudinal; 2 sessions	1.5-3	16	8 Non-Parkinson's	Movement of dominant upper limb (reach-to-eat): reach duration, eye movement latency, and movement scoring	UPDRS, MMSE, movement component rating scale, Peak Motus v.8.3.02-D digitizing system, MobileEye v.12 (Dark pupil tracking system)	Improvement in the latency to visually disengage the target

(continued on next page)

Table 1 (continued)

First Author and Year	Intervention	Type of Intervention: Longitudinal or Cross-sectional	Hoehn and Yahr Scale	Number of Participants	Controls: Parkinson's Disease or Non-Parkinson's	Variables Evaluated	Evaluation Methods	Results
Brown et al. (2010)[19]	Examine obstacle negotiation with and without music	Longitudinal; 12 trials	2-3	20	10 Non-Parkinson's	Step length, toe-obstacle distance, heel-obstacle distance, step height of lead foot, trail foot, and crossing velocity of lead limb	UPDRS (III), 6-camera motion analysis system (Pulnix TM-6701AN scan system) and Vicon Motus 9.2 software	With concurrent music, PD subjects crossed the obstacle slower (7.2% decrease); spatial parameters were maintained
Brown et al. (2009)[20]	Effect of music accompaniment (or not) in 4 different test conditions	Longitudinal; 6 trials	2-3	20	10 Non-Parkinson's	Gait velocity, stride length, and the percentage of the gait cycle spent in double-limb support	UPDRS (III), 6-camera motion analysis system (Peak Performance Technologies and Vicon Motus 9.0 software)	Adverse effect of music on gait for PD patients
Ma et al. (2009)[21]	Auditory stimuli (weather forecast or marching music) in a dual-task paradigm	Cross-sectional	1-3	20	Not specified	Dominant arm movement time, peak velocity, deceleration time and number of movement units	Five-point Likert scale, 3-dimensional ultrasound measuring system	Significantly more attention was directed toward the task in the no-sound condition; the effect of the weather forecast stimuli was significantly larger for movement time and deceleration time
Satoh et al. (2008)[22]	After music training, asses the effect of mental singing while walking	Longitudinal; 7 consecutive training tasks	2-3	8	Not specified	Gait, time to each step, festination	UPDRS, and video-counter	SSI in speed and steps taken while walking at a straight path and turning
Pacchetti et al. (2000)[9]	Active MT vs physical therapy	Longitudinal; once a week × 3 mo	2-3	32	16 Parkinson's	Motor function and QOL	UPDRS, happiness measure, PDQL	SSI in bradykinesia, rigidity, and QOL
Singing Intervention								
Stegemöller et al. (2017)[23]	Singing therapy	Longitudinal; 8 wk	Not specified	24	Not specified	Dysphagia	SWAL-QOL, UPDRS, and electromyography	Prolongation of laryngeal elevation during swallow in singing group
Stegemöller et al. (2016)[24]	Singing therapy	Longitudinal; 8 wk once/twice a week	Not specified	27	Not specified	Voice/speech, breathing problems (MIP, MEP) and QOL	MMSE, UPDRS; measures of vowels' sustainment, maximum phonation range, vocal intensity; portable respiratory pressure meter; V-RQOL; WHOQOL-BREF	SSI at MIP and MEP, phonation time, voice QOL, and whole health QOL
Shih et al. (2012)[25]	Choral singing therapy	Longitudinal; 12 sessions of 90 min, 1 per week	1-3	13	Not specified	Voice-related disorders	MMSE, UPDRS, V-RQOL	No significant changes due to the duration
Elefant et al. (2012)[26]	Group music sessions	Longitudinal; 1 h/wk × 20 wk	2-3	10	Not specified	Speech, singing and depressive symptoms	KayPentax Multi-Dimensional Voice Program, Voice Handicap Index, Montgomery and Asberg Depression rating scale	SSI in singing quality and voice range; no significant changes in depressive symptoms

Study	Intervention	Design	Duration (mo)	Sample size	Disease	Outcome measures	Assessment tools	Results
Di Benedetto et al (2009)[27]	Speech therapy and choral singing	Longitudinal; 2 sessions of 1-2 h/wk (26 h total)	1.5-2.5	20	Not specified	Speech, voice, prosodia, FVC, FEV1, FRC, RV, TLC, Raw, MIP, MEP, and maximum phonation time	UPDRS, MMSE, Hamilton Depression Scale; laryngeal videostroboscopy, voice analysis with Kay Computer Speech Lab Model 4300B, body plethysmography, mouth pressure meter, and visual analog scale	SSI in FRC, MIP, MEP, Maximum phonation time, quality of prosodia, and presence of fatigue reading a passage
Haneishi et al (2001)[28]	MT Voice Protocol sessions	Longitudinal; 12-14 sessions of 1 h 3 times a week (4-5 wk in total)	Not specified	4♀	Not specified	Speech intelligibility, vocal intensity, maximum vocal range, maximum of sustained vowel phonation, vocal fundamental frequency and variation, and mood	SIT: Self-Assessment Form, MultiSpeech™ analyzer, Rejeski Feeling Scale, PDQ music questionnaire	SSI in speech intelligibility and in vocal intensity; higher posttest scores evaluating mood
Rhythm intervention Pantelyat A et al (2017)[29]	Drum circle classes	Longitudinal; 6 wk, twice a week	Not specified	20	10 Parkinson's	QOL, motor symptoms, cognition, and mood	PDQ, Geriatric Depression Scale, at baseline, 6 and 12 wk	Drummers had significantly improved PDQ-39 scores from baseline to 6 wk
Cameron et al (2016)[30]	Beat-based timing over 2 sessions on and off medication	Cross-sectional; Each task twice the same day 30- to 90-min interval sessions	Not specified	142	70 Non-Parkinson's	Accuracy with rhythms	BAT, Goldsmiths Musical Sophistication Index, MMSE, UPDRS (III)	Both groups discriminated metric simple rhythms better; SSI on vs off medication
Del Olmo et al (2005)[31]	Effect of rhythm auditory cues on gait	Longitudinal; 1 h/ d × 5 d × 4 wk	1-2.5	30	15 Non-Parkinson's	Gait (velocity, length, and cadence)	Specific system of switches inside the shoes sending data to a computer	SSI in coefficients of variability for the preferred gait
Bernatzky et al (2004)[32]	Drumming music, off medication	Cross-sectional; 20 min	2-3	21♂	20 Non-Parkinson's	Fine motor coordination: steadiness, line tracking, aiming and tapping; coordination in legs	Vienna Test System; Powerforce working plate	SSI in line tracking and aiming; music effects more in precision than in speediness of movement
Thaut et al (2001)[14]	RAS	Longitudinal; 2 trial sessions	3	20	Not specified	Dysarthria	Assessment of intelligibility of dysarthric speech	SSI in speech intelligibility, being the most substantial enhancement in severely impaired speakers
McIntosh et al (1997)[33]	RAS on and off medication walking under 4 different conditions	Cross-sectional	2-4	41	10 Non-Parkinson's	Gait velocity, cadence, stride length, symmetry	Computerized food switch system	SSI in faster RAS in mean gait velocity, cadence, and stride length in all groups
Thaut et al (1996)[34]	RAS in a home-based gait-training program	Longitudinal; 3 wk	2,4	26	11 Parkinson's	Gait speed, stride length, step cadence	Electromyography, duty cycle index, correlation coefficient between amplitude-normalized average profiles	SSI in all parameters

(continued on next page)

Table 1 (continued)

First Author and Year	Intervention	Type of Intervention: Longitudinal or Cross-sectional	Hoehn and Yahr Scale	Number of Participants	Controls: Parkinson's Disease or Non-Parkinson's	Variables Evaluated	Evaluation Methods	Results
Mix Intervention								
Harrison et al. (2017)[35]	Uncued, music, singing, singing + music, and verbal task	Cross-sectional; a 5-min walk on instrumented, computerized GAITRite Walkway	2-3	23	Not specified	Gait variability: velocity, cadence, and stride length	UPDRS (III), FOG-Q, MMSE, BAT	Gait was less variable when singing than during other cued conditions
Bukowska et al. (2016)[2]	Combination of 3 neurologic MT sensorimotor techniques	Longitudinal; 45 min of MT 4 times a week × 4 wk	2-3	55	25 Parkinson's	Gait and stability	Gait (Optoelectrical 3D Movement Analysis, System BTS Smart-D); stability (Romberg test, Computerized Dynamic Posturography CQ Stab)	SSI in spatiotemporal gait parameters; improvement of proprioception was demonstrated based on stability test with eyes closed
Cancela et al. (2014)[3]	Auditory cues (rhythm, sounds and commercial music)	Cross-sectional	Not specified	101	97 Non-Parkinson's	Gait	Affinity diagrams (Beyer & Holtzblatt) and informal interviews carried out by a music therapist	Rhythm, melody, and harmony demonstrated beneficial effect in gait rehabilitation tasks
Nombela et al. (2013)[36]	Assessment of music effects	Cross-sectional	1-3	58	8	Motor function and QOL	Written structured music questionnaire designed by Cambridge University PD Research Clinic	No significant improvement

Variables: FEV1, forced expiratory volume in 1 s; FES-I, fear of falling; FVC, forced vital capacity; FRC, forced residual capacity; MEP, maximum expiratory pressure; MIP, maximum inspiratory pressure; MT, music therapy; QOL, quality of life; RAS, rhythmic auditory stimulation; Raw, airway resistance; RV, residual volume; TLC, total lung capacity.
Methods: BAASTA, Battery for the Assessment of Auditory Sensorimotor and Timing Abilities; BAT, Beat Alignment Test; BTS Smart-D, High Precision Digital Optoelectronic System for Analyzing all Types of Movement; FOG-Q, Freezing of Gait Questionnaire; MMSE, Mini-Mental State Examination; MoCA, Montreal Cognitive Assessment; PaSMO, Parallel Serial Mental Operations; PDQ, Parkinson's Disease Questionnaire; PDQL, Parkinson's Disease Quality of Life Questionnaire; PPFAOUEF, Purdue Pegboard for assessment of upper extremity function; SII, Speech Intelligibility Inventory; SIP, in-home music-contingent stepping-in-place; SCWT, Strop color/word test; SWAL-QOL, swallow quality of life; UPDRS, Unified Parkinson's Disease Rating Scale; V-RQOL, Voice-Related Quality of Life Questionnaire; WHOQOL-BREF, World Health Organization Quality of Life Questionnaire.
Results: SSI, statistically significant improvement.

significant improvement ($P < .05$) was obtained with music,[9,12,17] singing,[24] and rhythm.[16]

Discussion

The purpose of this review was to analyze the scientific evidence concerning the therapeutic effects of MT in PD. After a thorough examination of all the selected articles, we analyzed outcomes in motor, nonmotor, and quality of life according to the different types of MT (music, rhythm, and singing). Nevertheless, some trials looked at more than just 1 feature.

Of the 27 articles analyzed, most of the studies demonstrated beneficial effects of MT in persons with PD in motor symptoms (16 of 20 articles),[2,3,9,12,16–18,20,22,29,30,32–36] nonmotor symptoms (7 of 9 articles),[12,14,17,24,26–28] and quality of life and mood (6 of 8 articles).[9,12,16,17,24,28] Most trials reporting statistically significant beneficial effects used the active modality of MT for at least 1 month. This might indicate that MT should be an active and durable treatment for it to achieve positive long-term results.

Concerning motor symptoms, most of the studies with MT interventions resulted in improvement in gait,[2,3,13,31,33,34] motor timing,[13] coordination,[32] postural control, and balance.[2,15] Nevertheless, on account of the complex cognitive process involved in attention to both music and the different movements, MT has not always had positive outcomes in persons with PD.[20] Usually, the difficulty of the therapy was directly correlated with the outcome, so the feasibility and limitations of each therapy were factors that needed to be controlled.

Voice and speech disorders (dysarthria, loudness, fluency, and rhythm) occur in approximately 80% of persons with PD, and these are also some of the earliest symptoms of PD,[26] causing severe impairment. These deficits combined with other nonmotor symptoms like diminished facial expressions lead to lower self-confidence and lessen interpersonal communication. MT, such as a singing intervention, provides stimulation of the vocal and respiratory musculature and has the potential to improve these deficits.[37] Combining voice rehabilitation exercises with a correct posture ameliorates speech and respiratory conditions, providing greater thoracic expansion.[28] In addition, training persons with PD with simple therapies that they are able to reproduce when they have motor impairment, such as singing while walking to diminish gait disturbances, has been proven to be effective.[22]

Specific training methods that have shown positive effects can nevertheless have long-term limitations. This is due to the need for adherence to the therapy, home practice, and individual assessment by a clinician. Currently, many programs are dealing with these limitations and attempting to solve them with telepractice, specific software, and online help.[25]

The effect of music, however, is subjective. How it will affect the listener depends on his or her experiences, perception, and different tastes. Previous studies have analyzed the effect of familiar music and its relationship between the reward system and, specifically, the dopaminergic system. The dopaminergic system has been related with the experience of pleasure and expectations generated when listening to music. Some studies have demonstrated that dopamine release is higher when listening to familiar music rather than aleatory music.[38,39] As the individual response to music is unique and depends on several individual factors, therapies should be individualized in order to improve dopamine response to music. In our review, only 1 study used familiar music,[19] but the impact of the therapy on quality of life was not analyzed.

The main limitation concerns the heterogeneous designs of the studies. Some lacked a control group; some involved a small sample, thereby reducing the power to determine significance in some cases; the MT interventions applied used different protocols and different modalities; and a multiple battery of tests was used to evaluate the different symptoms.

Conclusions

As a nonpharmacologic therapy for persons with PD, MT presented benefits in motor and nonmotor symptoms and quality of life in most of the studies analyzed. Thus, MT should be included as a concomitant therapy in addition to conventional treatments in persons with PD. Nonetheless, further studies including longitudinal designs and homogenous MT protocols are needed to determine which type of MT is more suitable and which clinical manifestations are more susceptible to improvement according to the severity of the PD.

References

1. Hirtz D, Thurman DJ, Gwinn-Hardy K, et al. How common are the "common" neurologic disorders? Neurology 2007;68:326–337.
2. Bukowska AA, Krężałek P, Mirek E, et al. Neurologic music therapy training for mobility and stability rehabilitation with Parkinson's disease—A pilot study. Front Hum Neurosci 2016;9:1–12.
3. Cancela J, Moreno EM, Arredondo MT, et al. Designing auditory cues for Parkinson's disease gait rehabilitation. Conf Proc IEEE Eng Med Biol Soc 2014; 2014:5852–5855.
4. Alexander GE. Biology of Parkinson's disease: Pathogenesis and pathophysiology of a multisystem neurodegenerative disorder. Dialogues Clin Neurosci 2004;6:259–280.
5. Goetz CG, Poewe W, Rascol O, et al. Movement disorder society task force report on the Hoehn and Yahr staging scale: Status and recommendations. Mov Disord 2004;19:1020–1028.
6. Goetz CG, Tilley BC, Shaftman SR, et al. Movement Disorder Society-Sponsored Revision of the Unified Parkinson's Disease Rating Scale (MDS-UPDRS): Scale presentation and clinimetric testing results. Mov Disord 2008;23:2129–2170.
7. AlDakheel A, Kalia LV, Lang AE. Pathogenesis-targeted, disease-modifying therapies in Parkinson disease. Neurotherapeutics 2014;11:6–23.
8. Sarkar S, Raymick J, Imam S. Neuroprotective and therapeutic strategies against Parkinson's disease: Recent perspectives. Int J Mol Sci 2016;17.
9. Pacchetti C, Mancini F, Aglieri R, et al. Active music therapy in Parkinson's disease: An integrative method for motor and emotional rehabilitation. Psychosom Med 2000;62:386–393.
10. Amengual JL, Rojo N, Veciana de Las Heras M, et al. Sensorimotor plasticity after music-supported therapy in chronic stroke patients revealed by transcranial magnetic stimulation. PLoS One 2013;8:e61883.
11. Tsoi KKF, Chan JYC, Ng YM, et al. Receptive music therapy is more effective than interactive music therapy to relieve behavioral and psychological symptoms of dementia: A systematic review and meta-analysis. J Am Med Dir Assoc 2018;19:568–576.e3.
12. Pohl P, Dizdar N, Hallert E. The Ronnie Gardiner Rhythm and Music Method—A feasibility study in Parkinson's disease. Disabil Rehabil 2013;3526:2197–2204.
13. Dalla Bella S, Benoit CE, Farrugia N, et al. Effects of musically cued gait training in Parkinson's disease: Beyond a motor benefit. Ann N Y Acad Sci 2015;1337: 77–85.
14. Thaut M, McIntosh K. Auditory rhythmicity enhances movement and speech motor control in patients with Parkinson's disease. Funct Neurol 2001;16: 163–172.
15. Raglio A. Music therapy interventions in Parkinson's disease: The state-of-the-art. Front Neurol 2015;6:185.
16. Chomiak T, Watts A, Meyer N, et al. A training approach to improve stepping automaticity while dual-tasking in Parkinson's disease: A prospective pilot study. Medicine (Baltimore) 2017;96:e5934.
17. Spina E, Barone P, Mosca LL, et al. Music therapy for motor and nonmotor symptoms of Parkinson's disease: A prospective, randomized, controlled, single-blinded study. J Am Geriatr Soc 2016;64:36–39.
18. Sacrey LAR, Travis SG, Whishaw IQ. Drug treatment and familiar music aids an attention shift from vision to somatosensation in Parkinson's disease on the reach-to-eat task. Behav Brain Res 2011;217:391–398.
19. Brown LA, de Bruin N, Doan J, et al. Obstacle crossing among people with Parkinson disease is influenced by concurrent music. J Rehabil Res Dev 2010; 47:225–231.
20. Brown LA, de Bruin N, Doan JB, et al. Novel challenges to gait in Parkinson's disease: The effect of concurrent music in single- and dual-task contexts. Arch Phys Med Rehabil 2009;90:1578–1583.
21. Ma HI, Hwang WJ, Lin KC. The effects of two different auditory stimuli on functional arm movement in persons with Parkinson's disease: A dual-task paradigm. Clin Rehabil 2009;23:229–237.
22. Satoh M, Kuzuhara S. Training in mental singing while walking improves gait disturbance in Parkinson's disease patients. Eur Neurol 2008;60:237–243.
23. Stegemöller EL, Hibbing P, Radig H, et al. Therapeutic singing as an early intervention for swallowing in persons with Parkinson's disease. Complement Ther Med 2017;31:127–133.

24. Stegemöller EL, Radig H, Hibbing P, et al. Effects of singing on voice, respiratory control and quality of life in persons with Parkinson's disease. Disabil Rehabil 2017;39:594–600.
25. Shih LC, Piel J, Warren A, et al. Singing in groups for Parkinson's disease (SINGING-PD): A pilot study of group singing therapy for PD-related voice/speech disorders. Park Relat Disord 2012;18:548–552.
26. Elefant C, Baker FA, Lotan M, et al. The effect of group music therapy on mood, speech, and singing in individuals with Parkinson's disease—A feasibility study effects of music therapy on facial expression of individuals with Parkinson's disease: A pilot study. J Music Ther 2012;49:278–302.
27. Di Benedetto P, Cavazzon M, Mondolo F, et al. Voice and choral singing treatment: A new approach for speech and voice disorders in Parkinson's disease. Eur J Phys Rehabil Med 2009;45:13–19.
28. Haneishi E. Effects of a music therapy voice protocol on speech intelligibility, vocal acoustic measures, and mood of individuals with Parkinson's disease. J Music Ther 2001;38:273–290.
29. Pantelyat A, Syres C, Reichwein S, et al. DRUM-PD: The use of a drum circle to improve the symptoms and signs of Parkinson's disease (PD). Mov Disord Clin Pract 2016;3:243–249.
30. Cameron DJ, Pickett KA, Earhart GM, et al. The effect of dopaminergic medication on beat-based auditory timing in Parkinson's disease. Front Neurol 2016;7:19.
31. Del Olmo MF, Cudeiro J. Temporal variability of gait in Parkinson disease: Effects of a rehabilitation programme based on rhythmic sound cues. Park Relat Disord 2005;11:25–33.
32. Bernatzky G, Bernatzky P, Hesse HP, et al. Stimulating music increases motor coordination in patients afflicted with Morbus Parkinson. Neurosci Lett 2004; 361:4–8.
33. Mcintosh GC, Brown SH, Rice RR, et al. Rhythmic auditory-motor facilitation of gait patterns in patients with Parkinson's disease. J Neurol Neurosurg Psychiatry 1997;62:22–26.
34. Thaut MH, McIntosh GC, Rice RR, et al. Rhythmic auditory stimulation in gait training for Parkinson's disease patients. Mov Disord 1996;11:193–200.
35. Harrison EC, McNeely ME, Earhart GM. The feasibility of singing to improve gait in Parkinson disease. Gait Posture 2017;53:224–229.
36. Nombela C, Rae CL, Grahn JA, et al. How often does music and rhythm improve patients' perception of motor symptoms in Parkinson's disease. J Neurol 2013; 260:1404–1405.
37. Young-Mason J. Singing for the joy of it, singing for hope, singing to heal. Clin Nurse Spec 2012;26:343–344.
38. Salimpoor VN, Zald DH, Zatorre RJ, et al. Predictions and the brain: How Music sounds become rewarding. Trends Cogn Sci 2015;19:86–91.
39. Salimpoor VN, Benovoy M, Larcher K, et al. Anatomically distinct dopamine release during anticipation and experience of peak emotion to music. Nat Neurosci 2011;14:257–262.

Article

Music Therapy Self-Care Group for Parents of Preterm Infants in the Neonatal Intensive Care Unit: A Clinical Pilot Intervention

Esteban Roa [1,2] and Mark Ettenberger [2,3,*]

1. Berklee College of Music, Boston, MA 02215, USA; eroafuentes@berklee.edu
2. SONO—Centro de Musicoterapia, Bogotá 11021, Colombia
3. Clínica de la Mujer, Bogotá 11021, Colombia
* Correspondence: mark.ettenberger@gmx.at; Tel.: +57-311-284-7635

Received: 16 November 2018; Accepted: 13 December 2018; Published: 16 December 2018

Abstract: Background: The parents of preterm infants face major mental health challenges in the Neonatal Intensive Care Unit (NICU). Family-centered music therapy actively integrates and empowers parents in their infants' care. With the aim to better understand and address parental needs separately from their babies' needs, a music therapy (MT) self-care group was implemented as part of clinical practice at the hospital Clínica de la Mujer, in Bogotá, Colombia. **Methods:** The group was provided for both parents, twice a week, in the NICU. Music guided relaxations, breathing techniques, and self-expression were at the center of the MT group sessions. The parents completed a pre/post self-administered Numeric Rating Scale (NRS), including anxiety levels, stress levels, mood and motivation. **Results:** The parents highly valued the MT self-care group in the NICU. On average, there was a 37% improvement in anxiety levels, 28% improvement in stress levels, and 12% improvement in mood, restfulness and motivation. Being able to relax, to distract themselves from their worries and having time for themselves are amongst the most frequently mentioned benefits. **Conclusions:** Addressing parents' needs separately from their babies' treatment, with culturally sensitive interventions aimed at improving parental mental health, is essential for continuing the development of family-centered music therapy interventions in the NICU.

Keywords: music therapy; preterm infants; family-centered care; parents; self-care; wellbeing; Neonatal Intensive Care Unit (NICU)

1. Introduction

Having a newborn child is seen as a transformational and, often times, positive experience. However, having a preterm baby in the Neonatal Intensive Care Unit (NICU) can interrupt the transition into parenthood and cause parents to feel a surfeit of emotions, often leading to a sense of hopelessness, psychological distress, anxiety and symptoms of depression [1–5]. Uncertainties revolving around the infant's health, being in an intimidating and alien environment, the financial demands of hospitalization, and the physical appearance of the infant can all be potential stressors for the parents, putting their emotional and mental wellbeing at risk [5–7].

Mothers of preterm infants may show long-lasting signs of posttraumatic stress, depressive symptoms, and anxiety [8–10]. If the trauma experienced during the perinatal period is not addressed adequately, it may negatively affect the relationship between the mother and the child, specifically the mother's availability to recognize the infant's cues and needs [11,12]. Recently, fathers have been taking a more active role in the NICU [13,14] and, just like mothers, fathers are susceptible to various common stressors [15]. Having to care for both their infant and their partner, the pressures of keeping up with employment obligations and possible tensions related to cultural and societal expectations regarding 'masculinity', or gender roles are some of the primary stressors that are specific to fathers [13,16–18]. Unfortunately, follow-up on parental psychological wellbeing during and after hospitalization is not always included in the neonatal care settings. There is a need for culturally appropriate interventions that take into account psychological distress and wellbeing among parents in the NICU [15,17,19,20]. Understanding and addressing parents' needs as both connected to and distinct from their babies' needs may help parents not only as individuals, but it may also positively impact their journey towards parenthood and the relationship they foster with their baby.

Family-Centered Care and Family-Centered Music Therapy in the NICU

Family-Centered Care (FCC) is a growing approach to pediatric health care in which the family is recognized as the patient's primary source of support and as a fundamental part of their wellbeing [21]. The principles of FCC include information sharing, respect and honoring differences, partnership and collaboration, negotiation, and care in the context of the family and community [22]. This approach in health care has become a fundamental pillar in contemporary neonatal care [23] and has been shown to strengthen the parent–infant relationship [9,24], increase the wellbeing of preterm infants [25], and reduce parental stress [26].

Music therapy in the NICU is a well-established field of clinical practice and research [27–29]. Current literature suggests that music therapy is beneficial for both the neonates and caregivers [30–33]. Interventions directed towards the neonate aim to promote physiological and behavioral self-regulation [31,34], feeding success [31,35,36] and improve sleep or quiet alert states [31,37]. The positive impacts of music therapy on parents include relaxation [34], the reduction of anxiety and stress levels [30,31,38], and improved parent–infant bonding [30,33,39–41]. Qualitative analyses show that through the use of music parents can feel empowered by having a more active role in their infants' care [41–43], which is crucial for the transition into parenthood [44,45].

The recent shift in pediatric health care to actively integrate parents in their infants' treatment should also consider their individual wellbeing. Family-centered music therapy in the NICU is rooted in FCC principles and stresses the importance of both infant and parental wellbeing as being essential in neonatal care settings [30,43,46,47]. In order to further develop and detect new ways to help mothers and fathers cope with potential stressors and mental health risks, a music therapy self-care group for parents was implemented as part of the ongoing clinical practice at the NICU in the Clínica de la Mujer. This article highlights the development, process, and preliminary results of this clinical pilot intervention.

2. Materials and Methods

2.1. Context and Setting

The Clínica de la Mujer is one of Bogotá's (the capital of Colombia) most renowned maternity hospitals. Its Level-III NICU has space for 19 incubators located in individual rooms, with a few rooms reserved for twins. Parents have 24-h access to the unit and grandparents can visit the babies once a week. Kangaroo care is a standard intervention in the NICU and music therapy is part of an interdisciplinary therapy team, including respiratory therapy, speech and language therapy, nutrition, social work and psychology/psychiatry. FCC principles and a strong commitment to humanized care build the foundations of the hospital's care philosophy. Music therapy is provided twice a week for preterm and critically ill full-term babies and their families, focused primarily on parent–infant bonding, infant self-regulation and parental mental health.

The music therapy self-care group for mothers and fathers was integrated into a music therapy clinical practice as a pilot intervention in July 2018. Initially, the idea for the group developed in response to many mothers' concerns regarding their difficulties during breast milk extraction due to worries about their babies' health and the pressure to produce enough milk. It was hypothesized that a music therapy self-care group could help mothers to relax and thus reduce the stress perceived during breast milk extraction. After a few pilot sessions and in discussion with the parents and the health care team, it became clear however that not only mothers but also fathers could benefit from the self-care group. As a result, the group was opened for mothers and fathers in August 2018. With the aim to improve parental wellbeing during the NICU stay, the group is provided twice a week for 15–20 min on Wednesday afternoons and for 30 min on Friday mornings.

2.2. Music Therapy Self-Care Group: Procedure and Interventions

The group takes place in the NICU's breast milk extraction room before mothers are scheduled for their next time slot. Although participation in the music therapy self-care group is voluntary, the nursing and medical teams highly encourage both mothers and fathers to attend. The group usually starts with a short verbal introduction with the purpose of explaining the objectives and procedures for the new participants and to quickly assess current parents' moods or any specific stressors.

Live music therapy is at the center of the interventions. The music therapist regularly uses a nylon-string guitar, their voice, shakers, an ocean drum, and a 'Samafón' as the principal instruments. The 'Samafón' is an instrument that is shaped similar to a lyre, but instead of the strings, five hollow metal tubes hang from the top to the base of the instrument and are connected to each other with threads. Depending on the length of the tubes, notes are lower or higher and the instrument is normally tuned in variations of the pentatonic scales. The tubes are played either individually or quickly, one after another, with a mallet used for singing bowls and the sound is long-lasting. Additionally, the instrument can be rotated easily, holding it with one hand, creating ripples of sounds that project themselves in all directions. Short musical games with shakers, voices or movements serve as 'ice-breakers', seeking to activate the participants at the beginning of the session. Then, the music therapist provides verbal relaxation prompts focused on deep breathing, imagery (i.e., visualizing a place where participants feel safe and comfortable, or evoking a particular landscape, such as standing on a mountain top and looking over the horizon or sitting on the beach and contemplating the movement of the waves), and/or subtle movements with the objective to foster body awareness and to make conscious current moods, thoughts, or emotions. Subsequently, live music is provided, inviting parents to breathe with the music. Alternatively, parents are encouraged to use their voices with the music by either humming or singing vowels or closed consonants in order to achieve increased lengths of exhalation and to creatively explore their musicality.

Although there is debate on what music is best for relaxation [46], the music during the interventions is typically improvised and based on elements such as a slow tempo, repetition, and subtle melodic and harmonic variations or modulations. Often, chord intervals clearly indicating major or minor tonalities (i.e., major or minor thirds) are substituted with sus^9 or sus^4 chords, leaving it open to the music therapist's clinical improvisation skills to modulate between major or minor tonalities.

Once the intervention concludes, parents verbally reflect upon their experiences, thoughts, and feelings during the group session. The music therapist discusses music-assisted self-care techniques that participants can use in their own time. Such techniques include deep breathing techniques with music or voice, the use of recorded music for relaxation, and information sharing between parents.

2.3. Evaluation and Measurements

To evaluate the clinical pilot program and to better understand the potential benefits of the music therapy self-care group for parents in the NICU, the music therapy team designed a self-administered pre/post Numeric Rating Scale (NRS). It is important to highlight that the results gathered from the NRS are strictly used to evaluate the clinical pilot program and are not used for research purposes. The scale aims to detect changes in the perceived levels of anxiety, stress, and wellbeing before and after the music therapy intervention. An 'additional comments' section on the post-intervention sheet provides the opportunity for parents to share more personalized experiences and recommendations in regards to the group. Figure 1 shows the NRS that is currently used.

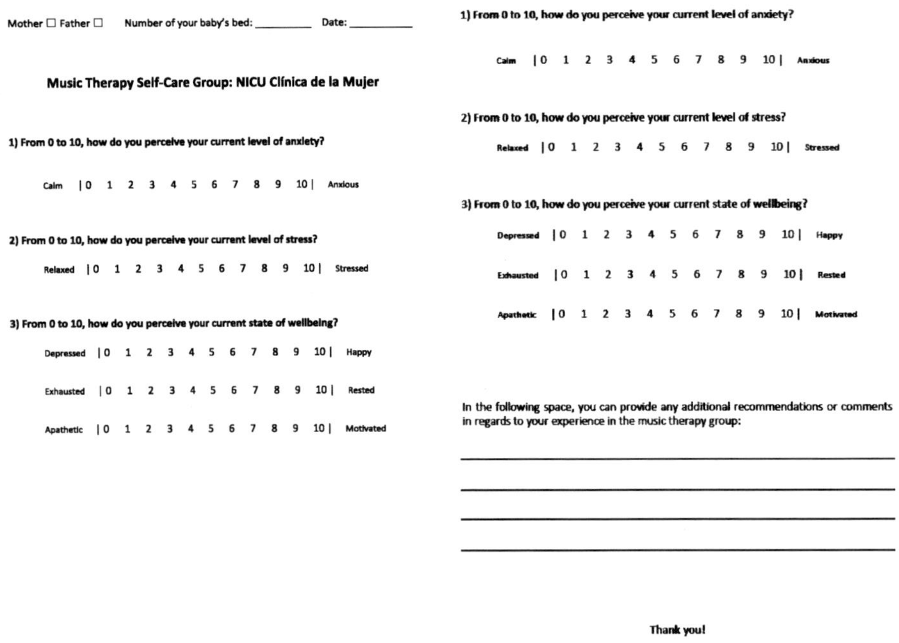

Mother ☐ Father ☐ Number of your baby's bed: ________ Date: ________

Music Therapy Self-Care Group: NICU Clínica de la Mujer

1) From 0 to 10, how do you perceive your current level of anxiety?

Calm | 0 1 2 3 4 5 6 7 8 9 10 | Anxious

2) From 0 to 10, how do you perceive your current level of stress?

Relaxed | 0 1 2 3 4 5 6 7 8 9 10 | Stressed

3) From 0 to 10, how do you perceive your current state of wellbeing?

Depressed | 0 1 2 3 4 5 6 7 8 9 10 | Happy

Exhausted | 0 1 2 3 4 5 6 7 8 9 10 | Rested

Apathetic | 0 1 2 3 4 5 6 7 8 9 10 | Motivated

1) From 0 to 10, how do you perceive your current level of anxiety?

Calm | 0 1 2 3 4 5 6 7 8 9 10 | Anxious

2) From 0 to 10, how do you perceive your current level of stress?

Relaxed | 0 1 2 3 4 5 6 7 8 9 10 | Stressed

3) From 0 to 10, how do you perceive your current state of wellbeing?

Depressed | 0 1 2 3 4 5 6 7 8 9 10 | Happy

Exhausted | 0 1 2 3 4 5 6 7 8 9 10 | Rested

Apathetic | 0 1 2 3 4 5 6 7 8 9 10 | Motivated

In the following space, you can provide any additional recommendations or comments in regards to your experience in the music therapy group:

Thank you!

(**a**) (**b**)

Figure 1. This figure shows the Numeric Rating Scale (NRS) the music therapy team designed to evaluate the clinical pilot program. (**a**) This is the pre-intervention sheet. Participants are given a few minutes prior to the intervention in order to fill it out. As shown above, the music therapy team considered anxiety, stress, and three areas of wellbeing, including mood, restfulness, and motivation. (**b**) This is the post-intervention sheet. The only difference is the 'additional comments' section at the bottom of the page. Participants are given a few minutes after the intervention in order to fill it out.

Parents are assured that their names and personal information are not used during the evaluation of the program. In addition to the NRS, a few semi-structured interviews were conducted with the participating parents to further understand their lived experiences with music therapy.

3. Results

As stated above, the music therapy self-care group took place twice a week. However, due to time restrictions on one of the days, data collection only took place before and after the thirty-minute sessions on Fridays. While the evaluation of the group is part of the clinical practice, it is hoped that the current data collection will help in the establishment of a research protocol in the near future. Table 1 shows the basic features of the group.

Table 1. Basic features of the music therapy self-care group since its implementation in July 2018 to November 2018.

Total Number of Sessions	Total Number of Participants	Total Number of Mothers	Total Number of Fathers
30	122	106	16

The results obtained with the NRS indicate a positive effect of the music therapy self-care group on parents' perceived anxiety and stress levels, and on their mood, restfulness, and motivation. Table 2 shows the mean scores for the pre- and post-intervention.

Figure 2 shows the results as bar charts. On average, there is a 37% improvement in anxiety levels, a 28% improvement in stress levels, a 6% improvement in mood, a 20% improvement in restfulness, and a 9% improvement in motivation. Being able to relax, to distract themselves from their worries and to have time for themselves are amongst the most frequently mentioned benefits parents left in the 'additional comments' section.

Table 2. The mean scores for anxiety and stress levels, mood, restfulness and motivation before and after the music therapy self-care group.

Intervention	Anxiety Levels	Stress Levels	Mood	Restfulness	Motivation
Pre-intervention	5.8	5.2	7.1	4.8	7.2
Post-intervention	2.1	2.4	7.7	6.8	8.1

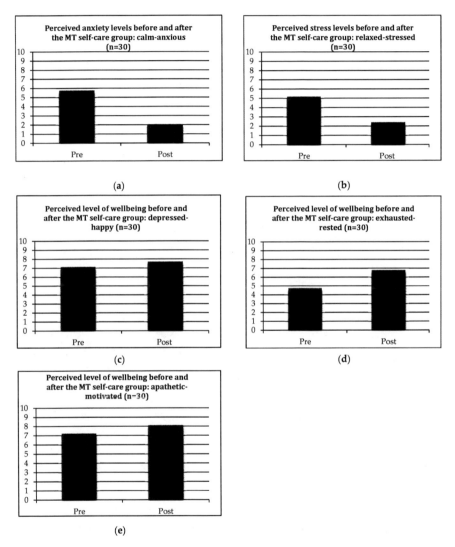

Figure 2. This figure shows the bar charts of the pre- and post-intervention results obtained with the NRS. Please note that the NRS was introduced at a later point, after the start of the clinical pilot program. This is why the data of 30 participants were collected via the NRS, but there were 122 participants in total. (**a**) This bar chart shows the perceived level of anxiety before and after the group sessions. A lower score indicates less perceived anxiety. (**b**) This bar chart shows the perceived level of stress before and after the group sessions. A lower score indicates less perceived stress. (**c**) This bar chart shows the perceived level of mood before and after the group sessions. A higher score indicates a better perceived mood. (**d**) This bar chart shows the perceived level of restfulness before and after the group sessions. A higher score indicates a better perceived feeling of restfulness. (**e**) This bar chart shows the perceived level of motivation before and after the group sessions. A higher score indicates a better perceived motivation.

4. Limitations

Although the evaluation of the music therapy self-care group was not part of the research protocol, the clinical pilot intervention faced the following limitations that should be considered for future investigations:

- The sessions take place in the breast milk extraction room between scheduled milk extraction time slots. Due to its size, it is currently the only available space in the NICU appropriate for group interventions. However, since breast milk extraction usually takes place continuously throughout the day, this caused difficulties with respect to the time restriction for the group on one of the days (Wednesday afternoon).
- The clinical pilot program aims to address the needs of both mothers and fathers. Bearing in mind the cultural norms, perceptions on gender roles, and employment obligations in Colombian society, there were not as many fathers present as mothers throughout the pilot program. Nonetheless, participating fathers regularly express having a positive experience with the group and encouraged that it be formalized in NICU care.
- Since mothers do not always schedule the same time slot for breast milk extraction and kangaroo care with their babies, participation in the group session was inconsistent. Some mothers joined the group several times, but others participated just once. To better assess the outcomes, it is suggested that the participants have a consistent and scheduled attendance for the music therapy self-care group.
- The music therapy team designed the NRS which was used to evaluate the clinical pilot intervention based on the experiences in clinical practice; it is not a standardized assessment tool and has not been validated. Nevertheless, it seems to be an intuitive and easily applicable tool to quickly assess some of the most important domains of parental wellbeing and the parents reported no difficulties in understanding the NRS.

5. Discussion and Conclusions

Parents in the NICU face many challenges that may have potential negative and long-lasting mental health implications. These challenges put not only the individual wellbeing of mothers and fathers at risk, but might also affect the evolving relationship with their baby [1,10–12,48,49]. Parents frequently communicate the need to access tools to better cope with the difficulties that a hospitalization in the NICU can imply and those parents who are provided with appropriate strategies feel empowered, which in turn can positively affect their personal wellbeing and their babies' development [50].

Despite the recent shift in NICU music therapy towards a more inclusive approach of mothers and fathers, studies that focus on relevant parental outcomes are still scarce [51]. Parental wellbeing is also influenced by many different factors, making it difficult to define and measure [52]. The music therapy self-care group at the Clínica de la Mujer was implemented to consciously try to address some of the most common parental stressors mentioned in pediatric health care literature [50] and to focus on parents' needs as individuals. The sessions aimed at providing a space for parents to work on their personal wellbeing using simple and transferable tools relevant for resilience and coping. The results gathered from the NRS are promising and indicate that mothers and fathers experience a decrease in perceived levels of anxiety and stress, and an improvement in mood, relaxation and restfulness after the intervention.

> *"A state of wellbeing is easily achieved with music therapy. Being in the NICU is stressful, but it becomes tolerable with this type of support."* (A participating mother)

Although no data were collected regarding our initial motive to reduce maternal stress and anxiety during breast milk extraction, a limited number of articles report a positive impact of recorded music on breast milk quantity and quality [53,54]. An improved relaxation response in mothers has been discussed as a potential mechanism in both of the aforementioned studies, and is in-line with the already documented anxiolytic and stress-reducing effects of music and music therapy interventions in the NICU [27–30,34,55,56]. Thus, a positive impact of the music therapy self-care group on maternal breast milk extraction seems to be a feasible hypothesis that needs to be investigated with a formal research protocol in the future.

"It is a great space because it allows us to rest and disconnect from the situation we are going through." (A participating father)

For this clinical pilot intervention, live music was considered the best practice due to the flexibility and ability to adapt the music depending on the parents' responses and current needs. Moreover, live music allows for a group dynamic in which participants can interact and share their experiences with one another. Considering that information sharing is at the core of the FCC principles [21,22], the music therapist regularly encourages and facilitates participants to share their experiences after the intervention and to use the space to build a support system amongst themselves. The time allocated for reflection and discussion after the intervention allows parents to share not only their current struggles and difficulties, but also ways to cope with them. Furthermore, considering the 'collective' nature of Colombian society, the active and interactive participation of parents was considered to be more culturally appropriate than individually using recorded music.

"It is a relaxing activity. It should be done more frequently. It allows us to alleviate the stress from this situation." (A participating mother)

This article highlights the impact of a music therapy self-care group on parental wellbeing in the NICU. The preliminary findings from this clinical pilot intervention indicate that this may be an appropriate intervention to help parents with stress reduction, coping, and relaxation. The pilot program aims to develop a research protocol in the near future to better evaluate the impact of the music therapy self-care group on parental mental health and on mothers' breast milk extraction. Addressing parents' needs separately from their babies' treatment, with culturally sensitive interventions aimed at improving parental mental health, is essential for continuing the development of family-centered music therapy in the NICU.

Author Contributions: All authors declare equal contribution for this article. Conceptualization, methodology, implementation, analysis, and draft preparation: E.R. & M.E. Supervision, review & editing: M.E.

Funding: This research received no external funding.

Acknowledgments: The authors are thankful to all the parents participating in the group sessions and to the NICU staff and the hospital's administration team of the Clínica de la Mujer for supporting this initiative.

Conflicts of Interest: The authors declare no conflict of interest.

References

1. Aagard, H.; Hall, E.O.C. Mothers' experiences of having a preterm infant in the neonatal care unit: A meta-synthesis. *J. Pediatr. Nurs.* **2008**, *23*, 26–36. [CrossRef] [PubMed]
2. Carson, C.; Redshaw, M.; Gray, R.; Quigley, M.A. Risk of psychological distress in parents of preterm children in the first year: Evidence from the UK Millennium Cohort Study. *BMJ Open* **2015**, *5*, e007942. [CrossRef] [PubMed]
3. Davis, L.; Edwards, H.; Mohay, H.; Wollin, J. The impact of very premature birth on the psychological health of mothers. *Early Hum. Dev.* **2003**, *73*, 61–70. [CrossRef]
4. Meijssen, D.E.; Wolf, M.J.; Koldewijn, K.; van Wassenaer, A.G.; Kok, J.H.; Van Baar, A.L. Parenting stress in mothers after very preterm birth and the effect of the Infant Behavioural Assessment and Intervention Program. *Child. Care Health Dev.* **2011**, *37*, 195. [CrossRef] [PubMed]
5. Singer, L.T.; Salvator, A.; Guo, S.; Collin, M.; Lilien, L.; Baley, J. Maternal Psychological Distress and Parenting Stress After the Birth of a Very Low-Birth-Weight Infant. *JAMA* **1999**, *281*, 799–805. [CrossRef] [PubMed]

6. Miles, M.S.; Funk, S.G.; Kasper, M.A. The neonatal intensive care unit environment: Sources of stress for parents. *AACN Clin. Issues Crit. Care Nurs.* **1991**, *2*, 346–354. [CrossRef] [PubMed]
7. Stefana, A.; Padovani, E.M.; Biban, P.; Lavelli, M. Experiences with their preterm babies admitted to neonatal intensive care unit: A multi-method study. *J. Adv. Nurs.* **2018**, *74*, 1090–1098. [CrossRef]
8. Kersting, A.; Dorsch, M.; Wesselmann, U.; Lüdorff, K.; Witthaut, J.; Ohrmann, P.; Arolt, V. Maternal posttraumatic stress response after the birth of a very low-birth-weight infant. *J. Psychosom. Res.* **2004**, *57*, 473–476. [CrossRef]
9. Jotzo, M.; Poets, C.F. Helping Parents Cope with the Trauma of Premature Birth: An Evaluation of a Trauma-Preventive Psychological Intervention. *Pediatrics* **2005**, *115*, 915–919. [CrossRef]
10. Hagan, R.; Evans, S.F.; Pope, S. Preventing postnatal depression in mothers of very preterm infants: A randomised controlled trial. *BJOG Int. J. Obstetr. Gynaecol.* **2004**, *111*, 641–647. [CrossRef]
11. Muller-Nix, C.; Forcada-Guex, M.; Pierrehumbert, B.; Jaunin, L.; Borghini, A.; Ansermet, F. Prematurity, maternal stress and mother-child interactions. *Early Hum. Dev.* **2004**, *79*, 145–158. [CrossRef] [PubMed]
12. Whitfield, M.F. Psychosocial effects of intensive care on infants and families after discharge. *Semin. Neonatol.* **2003**, *8*, 185–193. [CrossRef]
13. Mondanaro, J.F.; Ettenberger, M.; Park, L. Mars Rising: Music Therapy and the Increasing Presence of Fathers in the NICU. *Music Med.* **2016**, *8*, 96–107.
14. Arockiasamy, V.; Holsti, L.; Albersheim, S. Fathers' experiences in the neonatal intensive care unit: A search for control. *Pediatrics* **2008**, *121*, 215–222. [CrossRef] [PubMed]
15. Garten, L.; Nazary, L.; Metze, B.; Bührer, C. Pilot study of experiences and needs of 111 fathers of very low birth weight infants in a neonatal intensive care unit. *J. Perinatol.* **2013**, *33*, 65–69. [CrossRef] [PubMed]
16. Hugill, K.; Letherby, G.; Reid, T.; Lavender, T. Experiences of fathers shortly after the birth of their preterm infants. *J. Obstetr. Gynecol. Neonatal Nurs.* **2013**, *42*, 655–663. [CrossRef]
17. Sloan, K.; Rowe, J.; Jones, L. Stress and coping in fathers following the birth of a preterm infant. *J. Neonatal Nurs.* **2008**, *14*, 108–115. [CrossRef]
18. Ahn, Y.-M.; Kim, N.-H. Parental Perception of Neonates, Parental Stress and Education for NICU Parents. *Asian Nurs. Res.* **2007**, *1*, 199–210. [CrossRef]
19. Fabiyi, C.; Rankin, K.; Norr, K.; Shapiro, N.; White-Traut, R. Anxiety among Black and Latina Mothers of Premature Infants at Social-Environmental Risk. *Newborn Infant Nurs. Rev.* **2012**, *12*, 132–140. [CrossRef]
20. Turan, T.; Başbakkal, Z.; Ozbek, S. Effect of nursing interventions on stressors of parents of premature infants in neonatal intensive care unit. *J. Clin. Nurs.* **2008**, *17*, 2856–2866. [CrossRef]
21. Committee on Hospital Care; American Academy of Pediatrics. Family-centered care and the pediatrician's role. *Pediatrics* **2003**, *112 Pt 1*, 691–697. [CrossRef]
22. Kuo, D.Z.; Houtrow, A.J.; Arango, P.; Kuhlthau, K.A.; Simmons, J.M.; Neff, J.M. Family-centered care: Current applications and future directions in pediatric health care. *Matern. Child. Health J.* **2012**, *16*, 297–305. [CrossRef] [PubMed]
23. Gooding, J.S.; Cooper, L.G.; Blaine, A.I.; Franck, L.S.; Howse, J.L.; Berns, S.D. Family support and family-centered care in the neonatal intensive care unit: Origins, advances, impact. *Semin. Perinatol.* **2011**, *35*, 20–28. [CrossRef] [PubMed]
24. Cooper, L.G.; Gooding, J.S.; Gallagher, J.; Sternesky, L.; Ledsky, R.; Berns, S.D. Impact of a family-centered care initiative on NICU care, staff and families. *J. Perinatol.* **2007**, *27* (Suppl. 2), 32–37. [CrossRef] [PubMed]
25. Van Riper, M. Family-provider relationships and well-being in families with preterm infants in the NICU. *Heart Lung J. Crit. Care* **2001**, *30*, 74–84. [CrossRef] [PubMed]
26. Meyer, E.C.; Coll, C.T.; Lester, B.M.; Boukydis, C.F.; McDonough, S.M.; Oh, W. Family-based intervention improves maternal psychological well-being and feeding interaction of preterm infants. *Pediatrics* **1994**, *93*, 241–246.
27. Haslbeck, F.B. Music therapy for premature infants and their parents: An integrative review. *Nord. J. Music Ther.* **2012**, *21*, 203–226. [CrossRef]
28. Standley, J. Music therapy research in the NICU: An updated meta-analysis. *Neonatal Netw.* **2012**, *31*, 311–316. [CrossRef]
29. Bieleninik, Ł.; Ghetti, C.; Gold, C. Music Therapy for Preterm Infants and Their Parents: A Meta-analysis. *Pediatrics* **2016**, *138*. [CrossRef]

30. Ettenberger, M.; Cárdenas, C.R.; Parker, M.; Odell-Miller, H. Family-centred music therapy with preterm infants and their parents in the Neonatal Intensive Care Unit (NICU) in Colombia—A mixed-methods study. *Nord. J. Music Ther.* **2017**, *26*, 207–234. [CrossRef]
31. Loewy, J.; Stewart, K.; Dassler, A.-M.; Telsey, A.; Homel, P. The Effects of Music Therapy on Vital Signs, Feeding, and Sleep in Premature Infants. *Pediatrics* **2013**, *131*, 902–918. [CrossRef] [PubMed]
32. Loewy, J. NICU music therapy: Song of kin as critical lullaby in research and practice. *Ann. N. Y. Acad. Sci.* **2015**, *1337*, 178–185. [CrossRef] [PubMed]
33. Ettenberger, M.; Odell-Miller, H.; Cárdenas, C.; Serrano, S.; Parker, M.; Camargo Llanos, S. Music Therapy With Premature Infants and Their Caregivers in Colombia—A Mixed Methods Pilot Study Including a Randomized Trial. *Voices World Forum Music Ther.* **2014**, *14*. [CrossRef]
34. Teckenberg-Jansson, P.; Huotilainen, M.; Pölkki, T.; Lipsanen, J.; Järvenpää, A.-L. Rapid effects of neonatal music therapy combined with kangaroo care on prematurely-born infants. *Nord. J. Music Ther.* **2011**, *20*, 22–42. [CrossRef]
35. Standley, J.M. The effect of music-reinforced nonnutritive sucking on feeding rate of premature infants. *J. Pediatr. Nurs.* **2003**, *18*, 169–173. [CrossRef] [PubMed]
36. Vianna, M.; Barbosa, A.P.; Carvalhaes, A.S.; Cunha, A. Music therapy may increase breastfeeding rates among mothers of premature newborns: A randomized controlled trial. *Jornal de Pediatria* **2011**, *87*, 206–212. [CrossRef] [PubMed]
37. Olischar, M.; Shoemark, H.; Holton, T.; Weninger, M.; Hunt, R.W. The influence of music on a EEG activity in neurologically healthy newborns ≥32 weeks' gestational age. *Acta Paediatr.* **2011**, *100*, 670–675. [CrossRef]
38. Cevasco, A.M. The effects of mothers' singing on full-term and preterm infants and maternal emotional responses. *J. Music Ther.* **2008**, *45*, 273–306. [CrossRef]
39. Walworth, D. Effects of Developmental Music Groups for Parents and Premature or Typical Infants Under Two Years on Parental Responsiveness and Infant Social Development. *J. Music Ther.* **2009**, *46*, 32–52. [CrossRef]
40. Haslbeck, F.B. The interactive potential of creative music therapy with premature infants and their parents: A qualitative analysis. *Nord. J. Music Ther.* **2014**, *23*, 36–70. [CrossRef]
41. McLean, E. Fostering intimacy through musical beginnings: Exploring the application of communicative musicality through the musical experience of parents in a neonatal intensive care unit. *Voices World Forum Music Ther.* **2016**, *16*. Available online: https://voices.no/index.php/voices/article/view/874/721 (accessed on 30 November 2018). [CrossRef]
42. Palazzi, A.; Meschini, R.; Piccinini, C.A. Music therapy intervention for the mother-preterm infant dyad: Evidence from a case study in a Brazilian NICU. *Voices World Forum Music Ther.* **2017**, *17*. Available online: https://voices.no/index.php/voices/article/view/916 (accessed on 30 November 2018). [CrossRef]
43. Shoemark, H.; Dearn, T. Keeping Parents at the Centre of Family Centred Music Therapy with Hospitalized Infants. *Aust. J. Music Ther.* **2008**, *19*, 3–24.
44. Hutchinson, S.W.; Spillett, M.A.; Cronin, M. Parents' Experiences during their Infant's Transition from Neonatal Intensive Care Unit to Home: A Qualitative Study. *Qual. Rep.* **2012**, *17*, 1–20.
45. McLean, E.; McFerran Skewes, K.; Thompson, G.A. Parents' musical engagement with their baby in the neonatal unit to support emerging parental identity: A grounded theory study. *J. Neonatal Nurs.* **2018**. [CrossRef]
46. Haslbeck, F. Three little wonders. Music Therapy with families in neonatal care. In *Music Therapy with Families*; Lindhal, S., Ed.; Jessica Kingsley Publishers: London, UK, 2016; pp. 19–44.
47. Ettenberger, M. Music therapy in the neonatal intensive care unit: Putting the families at the centre of care. *Br. J. Music Ther.* **2017**, *31*, 12–17. [CrossRef]
48. Carter, J.D.; Mulder, R.T.; Darlow, B.A. Parental stress in the NICU: The influence of personality, psychological, pregnancy and family factors. *Person. Ment. Health* **2007**, *1*, 40–50. [CrossRef]
49. Pal, S.; Alpay, L.; Steenbrugge, G.; Detmar, S. An Exploration of Parents' Experiences and Empowerment in the Care for Preterm Born Children. *J. Child. Fam. Stud.* **2014**, *23*, 1081–1089. [CrossRef]
50. Melnyk, B.M.; Alpert-Gillis, L.; Feinstein, N.F.; Crean, H.F.; Johnson, J.; Fairbanks, E.; Small, L.; Rubenstein, J.; Slota, M.; Corbo-Richert, B. Creating opportunities for parent empowerment: Program effects on the mental health/coping outcomes of critically ill young children and their mothers. *Pediatrics* **2004**, *113*, e597–e607. [CrossRef]

51. Ettenberger. Family-Centred Music Therapy in the Neonatal Intensive Care Unit (NICU): Key concepts, research and examples of clinical practice. In *Music Therapy for Premature and Newborn Infants*, 2nd ed.; Nöcker-Ribaupierre, M., Ed.; Barcelona Publishers: Gilsum, NH, USA, 2018; in press.
52. Longo, Y.; Coyne, I.; Joseph, S. The Scales of general well-being. *Person. Individ. Differ.* **2017**, *109*, 148–159. [CrossRef]
53. Keith, D.R.; Weaver, B.S.; Vogel, R.L. The effect of music-based listening interventions on the volume, fat content, and caloric content of breast milk-produced by mothers of premature and critically ill infants. *Adv. Neonatal Care* **2012**, *12*, 112–119. [CrossRef] [PubMed]
54. Ak, J.; Lakshmanagowda, P.B.; G C M, P.; Goturu, J. Impact of music therapy on breast milk secretion in mothers of premature newborns. *J. Clin. Diagn. Res. JCDR* **2015**, *9*, 04–06. [CrossRef] [PubMed]
55. Lai, H.-L.; Chen, C.-J.; Peng, T.-C.; Chang, F.-M.; Hsieh, M.-L.; Huang, H.Y.; Chang, S.-H. Randomized controlled trial of music during kangaroo care on maternal state anxiety and preterm infants' responses. *Int. J. Nurs. Stud.* **2006**, *43*, 139–146. [CrossRef] [PubMed]
56. Schlez, A.; Litmanovitz, I.; Bauer, S.; Dolfin, T.; Regev, R.; Arnon, S. Combining Kangaroo Care and Live Harp Music Therapy in the Neonatal Intensive Care Unit Setting. *Isr. Med. Assoc. J.* **2011**, *13*, 354–358. [PubMed]

© 2018 by the authors. Licensee MDPI, Basel, Switzerland. This article is an open access article distributed under the terms and conditions of the Creative Commons Attribution (CC BY) license (http://creativecommons.org/licenses/by/4.0/).

Excerpts from: A History of the Music Therapy Profession

Chapter 1

THE DEVELOPMENT OF THE MUSIC THERAPY PROFESSION

Traditionally, music's role as a healing power has been assumed to be the profession's foundation. This perspective, however, ignores two details. First, music has historically served other purposes that are pertinent to current music therapy practice and account for some of its divisions and shared premises. Second, while music has always had a healing role, it was not until the 1940s that music therapy evolved as a distinct profession.

This chapter briefly addresses the historical influence of music's various social, spiritual/religious, and healing roles on current music therapy practice. How the field became established is then examined by reviewing its development within the United States, Europe, and other countries, particularly in the context of emerging psychology- and activity-based therapies. Shared premises for music therapy, as influenced by its historical evolution, are identified at the end of the chapter.

THE ROOTS OF MUSIC THERAPY: MUSIC'S HISTORICAL ROLES

Music has served various roles as civilization has evolved; music therapy mirrors this usage of music. In ancient societies, music fulfilled spiritual, religious, healing, and social roles in an integrated manner. Similarly, some approaches to music therapy focus on "wholeness," a term referring to the integration of all aspects of being: physical, spiritual, and social. In such approaches, music is understood to be an integral part of healthy living. Ancient preliterate societies also used music as a means to connect to their god(s). Contemporary music therapy reflects this use of music by making connections to god(s) and/or those parts of life that are most meaningful to a patient. For example, in palliative care, a connection to a higher being may be made when patients sing/listen to hymns or meditate to music, and music representing their family or community can help hospitalized patients connect to home. Also as in ancient preliterate societies, some contemporary music therapy techniques involve the use of music in ritual and ceremony. Rituals in music therapy include the use of consistent opening and closing songs and music to mark particular points in a therapy session, such as indicating when another group member is to assume leadership. Ceremony may be used in grief programs, as part of a memorial service, or to provide a formal ending to the client–therapist relationship at the end of music therapy involvement.

The ancient Greeks introduced the concept that music is an integral part of the cosmos, capable of affecting character development and health through the use of the "right" kind of music and through the balancing of one's passions. The ancient beliefs, that music is essential to human development and that music can be used to influence health, character and relaxation, are concepts that are integral to many music therapy approaches. For example, in various psychotherapeutic music therapy approaches, music's primary role is to create an emotional response in order to explore that emotion and to resolve related issues. The belief that the use of the "right" music can influence behaviours and emotions has also influenced the development of music therapy procedures, such as the "iso-principle." This technique involves matching particular music to a person's mood. Elements of the music are then gradually changed, thereby altering the client's emotions or energy levels (e.g., to calm or to energize).

The development of music's role in religion during the Middle Ages, and its emergence in the Renaissance and Baroque periods and subsequent establishment as a social entity in the 20th century, de-emphasized music's use as a healing power. Similarly, some music therapy approaches minimize music's role as a healing power and instead focus on music's social and spiritual aspects.

This brief review is far from comprehensive. Its purpose is to suggest that music fulfills an array of functions, not just that of "healer." These roles, with their roots in ancient thought, explain in part some of the divisions and shared premises that exist within music therapy. Divisions are found in the various roles that music fulfills in life: It serves ritual and ceremonial purposes; it is an integral part of spiritual, religious, healing, and social aspects of life; it provides connection to that which is meaningful; and it affects behaviours and emotions. These roles, and others, are all found in music therapy practice. Additionally, common to both ancient societies and music therapy are the assumptions that music is an integral part of life, and that music affects our lives.

THE DEVELOPMENT OF MODERN-DAY MUSIC THERAPY

From the ancient Greeks through to modern times, physicians have written about music as a form of medical treatment (Giola, 2006; Horden, 2000). Nearchus, Alexander the Great's physician, used music as an antidote for viper and scorpion bites (Licht, 1946). Roman Aulus Gellius (A.D. 125–180) believed that music could relieve the pain of gout, while fellow citizen Theophrastus thought that music could relieve epilepsy (McClellan, 1991). In the 1600s, physicians such as Med, Burette, and Baglivi recommended music for the treatment of melancholy (Licht, 1946) and physician Louis Roger, in 1748, published a book titled *A Treatise on the Effects of Music on the Human Body* (Soibelman, 1948).

While these and other writings recognize music's role in healing, an anonymous article published in *Columbian Magazine* in 1789 is the earliest written reference to music therapy (Davis, Gfeller, & Thaut, 1992; Heller, 1987). Davis, Gfeller, and Thaut (1992) claimed that this paper presented "basic principles of music therapy that are still in use today and provided evidence of music therapy practice in Europe" (p. 21). The document actually stems from the writings of the ancient Greeks: music and its effect on the regulation of emotions. The article's anonymous author asserted that music is a proven therapeutic agent and requires application by a trained practitioner. These beliefs were later expanded upon in a doctoral thesis written by Edwin Augustus Atlee in 1804. During the next 100 years, a number of articles referring to music therapy were published sporadically in various medical journals. Some of these papers looked closely at music's use in healthcare from a scientific perspective. Others advocated using music in modulating emotions or presented anecdotal evidence supporting music as a therapeutic agent.

While some writers in the late 1800s talked about music's therapeutic potential, others actively promoted music for the "betterment of life." For example, in England, the Guild of St. Cecilia, founded in 1891, provided live musical performers for the purpose of sedating or stimulating hospital patients (Bunt, 1994; Davis, 1989). By 1832, United States educational facilities, such as Boston's Perkins School for the Blind, began to integrate music into their curriculum specifically to assist the blind population. By 1880, 14 training schools had been established in the United States to support people with mental impairments. Each school integrated music into the curriculum, for purposes of socialization and physical well-being (Kraft, 1963).

In the late 1800s and early 1900s, there were a number of individuals who worked to establish music therapy as a profession. **Three noted practitioners were Eva Vescelius, Isa Maud Ilsen, and Harriet Ayer Seymour.** All three had specific beliefs, similar to those of the ancient Greeks, on how music should be used to facilitate health. For example, Vescelius (1918) felt that rhythm was of primary importance, postulating that, for fever, one should "play softly and rhythmically to bring the pulse and respiration to normal" and for "sluggish conditions of body and mind," one should use "the rhythmic waltz, polka, or mazurka" (p. 384).

THE DEVELOPMENT OF MUSIC THERAPY IN THE UNITED STATES

The endeavours of music therapy's early pioneers in both Europe and North America, while often extensive and impressive (e.g., Ilsen lectured on music therapy at Columbia University and founded the National Association for Music in Hospitals), tended to end with the death of each association/organization's founder. Thus, despite the work of early clinicians, the formation of the profession of music therapy is accepted as having begun during World War II with the United States Army's establishment of music programs for wounded servicemen. Historically, music had been used to entertain troops and to support mental and physical abilities (Rosenberry, 1944). The program developed during World War II, however, was the first to systematically implement and evaluate music to boost morale and, subsequently, to improve health outcomes. It was the duty of the Special Services Music Officer (Capt. Howard C. Bronson) to ensure the availability of music by encouraging its usage through the provision of songbooks, written music, and pocket instruments; by staging musical events; and by ensuring access to recorded music. In the words of Bronson (1942), the Army was learning that "music is one of the vital elements of a fighting Army" (p. 27). In 1943, the success of the music recreation service led to the development of the U.S. Army's Reconditioning Program, a program aimed at returning wounded men "to duty or civilian life in the best possible physical and mental condition" (Rorke, 1996, p. 190). In formulating the plan, the Surgeon General of the United States requested that a national survey be completed looking at the use of music in mental hospitals (Rorke, 1996). (According to Licht [1946], this survey was actually conducted by the National Music Council.) The results of this survey provided the basis for the Army's programs.

The program was based on the belief that music is effective in bringing people together, releasing emotions, and creating a feeling of community (Rorke, 1996). Three separate programs were devised: *active participation*, *passive participation*, and *audio reception*. The objective of the active participation program was to support social readjustment of the men, using music to accompany their rehabilitative exercises. Men with chest problems were taught to play wind instruments, while those with orthopaedic problems might learn the bass drum. Not only did they use the music to accompany their exercises, but also they participated in orchestras, glee clubs, and barbershop quartets and played for others in the hospital. Additionally, there were group singing events and individual lessons, focusing on harmonica or ukelele playing. An important element of the active participation program was the recording of performances.

The passive participation program involved listening to and discussing music, with the focus of the sessions being on musical appreciation. The purpose of this program was to support the men's social and mental ability to adapt to their altered circumstances, and it "stimulated physiological and psychological responses that contributed to the patient's sense of well-being" (Rorke, 1996, p. 193).

The audio reception program consisted of listening to music without any specific response being required. Activities included performances by the Red Cross and radio programs. The purpose of these activities was primarily entertainment. Additionally, there were "special activities" that did not fall within the parameters of any of the three programs. Such tasks included the making of musical instruments, songwriting, and musical quizzes.

While music therapists identify the Army's Reconditioning Program as the event that signaled the formation of the profession, the military was very careful to avoid using the term "music therapy" (Rorke, 1996). This stance was prompted by a lack of supporting scientific evidence. This led in 1944 to the commencement of a three-and-a-half-year study looking at the efficacy of the Army's program. The results, as evaluated by psychiatrists, suggested that 74% of patients within the programs attained improved health outcomes through involvement with music (Rorke, 1996).

By the end of the World War II, 122 Veterans hospitals were engaging the services of music therapy personnel (Rorke, 1996). Most of the therapists were unpaid volunteers or part-time staff members who worked under the supervision of medical personnel. The momentum gathered during the war thus continued after the war had ended, leading to the development of numerous university programs, with the founding of the National Association for Music Therapy occurring in 1950. Developments in the United States since then have included the establishment of the Registered (originally Regulated) Music Therapist (RMT) qualification, the institution of an examination based certification process, the establishment of degree programs and requirements, the publication of the *Journal of Music Therapy* and *Music Therapy Perspectives*, and the gradual expansion of the scope of practice to include various client populations.

THE DEVELOPMENT OF MUSIC THERAPY IN THE UNITED KINGDOM AND EUROPE

While music was used during World War II in European hospitals, as in America, to entertain the troops and to support morale and facilitate recovery, the profession of music therapy did not formally develop in Europe until the 1950s. Juliette Alvin is recognized as being the primary pioneer responsible for developing music therapy in Britain. Alvin worked primarily with children who were autistic, mentally impaired, and/or physically handicapped. In 1958, she founded the Society for Music Therapy and Remedial Music Therapy (soon after renamed the British Society for Music Therapy). This development was followed 10 years later by the founding of the first training program at the Guildhall School of Music and Drama. Many well-known European music therapists trained under Alvin's supervision, including Mary Priestley,

Tony Wigram, Leslie Bunt, Amelia Oldfield, and Helen Odell-Miller. It is generally recognized that during her lifetime, Alvin maintained strict control over the development of the field in the United Kingdom (Durham, 2000; Loth, 2000; Simmons, 2001; Tyler, 2002). Alvin's domination, however, was not readily accepted by all therapists. Resultant tensions have been referred to in published online interviews (Simmons, 2001; Darnley-Smith, 2001).

In 1976, the field was officially recognized by the British government with the formation of the Association of Professional Music Therapy (a government organization responsible for the regulation of the profession). By 2005, the United Kingdom had six established training programs (Sekeles, 2005), with the first university program opening in 1991 at Bristol University. In general, music therapy practice in the United Kingdom today is largely based upon the use of improvised music and reflects the existence of two primary theories (Darnley-Smith & Patey, 2003): The first considers music as a medium through which therapy occurs, and the other, based upon psychodynamic theories, emphasizes the therapeutic relationship.

Development of the field in other European countries soon followed that of the United Kingdom, most integrating psychoanalytic, psychodynamic, humanistic, developmental-integrative, or Gestalt approaches (Sekeles, 2005). By the end of the 1970s, music therapy could be found in the Netherlands, Norway, Sweden, Denmark, Germany, Austria, France, Switzerland, Yugoslavia, and Belgium. The numerous countries with established music therapy services and supportive associations led, in 1989, to the formation of the European Music Therapy Confederation. By 2005, membership in the Confederation included those countries listed above as well as Italy and Spain (both founding members), Cyprus, Estonia, Finland, Greece, Hungary, Israel, Lithuania, Malta, Poland, Portugal, Switzerland, and the Republic of San Marino (Loth, 2000; Sekeles, 2005).

THE DEVELOPMENT OF MUSIC THERAPY WORLDWIDE

While music therapy began in the United States, it soon spread across the globe. In general, therapists trained in either the United States or England and then returned to their home country, bringing with them what they had learned, or leaders in the field of music therapy visited a country and introduced their ideas through a presentation. Once music therapy was introduced in a new region, the number of practitioners tended to grow in number, associations were formed, and training institutions were established.

The music therapy approaches established within each country depended upon the initial pioneers with whom therapists trained. Work was also shaped by the cultural and political contexts of each country (Maranto, 1993). In both Poland and the Netherlands, for example, music therapy began in psychiatric hospitals. Thus, music therapy in these countries is now based upon psychodynamic models (Aldridge, Ruud, & Wigram, 2001; Janicki, 1993; Smeijsters & Vink, 2003). In Finland, music therapy was initially used to support children with developmental disabilities and now continues to focus on supporting children and adults with mental impairments (Lehikoinen, 1989). In New Zealand, music therapy was introduced by a student of Juliette Alvin. Today, the country's therapists continue to work according to Alvin's approach (Croxson, 1993). South African music therapists either embrace an eclectic approach or base their work on Nordoff-Robbins Music Therapy, a model that values creativity. Music therapy in Australia is characterized by an eclectic approach that embraces psychodynamic concepts but rarely makes use of improvisation (Erdonmez, Bright, & Allison, 1993). Music therapy in Argentina was initially pioneered by Benenzon, an American-trained psychiatrist who merged his knowledge with that of his understanding of music therapy and Dalacroze's eurhythmics approach to music education (Benenzon, 1981). There are now many models of music therapy that are utilized in Argentina, but they all share a common use of Benenzon's body–sound–music techniques (Wagner & Benenzon, 1993, pp. 7–8). In some countries (e.g., France, Spain, and Israel), a multitude of approaches derived from psychodynamic, behavioural, and medical foundations coexist (Blasco & del Campo san Vincente, 1993; Lecourt, 1993; Sandbank & Sekeles, 1993). Similarly, the divisions in music therapy in Japan can be traced to historical roots. Music therapy was initially fostered in that country by two different, competing organizations: the Japanese Association of Clinical Music Therapy, founded by musicians and music therapy practitioners, and the Bio-Music Association, founded by medical doctors (Ikuno, 2007).

Music therapy not only has spread throughout the Americas, Europe, and Australia/New Zealand, but in the past 20 years has also gained a foothold in the Far East, with practitioners integrating their own cultural beliefs into clinical work. Music therapists in India have researched the use of ragas to affect specific illnesses and disorders (Desmukh et al., 2009; Jagdev, 2008). In Japan, the theories of traditional healers and their use of techniques such as acupuncture, herbal medicine, and breathing exercises have been integrated into music therapy practice (Maranto, 1991; Nishihata, 1993). Similarly, in China, music therapists have been interested in combining music with electro-acupuncture treatment (Hongshi, 1989) and readily integrate traditional Chinese medical theory (Zhang & Miao, 1993).

As music therapy grew around the world, the organization of an international conference was inevitable. The first occurred in Buenos Aires in 1974, although there is some debate over this claim. (See chapter 4, Multinational Symposia.) Since then, world congresses have been held approximately every four years. Soon after the first congress, the American Association for Music Therapy began to publish an international music therapy journal titled *Music Therapy International Report* (Kenny & Stige, 2002). This later led to the development of the online journal *Voices: A World Forum for Music Therapy*. In 1985, after the presentation of additional world congresses, the World Federation of Music Therapy was established.

MUSIC THERAPY WITHIN THE CONTEXT OF MODERN HISTORY

The outline provided thus far explains the general understanding that music therapists have concerning the development of the field, with the United States being the acknowledged birthplace. What has been left out in this narrative is an examination of the contextual development that occurred prior to and simultaneous with the evolution of music therapy. An exploration of this literature helps answer the question, "Why did music therapy develop when it did?"

Music therapy's development in the United States was clearly affected by two professions: medicine and music education. Interactions between music education and music therapy began in the early 1800s. Various schools (e.g., Perkins School for the Blind, New York School for the Blind, and American Asylum for the Deaf) incorporated music into their curriculum with the belief that students would benefit from the integration of music with their studies (Giola, 2006). Further influence came from the National Music Council, which conducted the survey upon which the Army's program was based and sponsored the committee that resulted in the formation of the National Association for Music Therapy. Prior to the establishment of the Association and its regulatory qualification, music therapists were often music educators or professional musicians who worked with people with mental health needs. The influence of music education on the field can clearly be seen in the integration of Orff Schulwerk, Dalacroze, and Kodaly concepts into some therapists' work (Darrow, 2004; Peters, 1987).

Similarly, the medical community influenced the development of music therapy as nurses also worked as music therapists in the early years. In the first 10 years of the profession, music therapy personnel were supervised by physicians. Their influence was felt in the demands that music therapy be investigated through vigorous scientific examination. For example, in the 1960s, the American Psychiatric Association refused to acknowledge music therapy as a viable treatment approach due to a lack of evidence supporting the claims of the field (Clair, 2007). Thus, in the United States, quantitative research became of primary importance to the development of the field (Bonny, 1997; Clair, 2007; Rorke, 1996).

Two additional influences significantly affected the evolution of music therapy as a profession: the development of psychotherapy and occupational therapy, both of which preceded the establishment of music therapy. A review of their history suggests that both were directly responsible for spawning the establishment of music therapy as a profession.

THE DEVELOPMENT OF PSYCHOTHERAPY AND ITS IMPACT ON MUSIC THERAPY

Three primary approaches to psychotherapy developed over the first 50 years of the profession's existence: psychodynamic therapy, behaviour therapy, and humanistic-based therapy. Psychodynamic therapy developed from the work of Sigmund Freud, primarily from 1890–1910. Freud was a physician whose investigation of patient symptoms led him to search for hidden motives and unconscious thoughts. From his analysis, Freud concluded that most problems suffered in adulthood stem from painful events, perceptions, and feelings that occurred during childhood. The job of the psychodynamic psychotherapist then is to release, through free association and dream interpretation, the resultant repressed emotions. Numerous variations, either providing a modification or an abandonment of Freud's ideas, followed, leading to the evolution of other important psychological therapies (e.g., Jungian analysis). By the 1950s, interaction between the various schools of thought had developed into an intense debate within the area of psychodynamic psychotherapy. American Psychoanalytic Association president Robert P. Knight remarked that, "The spectacle of a national association of physicians and scientists feuding with each other ... and calling each other orthodox and conservative or deviant and dissident is not an attractive one, to say the least" (Feder & Feder, 1981, p. 35).

Behaviour therapy developed in the 1950s, focusing on learned behaviours rather than on unobservable subjective mental experiences and involving the clinical application of techniques developed in behavioural psychology research. Early roots of behaviourism are found in the work of Wundt, who in 1874 published a book titled *Principles of Physiological Play*, in which he argued for scientific study of the mind.

There are three recognized stages to the history of behaviour therapy. The first began with Watson (1913), who outlined principles of behaviour psychology. Stage one is dominated by the concept of "classical conditioning." Stage two, which began in the late 1920s, is characterized by the concepts of "operant conditioning," as formalized by B. F. Skinner. Stage three (1960–present) is characterized by the integration of social learning theories (e.g., Maslow, Bandura) into behaviour therapy. These introduced the concepts of "modeling" and "shaping." All behaviour therapy involves observing, modifying, and developing behaviour.

The third major approach to psychotherapy, based on humanistic philosophy, emerged in the 1960s, primarily through the work of Abraham Maslow and Carl Rogers. This approach originally placed an emphasis on positive abilities and aspirations, free will, wholeness, and fulfillment and was characterized by the concept of "self-actualization." There are five key values of this approach: (1) a belief in the worth of persons and dedication to the development of human potential, (2) an understanding of life as a process (e.g., change is inevitable), (3) an appreciation of the spiritual and intuitive, (4) a commitment to ecological integrity, and (5) a recognition of the profound problems affecting our world and a responsibility to hope and to promote constructive change.

Internal tensions within psychoanalysis and between the three primary approaches gradually calmed after the 1950s as therapists adopted an eclectic approach to their work. Nonetheless, tensions still existed. In 1997, Messer and Wachtel described the profession in this manner:

> ... proliferation of "brands of psychotherapy," each claiming to be more effective and to have discovered an important and theretofore unrecognized or suppressed truth. ... They differ in practice, in values, in the training and temperaments of their practitioners and advocates, and in the intellectual traditions to which they link themselves. (p. 2)

Despite the existence of a multitude of "therapeutic schools" and their multiple differences, Frank (1974) argued that the various approaches have much in common, suggesting that they all attained equivalent results and utilized the same processes. Specifically, Frank identified four common features:

(1) a relationship in which the patient has confidence that the therapist is competent and cares about his welfare;

(2) a practice setting that is socially defined as a place of healing;

(3) a rationale of "myth" that explains the patient's suffering and how it can be overcome; and

(4) a set of procedures that require the active participation of both patient and therapist and which both believe to be the means of restoring the patient's health.

A more recent development (Messer & Wachtel, 1997) has been the demand for evidence-based practice in healthcare. Evidence-based practice refers to basing therapy upon research evidence that supports efficacy and defines best practice (Harper, Muluvey, & Robinson, 2003, p. 158). This evolution has brought with it a demand that public monies fund only those therapies that are proven to be effective. The requirement raises many questions: "Do practitioners really base what they do on the research literature?" "What kind of knowledge counts as evidence?" "Is current

Multiculturalism

"Multiculturalism" is used here as an inclusive term, addressing awareness and sensitivity to one's culture and issues of disability, feminism, gender constructs, race, and religion. Music therapy developed in the Western world as a service to its citizens. Since its inception as a profession, the field has grown to be a global entity. In turn, interaction amongst differing peoples has increased, with the ease of travel and communication. Yet, a survey conducted in 2000 by the American Association of Music Therapy revealed that "... our profession is not representative of the current racial, ethnic, and gender demographic of our country" (Croene, 2003, p. 12). In fact, it is dominated by white women.

Early indications of a slow-growing awareness of cultural differences were seen in the field as early as 1990, with the publication of *Music Therapy Perspectives'* regular column, "International Perspectives," written by Joseph Moreno. The column focused on introducing both global developments in music therapy and gently stimulating thought concerning multiculturalism in music therapy. In 1996, Sloss (1996) published a survey of Canadian music therapists and multicultural practice. By 2003, enough had been published on the topic for Chase to write a review of the literature (Chase, 2003). In 2014, the *Australian Journal of Music Therapy* devoted a whole issue to multiculturalism.

Cultural awareness impacts music therapy on many levels, from that of global interactions to training, to the establishment of a therapeutic relationship (Bradt, 1997; Kim & Whitehead-Pleaux, 2015). Issues encountered clinically include communication problems, ignorance, ethnocentric attitudes, power dynamics, and misunderstandings (Kim, 2008; Sloss, 1996). Application of music without an understanding of the music's importance in a client's life can also have severe adverse effects, as "Music is deeply rooted in culture" (Kenny & Stige, 2001, p. 1). Thus, how music functions is often culturally dependent, and it is essential that music therapists understand the role of music in the client's culture (Brown, 2001; Darrow & Molloy, 1998; Froman, 2009; Mahoney, 2015).

While acknowledging the importance of multiculturalism, it must be recognized that it is a difficult aspect to effectively address in clinical practice. A therapist must first have a clear comprehension of his own culture, values, and beliefs and how each impacts his work (Bradt, 1997; Chase, 2003; Kim & Whitehead-Pleaux, 2015; Mahoney, 2015). A therapist must also then develop an understanding of the client's culture. This includes an understanding of music's role: how it is used and its meaning (Bradt, 1997). Yet, a therapist cannot know and understand every culture (and its music) encountered in clinical practice. This presents a challenge to clinical work. This challenge is beginning to be addressed through the sharing of stories concerning clinical work and student supervision and issues encountered in that work (e.g.,

Brotons et al., 1997; Euper, 1969; Froman, 2009; Kim, 2011; Kutana, 1985; Lee, 2008; Rilinger, 2011; Rykov, 2001; Swamy, 2001); the development of guidelines and policies, protocols, training programs, and courses; and the dissemination of information about localized music therapy work throughout the world (Chase, 2004; Kenny & Stige, 2001; Whitehead-Pleaux et al., 2012).

An additional issue of concern is seen in how music therapy spread and developed around the world. Western ideas were imported into non-Western countries. These ideas then formed the basis of clinical work in those countries. As Whitehead-Pleaux et al. (2012) pointed out, current music therapy theory and practice were originally conceived to meet the needs of middle and upper classes in Europe and America.

Futamata (2005) wondered if Asian music therapists should simply be "copying" what exists in the Americas and Europe. This question arose when she realized that she herself had ignored Japanese resources. Futamata repored that there are some unique models of practice in Japan, but that these ideas have not been shared extensively, and definitely not with the music therapy community at large (Futamata, 2005). *Voices: A World Forum for Music Therapy*, the online journal, has done much to improve this situation through the publication of articles from therapists from all over the globe. Through this resource, the profession is able to gain a basic understanding of how music therapists are working in countries such as India (Sundar, 2009) and Kenya (Kigunda, 2004). It is, nonetheless, an issue that requires much more attention, with the development of resources and guidance for clinicians.

THEORETICAL DEVELOPMENTS (MODELS OF PRACTICE)

Community Music Therapy

While music therapy programs based in the community (i.e., not in a hospital or school) have been referred to in the literature as early as 1974 (Ragland & Apprey, 1974), this model of practice was not formally identified, defined, and provided with a theoretical basis until the early 2000s by European writers. The Community Music Therapy model is characterized by a concern for context and sociocultural factors. Examples of Community Music Therapy programs range from Venja Ruud Nilsen's work with female inmates in a woman's prison (Ruud, n.d.), to shared music-making in culturally and situationally tense encounters (Pavlicevic, 2004), to a three-stage program where clients move from individual music therapy to small group work, eventually joining the wider community in music-based activity (Wood, Verney, & Atkinson, 2004).

Community Music Therapy is concerned with context, both cultural and social, in which people are actively engaged in making music for purposes of supporting health, human development, equity, and social change (Pavlicevic, 2012; Stige, 2010). It takes into consideration the needs of the individual while simultaneously attempting to develop a musical community. The model is "participatory based," involving group music-making while acknowledging each individual's "voice"; "performative," involving the creation and performing of music; "resource-oriented," with strengths of individuals and their community rather than their problems being the program's focus; and "actively reflective," in that each program reflects its sociocultural community (Stige, Ansdell, Elefant, & Pavlicevic, 2010). Since Community Music Therapy's initial conceptualization, clinicians and researchers have gone on to identify further features of the model. These components include a concern for an "ecological perspective," meaning that relationships between individuals, systems, organizations, and networks are integral to the process; the process is participatory, in that it is not expert-directed but is a group process; activism is an integral part of the process; and the entire process is "ethics-driven" (Stige, 2015a; Stige et al., 2010).

This model has led to many queries on the boundaries of music therapy. For example, the boundaries between Community Music Therapy and Community Music are difficult to discern. There are many illustrations of this overlap. For example, Bowers (1998) referred to a group of senior citizens who joined together with university women students to sing. The choir was conducted by music educators, but guidance on music selection was provided by a music therapist. Myers (2005) talked about a Kansas intergenerational choir, a program based on music education. Yet, intergenerational programs are also promoted under the guise of music therapy (Darrow, Johnson, & Ollenberger, 1994; Shaw & Manthey, 1996). Powell (2004) suggested that the difference between community music used for educational purposes and music therapy's conceptualization of community music is that, within the former, the product (the performance) propels the program, whereas in music therapy, "the performance is the by-product or added bonus" (Powell, 2004, p. 181).

It can also be difficult to discern the difference between Community Music Therapy and the natural occurrence of music interaction in the community. Consider Pavlicevic's (2004) depiction of a music therapy encounter in Africa. She described tension that exists between herself and a group of women whom she was "supporting" within a community health agency. Pavlicevic did not define what she meant by "support," and she clearly stated that no specific outcome was sought in regard to health. Pavlicevic and the women simply engaged in making music, taking turns in leading the process. Pavlicevic conceptualized this experience as Community Music Therapy. This experience, however, can also be interpreted as a natural musical interaction between people from two different cultures. Pavlicevic herself recognized this in stating, "... performance situations often grow pragmatically out of the needs of patients and institutions" (Pavlicevic & Ansdell, 2004, p. 30).

Within the field of music therapy, Community Music Therapy stands in contradiction to traditional standards of practice, which require confidentiality, closed sessional work, and definitive session parameters, with goals, objectives, and evaluation. Community Music Therapy does not occur behind closed doors, thus making confidentiality difficult to attain, and it rarely incorporates goals, objectives, and formal evaluation. Community Music Therapy also differs from other approaches as it is founded not upon psychological theory but on systems theory and theories from anthropology, sociology, and community psychology (Stige, 2002a). As a result, this model has been met with controversy, particularly in Europe. Nonetheless, it is representative of the field's traditional developmental process: It evolved in response to client needs.

Philosophical Developments

Philosophical literature in the 2000s–2010s primarily addresses the philosophy of music therapy, with a multitude of authors writing on the topic. Related philosophical concepts frequently addressed in these decades center on cultural and environmental concerns and the relationship between health and music.

Models of Practice

Clinical work in music therapy and models of practice have evolved from client needs, philosophical and theoretical environments, governmental systems, economic demands, and societal pressures. Each model of practice developed from a differing mix of needs and influences:

> As far as I have observed and investigated, models of music therapy were established and assembled by professionals based on and influenced by their personal history and culture, as well as by practical and theoretical thinking that connected music to relevant subjects and developed into one body. (Sekeles, 2011, p. 674)

In 1984, Maranto identified over a 100 models in use worldwide. This has since continued to increase.

There is an almost universal conviction among music therapists that clinical practice develops in response to client needs. There are many examples of this. Consider De Backer and Sutton's explanation of how one's work situation affects the development of clinical skills and perspective:

> The work setting, and its philosophy and ethos, has affected how the profession has developed. For example, therapists working within occupational therapy departments may make use of behavioural observations, develop an interest in rehabilitation processes or in holistic approaches. Those working within education may find developmental theory the most appropriate for their work, while therapists who have a post in centres treating patients with neurological symptoms discover an interest in the complexity of the brain. (De Backer & Sutton, 2014, p. 38)

There are, however, many factors beyond work environment and personal culture which have influenced, and continue to influence, the development of models of practice. As an example, consider the development of Nordoff-Robbins Music Therapy. It developed in response to a perceived need to enable children with intellectual disabilities to engage in musical experiences. The opportunity was presented by a school that was willing to allow two people to explore this concept. The model grew as others became excited by the idea and by what they observed: This led to more opportunities (Robbins, 2005). As the model was presented around the world, other countries embraced it. Nordoff-Robbins Music Therapy, for example, is now firmly established in Japan (Futamata, 2005). As the model continued to evolve, economic demands altered the original conceptualization of the model's process; hence, the use of two music therapists per session was made optional. The model also continued to develop in response to client need and demand. Originally used for children with autism and/or intellectual disabilities, the model then embraced work with children with hearing impairments. It is now used with a wide range of clientele, from psychiatry to neurology, intensive care, and palliative care. Likewise, it now integrates components of other models of practice as needed in accordance with the clinician's work and the client's needs. Hence, a Nordoff-Robbins practitioner working with a person with abuse issues may integrate psychodynamic principles into his/her practice.

Models of practice have also evolved in response to other demands. Consider the development of Orff Music Therapy, in Germany, where a physician requested that a music therapist develop a model of practice based on Orff-Schulwerk (Voight, 2003), or that of Integrative Music Therapy, which developed from a plethora of philosophies and theories which infused the German climate (Frohne-Hagemann, 2011). Both of these models grew out of a philosophical and theoretical environment which was open to integrating music therapy as a component of its work. As Doherty and McDaniel (2010, p. 6) explained, "Every therapy model is shaped by the culture of its origin and is challenged to adapt to cultural change."

The development of models of practice has also been influenced by politics. Schwabe's work provides an excellent example of how the dominance of a governmental system influences clinical work (Schwabe, 2005). Schwabe grew up in a country dominated by Nazi thought, developed his work as a music therapist in a communist regime, and then had to adapt and revamp his model of practice when his country embraced democracy and capitalism. As he stated:

> One consequence of this radical social event was the collapse of many psychotherapy and music therapy structures in Eastern Germany as they had to adapt rapidly to Western German standards. ... As the psychotherapeutic context broke down, important and well-developed music therapy treatment structures vanished. (Schwabe, 2005, p. 51)

As a result, Schwabe had to change his approach, resulting in the development of Resource-Oriented Music Therapy.

Economics have influenced which models of practice thrive. For example, in the current healthcare climate in which evidence-based practice predominates, Neurological Music Therapy is growing in usage and influence as it is a model firmly developed upon scientific research and randomized controlled trials.

Societal developments are yet another element that has implications for the development of models of practice. Guided Imagery and Music is an early example of this tendency, as it evolved when the use of lysergic acid diethylamide (LSD) was deemed socially unacceptable and was then subsequently outlawed. A more recent example is Community Music Therapy, which is a model of practice that is reflective of, and responsive to, demands for inclusivity and consideration for issues of social justice.

Thus, the evolution of music therapy's models of practice has been influenced by many needs, demands, and external influences. The resultant myriad of approaches, techniques, and purposes reflects the chameleon nature of music therapy.

GOVERNMENT POLICY AND POLITICS

The music therapy profession in the United States grew out of government-sanctioned work within the Army. Since then, its development has continued to be shaped by government policy. Possibly the most influential policy change, worldwide, has been the move toward deinstitutionalization. As Bibb (2013) explained, the closure of large institutions resulted in the loss of many professional healthcare jobs as, while community programs were created, they were not mandatory. (Ironically, the lack of mandatory programs is seen to be unhealthy for those with mental illness, as a lack of motivation is one of the symptoms of their illness.) Additionally, professionals had less opportunity to develop their skills, as work was less secure and service provision was shortened.

Arguably, this change in perspective is rooted in 19th-century France, with Phillippe Pinel's work in promoting the belief that those in custodial care deserved to be treated as human beings. It was not, though, until the 1950s that governments began to consider and to implement the closure of residential facilities. Deinstitutionalization policies forced health professionals to reconsider clinical care as services were moved to the community. Some established centers for music therapy (e.g., Florence Tyson in New York, the Cleveland Music School Settlement). Clinical work gradually morphed to embrace short-term programs, family inclusion, and consultative modes of service provision. Within music therapy, models such as Community Music Therapy and Interactive Music Therapy (Oldfield) developed, undoubtedly for many reasons, but in part due to the need to provide services outside of a residential facility.

Other policies that have affected work include Australia's Sing&Grow program ("About Sing&Grow," n.d.; Baker, 2009); bill PL94-142 in the United States, which affected service provision in schools for children with intellectual and/or sensory disabilities and/or mental illness (see chapter 5); and the American Senate hearings that impacted the development of services for the geriatric population both in America and Canada (Crowe, 1992; Forever Young, 1992). As already mentioned, a fascinating example of how politics affects clinical work is found in the career of Christoph Schwabe.

ECONOMICS

Any music therapist who works in private practice is very aware of how economics influence clinical work on a very pragmatic level. This is also true for employees. "In work with severely disturbed adult psychiatric patients, the music therapist's role has been largely the outcome of situational necessity and professional opportunity" (Stein, 1965, p. 53). Stein elaborated through an example, explaining that as money was not available to support intensive music therapy work in large, continued-care wards, clinical work changed in these facilities to focus on the provision of "simple group activities to socialize patients and to normalize their environment" (Stein, 1965, p. 53). Stein wanted to develop more skills and to do more than "social entertainment" but had to fill the need that was there, which was, at least in part, dictated by economics.

A clear example of the effect of economics on healthcare provision has been the development of evidence-based practice. While this model was not developed for economic reasons, factors outside of healthcare (e.g., insurance companies) saw in evidence-based practice a way to measure service effectiveness and therefore determine where and how to spend money. The pressure on all healthcare professions to develop interventions supported by randomized controlled trials (RCTs) is immense. Within music therapy, it has strengthened some models of practice, such as Music Medicine, which is supported by scientific research, while simultaneously threatening the existence of models of practice that focus on the creative aspect of music. Proponents of these models are working, however, to propose alternative perspectives and standard measures of effectiveness. Of particular note, Procter (2011) proposed the adoption of social capital theory as a basis for music therapy. This theory allows for the full breadth of music therapy practice to be seen as being economically viable.

SOCIETAL CHANGES

Bunt and Stige (2014) argued, "Areas of practice are shaped not only by the possibilities of the profession but also by the needs and structure of a society" (Bunt & Stige, 2010, p. 22). Furthermore, the profession itself is shaped by society's needs and by society itself. The development of music therapy as a profession occurred due to opportunities created by society as well as the social evolution of the concept of "professions." Music therapy's growth has continued to mirror changes in society. For example, in the United States, the prevalence of Behavioural Music Therapy in the 1960s and 1970s is reflective of the then dominance of behavioural psychology in both healthcare and education.

A social advancement that has influenced music therapy has been the rise of technology. This development has affected both clinical work and research. Neurological Music Therapy research uses technical apparatus such as electroencephalograms (EEGs) and functional magnetic resonance imaging (fMRIs) in order to understand how rhythm affects the brain and the central nervous system. Clinical work in Neurological Music Therapy is dependent upon technology for portable recorded music that can accompany clients while they walk. Streeter's (2011) computer program records and analyzes the musical output of the client and therapist. The resultant data provides insight about what is occurring in the musical interaction (e.g., length of play, both shared and individual, and the quality of that playing in terms of exact or approximate imitation). In palliative care, clinicians often work with a client to develop and record "legacy" CDs, which contain meaningful music (both unique and precomposed) that the client wishes to leave as a gift for his/her family and friends. The use of technology thus enables clinicians to offer enhanced services and provides researchers with effective tools for data collection and analysis.

Twenty-first century scientific research, in the form of evidence-based practice, is another societal development that continues to exercise a strong influence on the field. However, a competing force in society is also exerting its claims: "Lately ... music as a universal kind of therapy ... seems to have one popularity, due to such factors as changing concepts of science, a more holistic-based approach to life, influences from other music cultures, and increased understanding of the breakdown of linear logic or [the] instrumental type of reasoning" (Ruud, 1988, p. 35). An initial emphasis on wholeness and client-centered practice within healthcare has now expanded to include a respect for, awareness of, and responsiveness to cultural, gender, race, ethnic, and sexual orientation elements of the human condition. Clinicians are expected to integrate these concerns. Stige's *Cultural Music Therapy* (2002) and the advent of Community Music Therapy are reflective of this. Societies have taken an interest in music and health and the role music plays in general life (e.g., Ansdell, 2014; DeNora, 2000). Beyond the publication of a number of academic books, the growth of music-based healing work outside of the parameters of music therapy is occurring, from nurses using music to modern-day "sound healers," to neuroscientists developing centers to study the phenomenon of music and to develop their own interventions. Music therapy's already fluid boundaries are, as a result, becoming even more difficult to discern.

Excerpts from: Biomedical Foundations of Music as Therapy

MUSIC AND PSYCHOTIC SYMPTOMS

As described above, positive and negative symptoms of schizophrenia as those that are known by their presence or their absence respectively. Positive symptoms include *thought disorders* such as disorganized or irrational thinking, *delusions* consisting of beliefs that are contrary to fact, and *hallucinations* that appear as stimuli that are not being presented by the external environment. These symptoms generally result in impaired cognitive behavior. Negative symptoms include flat affective responses, diminished speech capacity, lack of perseverance, decreased ability to experience pleasure, and social withdrawal.

Ruud (1978) described psychotic patients as inattentive, distractible, confused, depressed, hallucinated or in such an anxiety state that verbal contact is ineffective. Music makes contact through the thalamus which relays sensations and feelings directly to the emotional centers--the hypothalamus and limbic system--thereby reaching cranial emotional centers without prior need for higher cortical analysis of the sensation.

In his meta-analysis of quantitative research into musical influences on the symptoms of psychosis, Silverman (2003) found that music had proven to be "significantly effective" in combating psychotic symptomatology. Both live and recorded music and both structured and passive listening music therapy groups were equally effective. While the effects of patient-preferred music versus therapist-selected music did not differ, it was found that non-classical music proved to be more effective than classical music. Statistical analysis of the findings indicated that results were inconsistent among the 19 studies that were included, although it did not specify the source of the inconsistency. The analysis did show that catatonic patients yielded different results from patients exhibiting cognitive or general symptoms. Also, the use of both live and recorded music in the same study yielded different results from studies in which these types of music were used separately.

The report by Morgan (2007) discussed above included data on the effects of music on the symptomatology exhibited by subjects experiencing psychotic episodes. Comparison of the decreases found among music group subjects and those observed in control subjects showed significantly greater pretest to posttest decreases in treatment group subjects in BPRS and Calgary scores, depression, disorientation, mania, and in both positive and negative symptoms.

MUSIC AND REALITY CONTACT IN SCHIZOPHRENICS

To bring psychotic patients into contact with the reality of their immediate external perceptual environment, it is often effective to involve them in active physical interaction with that environment. Through playing, singing, or otherwise participating in the production of music itself, the brain must act in direct relationship to the concurrent musical stimuli that enter the realm of the brain's perception. Participation in a musical act requires behavior based on adequate perception of tempo, key center, rhythmic patterning, musical selection, and numerous other basic as well as more subtle aspects of the musical product. Such behaviors preclude conscious reaction to hallucinatory, delusional, or disorganized thought patterns that are characteristic of the schizophrenic patient. Sustained musical interaction, therefore, may be quite effective in helping the brain of the psychotic person regain its ability to receive, organize, and react appropriately to sensations perceived from the external environment, thereby enhancing cognitive performance.

One-to-one musical interaction through improvisation was used by Pavlicevic et al. (1994) in the rehabilitation of persons with chronic schizophrenia. Participants who exhibited social withdrawal and emotional flattening were assessed using the BPRS and other assessment measures to determine that they met project criteria for chronic schizophrenia. The 21 Treatment Group subjects attended weekly individual music therapy sessions and the 20 Control Group subjects received one individual music therapy session at the beginning of the ten weeks of treatment and another such session at the end of that time. The initial and final improvisation sessions utilized an untuned percussion instrument such as a bongo drum and a tuned percussion instrument such as a marimba. However, when the subject improvised using the bongo, the therapist played along on piano. When the subject played marimba, the therapist and subject took turns playing the same instrument. For the other Treatment Group sessions, additional tuned and untuned instruments were made available for the subjects to choose from. A nine-level scale developed by the investigators called the Music Interaction Rating for Schizophrenia was used to assess levels of contact exhibited by the subjects. Statistical analysis of results indicated that Control subjects did not increase significantly in level of contact or length of musical engagement while Treatment subjects had significant increases on both measures. Noting that lower BPRS scores mean less symptomatology, the latter group also showed a significant drop in BPRS rating when comparing their scores at the beginning and end of the ten sessions. The higher the initial score, the greater was the drop in score, meaning the greater the degree of improvement. Treatment group subjects generally improved in their capacity to respond to and interact with the music therapist.

In a psychoanalytically based explanation of the therapeutic effects of music on autistic and schizophrenic children, Hudson (1973) described the autistic ego as not having developed, and the schizophrenic child as having developed with a distorted ego. He then characterized rhythm in music as a language having physiological appeal in the process of ego restructuring with autistic and schizophrenic children. The neurophysiological mechanism for this effect was addressed in Roederer's (1975) discussion of the psychophysics of music when he theorized that "the propagation through neural tissue of a cyclically changing flux of neural signals triggered by rhythmic sound patterns may . . . enter into 'resonance' with the natural 'clocks' of the brain that control body functions and behavioral response" (p. 165).

MUSIC THERAPY WITH ALZHEIMER'S DISEASE & OTHER DEMENTIAS

The large number of published papers written by music therapists on the topic of music therapy for Alzheimer's disease tends to support the hypothesis that brain stimulation through music may prompt the use of alternative processing circuits in the brain of the **Alzheimer's** patient. In a review of the literature on music and dementias, Brotons and Pickett-Cooper (1997) observed that results indicated that patients with Alzheimer's disease and related disorders (ADRD) exhibited impairment in recognition memory for well-known tunes, and that these deficits are not continuously related to age or ADRD severity. They concluded that the "functional dissociation of declarative and procedural memory implies differential underlying neural substrates, with ADRD affecting some brain systems more than others" (p. 210). Also observed was dissociation between musical and language abilities in ADRD which could reflect differential hemispheric degeneration. Research was cited that offers support for the idea of dissociation between right and left cerebral hemispheres in terms of their respective contributions to music and language functions.

Silber and Hes (1995) drew a related conclusion in suggesting that, "Creative [song] writing appears to utilize an intact portion of the brain and thus partially compensates for the affected areas" (p. 33). They reported that songwriting provided an opportunity to counteract some of the negative emotional, social, and cognitive aspects of the disease. The patients socialized, interacted, and pleasure, and initiative by leading singing, dancing, or by playing piano. Improvised harmonic, melodic, rhythmic, and dance movements revealed musical skills preserved from early years of life. Increases in nonverbal, verbal, indirect interaction, and motor activity accompanied by decreases in active sensory and passive behavior prompted the authors to suggest that subjects may have been predisposed to interact socially after music due to the state of increased alertness generated by the music. This observation reflects and reinforces the continuing need for research and application of findings reported above regarding enhanced cognitive capability after music due to musically stimulated cortical arousal.

Although much of the research attention in recent years has been focused on Alzheimer's dementia, some researchers are continuing to study the effects of various interventions on elderly subjects who also suffer from other forms of dementia. Takahashi and Matsushita (2006) studied the long-term effects of music therapy on changes in salivary cortisol levels, blood pressure, and intelligence assessment scores among elderly patients who exhibited moderate or severe dementia. The 24 experimental subjects participated in group music therapy once weekly during a 2-year period and were compared to a control group of 19 subjects who did not have music therapy. Each group consisted of subjects who had one of three forms of dementia including Alzheimer's disease, cerebrovascular dementia, and Parkinson-type dementia. Although systolic blood pressure normally increases with aging, it increased significantly more in the nonmusic group than in the music therapy group. Salivary cortisol level and intelligence scores did not show significant differences between groups, but the music therapy group showed better maintenance of physical and mental states during the two years of the study. The authors, both of whom were medical faculty members, concluded that the singing and playing of musical instruments in a concert setting was effective in preventing heart and brain diseases.

In another study by Pollack and Namazi (1992), Alzheimer's patients exhibited significant increases in direct verbal, direct nonverbal, and indirect social behavior. Of all social behaviors recorded, 62% occurred after music. Cooperation and attentiveness were exhibited during sessions involving music. Only four of the eight subjects exhibited instances of distraction or apathy in only seven of the 48 sessions. Subjects participated, displayed physical energy, positive affect, increased and more fluent verbalization, communicated while writing, correcting, improving, and adding to what had been written. Through changes in brain functioning generated by musical intervention, Alzheimer's patients partially and temporarily overcame apparent cognitive, memory, and language deficits. O'Callaghan (1999) cited similar results indicating that subjects with difficulty learning and remembering new material could remember song lyrics written during music therapy, and that cognitively intact participants could recall text better when accompanied by a simple melody than when the text was presented without music.

Other work reported by Prickett & Moore (1991) demonstrated the effectiveness of using long-familiar songs to stimulate successful use of memory skills in patients diagnosed with probable Alzheimer's disease. Patients exhibited better recall for words of songs than for spoken words or spoken information. Even when words could not be remembered, patients attempted to sing, hum, or keep time with the singing of the therapist. With consistent practice, some patients showed the capability for learning new song material even in the absence of ability to learn or recall new spoken material. Perhaps a general conclusion concerning observed effects of music on brain functioning in Alzheimer's patients is best summarized in a statement by Walton, et al. (1988) who noted that, "In the face of their impaired cognitive abilities the responsiveness to music is quite remarkable" (p. 135).

TRAUMATIC BRAIN INJURY AND MUSIC THERAPY

Whether in a hospital or other clinical setting, music therapists often work with patients who have suffered traumatic brain injuries. Because referral information often includes data on the injury as well as the diagnostic tests used to determine a diagnosis, it is important for the music therapist to understand what the various tests are designed to examine. Although there are numerous testing procedures for suspected brain trauma, there are only two basic types of tests, those that examine brain structure and those that examine brain functioning. CT scans and MRI tests are used to look at brain structure. EEG, fMRI and PET scans examine brain function.

Whether caused by physical trauma, stroke, or anoxia, damage to the brain may impair any of the numerous cognitive, physical, emotional, communication, or perceptual functions that humans use to interact and survive. The **functional disorders** resulting from brain trauma depend on where on the brain the injury occurs. See Figure 4e for brain lobe locations referred to below.

- Frontal lobe: Paralysis of some body parts; sequence planning; thought perseveration; personality and mood changes; attending to a task; problem solving difficulty; and Broca's aphasia.
- Parietal lobe: Problems with naming, writing, reading, or drawing; difficulty with eye-hand coordination or visual focus; lack of awareness of some body parts or surrounding space.
- Occipital lobe: Visual defects such as locating or identifying objects; recognizing colors, words, drawings or object movement; difficulty with reading and writing.
- Temporal lobes: Difficulty with recognizing faces, understanding words, categorizing or verbalizing about objects; short term memory loss and long term interference; decreased sexual interest; increased aggressive behavior.
- Brain Stem: Decreased vital capacity for breathing; problems with environmental perception and organization; difficulty with swallowing, balance or movement; nausea and sleep difficulty.
- Cerebellum: Loss of ability of coordinate fine movements, walk, make rapid movements, or reach and grasp objects; dizziness, tremors and slurred speech (Igou, 2010).

A common problem with traumatic brain injured clients occurs with **attention deficits**. To approach treatment of this area, it is essential that the music therapist have an understanding of attention as a concept and a behavior, and know that attending is necessary for effective perception, essential for accurate memory, and a precursor to cognition. Knox et al. (2003) have cited five levels of attention including a) *focused attention* which allows one to respond discretely to specific stimuli, b) *sustained attention* or the ability to maintain consistent response behavior during repetitive or continuous activity, c) *selective attention* which is the ability to maintain cognitive processing that involves activating and inhibiting responses based on discrimination between stimuli, d) *alternating attention* in which one demonstrates mental flexibility by moving between tasks that have different cognitive requirements, and e) *divided attention* or simultaneously responding to multiple tasks. Functioning at any or all of the five levels may be problematic for the TBI patient.

Focused attention was found to improve significantly among stroke victims as a result of listening to self-selected music daily for two months in research conducted by Sarkamo et al. (2008). Music group subjects were compared to a language group that listened to audio books and a control group that had no listening material. All sixty participants were middle cerebral artery stroke victims. Verbal memory also showed significant improvement over the other two groups, and the music group experienced less confused mood and depression than the control group. The authors concluded that their study demonstrates that listening to music in the early stage following stroke can improve cognitive recovery and contribute to prevention of negative mood states.

In order to be effective in treating TBI, **music therapy treatment** must be planned in terms of needed increases in specific brain functions. When focus of attention is the problem, music in the form of directed handbell or tone chime playing will activate areas of

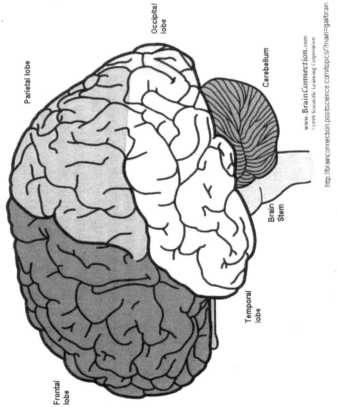

Figure 4e: Brain Areas

Examples of damage locations and associated loss of functions are as follows:

need to change their own behavior in hopes of a better future, and finding a place in society; 7) *Imagery*: Lyrics using metaphors to express feelings about their situations were found only in the songs of older adolescents and young adults; 8) *Spirituality*: There were references to prayers, God, religion, spirituality, or fate found within only a few songs.

Memory deficits resulting from brain injury may take the form of **Post Traumatic Amnesia** in which part or all of a person's stored memory becomes inaccessible. It is not uncommon for damage to temporal or parietal areas of the brain to result in some memory loss. Full recovery of information from damaged areas may be difficult to achieve, although related memory may be still intact in other areas of the brain. Stimulating motor memory, visual and auditory recall, verbal pattern recall, or emotional cognition through musical experience becomes the goal of music therapy intervention. Early intervention may take the form of simple improvised songs about the person's immediate environment to activate the person's working memory capabilities. The therapist also should gather as soon as possible information from family and others about the person's musical knowledge, preferences, and background. Once obtained, this information should be used to sing with simple or no accompaniment songs that the patient has sung in the past, or to utilize undamaged cranial areas to rekindle former musical interests or generate new motivation. If Broca's area functions are intact, these songs may begin to activate previously stored sequences of motor activity needed to articulate song words that are stored in reference memory. When this does occur, the patient may start to participate on some level. It is also quite probable that associated memories may accompany the person's participation. However, the music therapist must be aware that the location and extent of trauma may prevent or delay the appearance of such participation and associations.

As a result of her work with brain injury clients, Magee (1999) addressed the issue regarding the music therapist's focus on functional goals of a physical and medical nature as opposed to addressing the person's emotional and expressive needs resulting from the traumatic event. Most of the music therapy literature was characterized as identifying outcomes in the areas of physical and speech rehabilitation. The use of familiar precomposed music is reported overwhelmingly while improvisatory models are used less frequently in clinical work with this population. However,

the brain not normally used for attending and will bring that brain power to bear on the immediate task. Motivation will be generated by simplifying instructions, thereby avoiding confusion and aiding sensory processing. Singing uses working and reference memory to access words and word sequences, thus aiding in recovering organized cognition that requires pattern processing skills. Use of specially designed printed or gestured visual cues for playing or singing will be determined by the patient's need for recovery of visual perception, color recognition, motion detection, or visual pattern recognition.

Songwriting enhances the brain's use of sensory organization, memory, emotional expression, and stimulates motivation and initiative. Baker et al. (2005) conducted a study to determine if age differences are represented in the themes of songs written by TBI patients. Data consisted of 82 songs written by 32 music therapy patients during a ten month period. Six separate age groups were identified and their song themes analyzed. Many different forms of songwriting were used with various levels of therapist support provided. Although therapist support levels may have influenced patient responses, documentation was not sufficient to include this influence as a variable in the analysis. Eight basic theme groupings were identified and were represented in song lyrics as follows: 1) *Self-Reflections*: Early adolescents and late adolescents showed the greatest incidence of this theme with middle adolescents showing the least self reflection; 2) *Messages*: The middle adolescent group most frequently included in their lyrics messages to others about feelings, experiences, or wishing to be together; 3) *Memories*: The songs of children and early and middle adolescents described memories of relationships with pets, people, and related events; 4) *Reflections Upon Significant Others*: Patients across the lifespan used songs to reflect upon feelings toward significant others, and on the meaning of significant people or events in their lives; 5) *Expression of Adversity*: Although this theme did not appear in the songs of the middle adolescent group, late adolescents and young adults focused on their disabilities or hospitalization experiences such as the pain and frustration at their lack of desired progress in therapy, and their chances of finding a partner and having a career or starting a family; 6) *Concern for the Future*: Early and late adolescents most frequently expressed their hopes and dreams regarding life in the future with impairments, the need to modify pre-trauma hopes and dreams, the improvisation is considered important in addressing low self esteem after stroke, recognition of structure and intentionality for patients in a vegetative state, and accessing self awareness through improvised singing. Little commonality in music therapy procedures was found within brain injury rehabilitation, making it difficult to anticipate music therapy outcomes or formulate outcome measures. The author concluded that the absence of outcome projections and assessment measures makes it difficult to determine the important role played by music therapy in providing continuing emotional support and an expressive outlet through music.

CHAPTER V

THE BIOMEDICAL THEORY OF MUSIC THERAPY AND PAIN MANAGEMENT

The effectiveness of music in lowering pain awareness has long been observed in medical and other settings, which has led to the use of music as an alternative intervention in managing pain. However, until near the end of the twentieth century, music therapists have not had an acceptable scientifically sound explanation for how and why this effect occurs. The present chapter, therefore, contains a compilation of research findings, clinical applications, and conclusions to be drawn in order to provide a clear explanation as to how music raises the pain threshold thus resulting in less pain perception. The second of the five hypotheses that form the Biomedical Theory of Music Therapy deals with pain:

Hypothesis 2:

Because all sound stimuli are accessed by all parts of the brain, sound as music affects pain perception through its direct effect on the ability of the somatosensory cortex to receive pain sensations ascending through the spinothalamic tract following reception by sensors in the peripheral nervous system.

The applicability of this principle is reflected in the work of numerous investigators who have reported uses of music which resulted in decreased overt pain responses, reduced pain sensations as indicated in patient reports of music's analgesic effects, and decreased amounts of anesthetic or analgesic medication needed both during and following surgical and obstetrical procedures. What causes these effects? Some descriptions have relied on a distraction hypothesis, which explains music as a distracter that draws attention away from awareness of pain and refocuses it on musical stimuli (Mandel, 1988; Clark, et al., 1981; Hanser et al., 1983). Mitchell and MacDonald (2006) used the distraction theory to help explain why female participants reported significantly reduced pain intensity ratings while listening to preferred music as compared to results achieved while listening to experimenter selected relaxing music or to white noise. The analysis also indicated that both genders showed significantly greater tolerance for pain stimuli with preselected relaxing music than with white noise.

Since the early 1970s, investigators have known that pain perception can be modified by a variety of environmental stimuli. Volumes of reports from medical and dental uses of music have established that music is one of the more reliable of these environmental stimuli. By activating analgesia-producing neural circuits, these stimuli induce the release of endogenous opiates (explained below) which then stimulate opiate receptors on neurons in the periaqueductal gray matter of the thalamus. These thalamic neurons also may be activated directly through synaptic connections with various neural pathways including the central nucleus of the amygdala which regulates expression and modulation of pain behavior and activates neurons located in the nucleus raphe magnus of the medulla. These neurons then send axons to the gray matter of the dorsal horn of the spinal cord (red pathway in Figure 5a) where their function is to inhibit the activity of afferent neurons bringing pain information into the CNS for transmission to the brain. Neurons such as those in the locus coeruleus that contain norepinephrine connect with brainstem pathways that descend to the spinal cord to inhibit synaptic conduction of pain stimuli.

Endogenous opiates, similar to opiate drugs such as opium, morphine, heroin, codeine, and methadone, produce analgesia (not 'anaesthesia' because the patient remains conscious) by stimulating specialized receptors in the brain. These receptors are "opiate receptors" and their normal function is to monitor the presence of "endogenous opioids" such as dopamine or norepinephrine. Opioids bond with opioid receptors - particularly in the gray matter of the midbrain to 1) produce analgesia and 2) stimulate the neuronal system involved in "reinforcement." Any stimulus or sensation, such as music, which can stimulate or increase endogenous opioid (endogenous morphine or "endorphine") production will produce an analgesic effect by activating opioid receptors in the periaqueductal gray matter of the midbrain. There is ample literature affirming that music has been found to enhance endorphine production (Scarantino, 1987). There also are many studies reporting success in applying music for analgesia.

Heightened responsiveness to incoming sensory stimuli by afferent PNS and CNS nerves is called *sensitization* and it is inherently involved in persistent pain states (Neugebauer et al., 2004). Continuous or repeated stimulation of nociceptors does not result in a reduction in their firing intensity, and may actually lead to

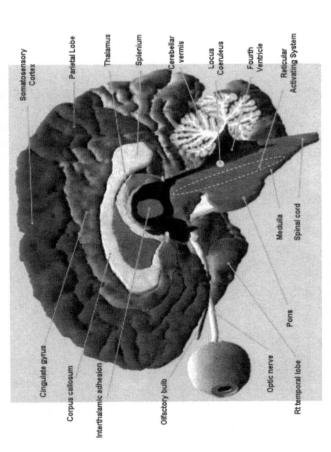

University of Washington Digital Atlas of Brain Structures
http://da.biostr.washington.edu:80/cgi-bin/DAPageMaster?atlas:Neuroanatomy+fflpath!index3D'Object'Composits'Midline'^objects+2

Figure 5b: Midline Objects Composite

An injury also results in rupture of capillary and tissue cells, thereby stimulating mast cells to release *bradykinin*, a peptide consisting of nine amino acids that acts to dilate blood vessels, lowering blood pressure and facilitating actions of the immune system (Neugebauer et al., 2004; Carlson, 1992; Mader, 1995). See Ch. 8 for a thorough discussion of the effect of music on the immune system.

MUSIC AND MODULATION OF PAIN PERCEPTION

Pain perception is not an inevitable result of stimulation of pain receptors. Rather, "it is a complex phenomenon that can be modified by experience and the immediate environment" (Carlson, p. 201). It is generally believed among investigators that peptide neurotransmitters are active in the control of sensitivity to pain. Serotonin, a monoamine transmitter, is released at most synapses and participates in the regulation of pain by producing inhibitory postsynaptic potentials.

sensitization or a lowering of the response threshold. Neurotransmitters produced within the neural cell body are released at both ends of the nerve fiber, thereby helping to produce pain centrally as well as promoting additional peripheral pain sensation (De Leon-Casasola, 2007). Any environmental stimulus, such as music, that interferes with this process acts to *desensitize* the brain to the awareness of pain stimuli, an important process in dealing with chronic pain.

ANALGESIC MUSIC IN SURGERY

The effects of music in the process of surgery are often vital in increasing the chances of survival for surgical patients. As Spintge (1989) has explained, patients undergoing surgery often experience a reduction in general immune response, impaired resistance to infectious diseases, unsatisfactory healing of wounds, increased basal metabolic rate and heightened risk of cardiac infarction, heart attacks, cardiovascular collapse and death. Under these conditions, the demand for analgesics, sedatives and anesthetics increases. The author observed that the emotional state of the patient is responsible for the amount of postoperative pain sensation, which has a direct effect upon patient compliance and cooperation during rehabilitation. Shapiro and Cohen (1983) also observed that a neurophysiological response to a specific painful stimulus varies according to individual personality and pain threshold. They also concluded that anxiety associated with a painful experience serve to implicate the limbic system as a consistent player in pain awareness and response. Neugebauer et al. (2004) report that the amygdala, a very active limbic system structure (Figure 5c), is strongly implicated in pain modulation, having been shown to be involved in both pain enhancement and pain reduction. Experimental inactivation of the amygdala has been shown to decrease emotional reactions to pain while not affecting normal behavior or nociceptive responses. It follows, therefore, that the use of music to decrease neural impulse activity in the amygdala may be effective in decreasing pain awareness and pain response behavior.

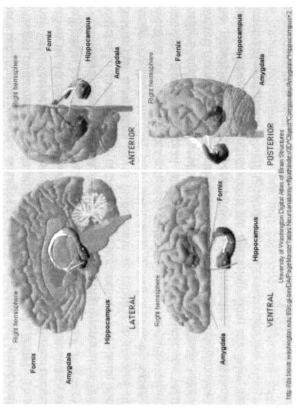

Figure 5c: Hippocampus & Amygdala

Frequent observations of a close relationship between emotional state and pain experience serve to implicate the limbic system as a consistent player in pain awareness and response.

A Yale University School of Medicine study (Ayoub et al., 2005) confirmed earlier work showing that patients who listened to music during surgery required significantly less sedation than patients who listened to white noise to simply block out the sounds of surgical instruments and other operating room noises. Researchers wanted to determine whether the effect was due to the music itself or to the masking effect of sound, a question which had been left unanswered in their earlier research (Koch et al., 1998). They studied 90 surgical patients all of whom were equipped with occlusive headphones. Some listened to Patient-Selected Music while others listened to white noise. A third group was fed operating room sounds via a mini-amplifier and mini-microphone that picked up real ambient room noises. Results showed that there was no decrease in sedative or pain-reducing requirements among patients in the groups that had white noise or ambient sounds. To understand the neurobiological basis for such findings, it is helpful to look to the amygdala and to research showing that bilateral amygdala activation in humans correlates with perceived pain intensity. See Figure 5c for bilateral amygdala positioning.

Pain response functions have shown positive correlations between neural impulse changes in the amygdala and perceived changes in intensity of pain stimuli (Neugebauer et al., 2004). This may be interpreted to show that as appropriately chosen music serves to decrease anxiety-related neural discharge patterns in the amygdala, perceived pain intensity also decreases.

Music has been found beneficial during preparation for surgery, in the operating room, and during recovery. Among the factors that have been found to decrease in relation to the use of music are fear, anxiety, pain awareness, use of anesthetic agents, rejection of anesthesia, surgical team tensions, mortality rates, recovery periods, hospital stays, postoperative medications, and medical costs. Before reviewing published reports of such values derived from music in the surgical suite, it is important to understand the anesthesiologist's responsibility in maintaining the delicate balance between life and death in the operating room and how the introduction of music is helping to manage that responsibility.

ANESTHESIOLOGY

One of the major applications of music during a surgical procedure is to assist in pain abatement. However, the history of attempts to avoid pain during surgery reveals the use of much more intrusive and dangerous techniques. Centuries ago, a person was rendered unconscious to avoid pain by striking hard a wooden bowl placed on the individual's head, strangling until the person passed out, or administering large quantities of alcohol or opiates. No procedure was reliable and the amounts of alcohol or opiates needed were dangerously close to the amounts that would cause death. Also, these drugs do not suppress the brain's ability to respond to bodily injury with "surgical shock" which results in intense activity of the parasympathetic nervous system that dilates blood vessels and greatly reduces blood pressure, often leading to fatal heart failure. In the mid-nineteenth century, experimentation with the newly discovered anesthetics ether and nitrous oxide led to their use in dentistry and surgery because they could produce both unconsciousness and pain desensitization. While ether was preferred due to the greater stability of its effects and to its ability to produce deep prolonged anesthesia, it is extremely flammable and has been replaced by more recently discovered nonflammable anesthetics that also reduce the occurrence of surgical shock (Carlson, 1992).

APPLIED PAIN AND ANXIETY REDUCTION WITH MUSIC

Some investigators have measured pain and anxiety reduction by measuring the amounts of patient-controlled medication needed to manage these conditions during surgery. For example, Koch et al. (1998) conducted two randomized controlled trials to determine whether music influences intraoperative sedative and analgesic medication requirements. In phase 1, 35 adults undergoing urologic procedures with spinal anesthesia and patient-controlled intravenous propofol sedation were randomly assigned to hear music via headset or to have no music during surgery. In phase 2, 43 adults undergoing renal or ureteral treatment and receiving patient-controlled intravenous opioid analgesia were randomly assigned to either a music or no-music group. Results showed that patients in the music groups required significantly less propofol for sedation than control group patients and showed significant reductions in requirements for the analgesic alfentanil. The investigators concluded that use of intraoperative music in awake patients decreases patient-controlled sedative and analgesic requirements.

Spintge (1989) reported on an extensive study using pre- and postoperative standardized questionnaires to determine the effectiveness of perioperative applications of music. The music was selected in advance by the patient and was administered using earphones and music from compact disc players. The earphones were given to each patient in the preoperative waiting room and worn until the patient was asleep when general anesthesia was used. During an operation using local or regional anesthesia, the patient was able to listen to the music during the entire procedure. Among the reported results were a rise in the pain threshold, increased pain tolerance, and an approximate 50% reduction in the usual dosage of sedative and analgesic drugs.

Semelka (1983) reported numerous general hospital uses of music in anesthesiological practice. Among these was a report of an older lady who enjoyed hearing music during spinal anesthesia. One young man who had become a paraplegic as a result of an automobile accident, claimed to be resistant to anesthesia and therefore felt pain regardless of the medications. He agreed to have music played during preoperative administration of the anesthetic and he subsequently exhibited no pain awareness during removal of a skin ulcer. The surgical team discontinued the narcotics, but continued the operation with music. The patient did not complain of pain until three days after the operation had been completed.

In a study of forty-eight male patients between the ages of 40 and 90, the patients underwent prostate or bladder surgery with either a standard i.v. dose of the anesthetic Diazepam as the operation began or music through headphones throughout the operation. Music was generally slow in tempo with restrained dynamics, soft timbres, small intervals, nonsyncopated rhythm, and uniform ascending and descending melodic contour. The surgical team concluded that anxiety was reduced to a level equal to that of an additional dose of a tranquilizer without undesirable side effects, and that music was a technically simple and effective method that could be used with "good success" especially in conjunction with regional anesthesia (Sehhati-Chafai & Kau, 1985).

Susan Mandel (1988), a Registered Music Therapist, has reported on the planned use of music for postoperative pain abatement during her own spinal surgery experience. Music that had been pre-selected included ballads (songs with lyrics that told a story), music with a strong beat, and music that carried positive emotional associations with people or experiences. Although the writer had undergone two prior spinal operations with a "long and difficult" first night following each one, she reported no memory of post-surgical pain while regaining consciousness from the anesthetic following the third procedure. She reported also that the use of taped music during the administering of pain medication resulted in decreased need for the medication and in her ability to be discharged two days earlier than expected.

At the Seventh World Congress of Music Therapy in 1993, Sabina Puppo, then Secretary of the Governing Board of the Music Therapy Foundation in Buenos Aires, Argentina, provided a synopsis of the objectives and values to be gained from music in the surgical process. After observing that music therapy has made important advances in surgical applications, she proposed that music be used in the pre-operative stage to de-mystify the operation, balance internal rhythm, encourage relaxation and body awareness, raise the pain threshold, diminish anxiety levels, and prepare the patient for the anesthetic and operation. Immediately prior to surgery, music was proposed as a means of diminishing muscular tension and regulating blood pressure, body temperature and pulse in order to allow the maximum effect of the anesthetic and use the least amount of it as possible. During surgery, the music would have an enabling effect on the patient under anesthesia by masking the sounds of surgical team conversations and other operating room noises. In the postoperative phase, it was proposed that the music be administered to facilitate the general recovery process through its positive effects on post-shock reactions and homeostatic maintenance.

Also at the Seventh World Congress, Alain Carre of Rennes, France, reported in the abstract of his presentation the results of a recent research project conducted in the Children's Surgery Service of Rennes Regional Hospital Centre. There was a high incidence of satisfaction with 90% of the patients who had been subjected to music reporting feeling "happy." The investigators noted also an approximate 32% decrease in the amount of anesthetic substances used during the operations. Music also helped reduce anxiety prior to the operations. Specific analgesic effects were noted during the post-operative period with less awareness of pain upon awakening from the anesthesia, and in some cases, total absence of pain.

In addition to the positive effects of music on pain abatement for the patient, the effects of music on the surgical staff have been noted. Puppo, whose work is mentioned above, has observed that music helps the anesthetist and other surgical staff members work in a relaxed atmosphere. Cook (1981) also has reported the work of investigators who indicated that the professional staff may benefit from the warmer and more pleasant atmosphere, closer harmony within the team due to decreased tension and fatigue, rhythmic stimulation of coordinated movements, and improved staff morale and efficiency through reduction of monotony during preparation and cleanup. Numerous writers have asserted that a patient with reduced pain awareness and decreased anxiety presents far fewer problems for the anesthetist and surgical team than one whose anxiety level and fear of pain are elevated.

Please see Chapter 8 for more on the use of music to reduce anxiety, tension, and stress during the surgical experience.

Excerpts from: Music Therapy Treatment Process

PART I: THE CLINICAL PROCESS

According to Cohen and Gericke (1972), "The cornerstone upon which to develop a responsible and meaningful treatment-rehabilitation program is the accumulation and synthesis of accurate, significant patient data" (p. 161). After this information has been collected and analyzed, it is used to formulate treatment goals, objectives, and strategies. Assessment of client needs also assists the therapist in evaluating and documenting clinical change that occurs during treatment (Cohen & Gericke, 1972; Douglass, 2006; Hanser, 1987; Isenberg-Grezeda, 1988; Punwar, 1988). This chapter will discuss areas of professional accountability, including assessment of client needs, development of the treatment plan, evaluation of clinical change, and documentation of progress. In addition, several other key components to professional competence will be addressed: professional ethics, cultural competence, and personal qualifications.

> *Donna is a 68-year-old woman with chronic lower back pain. Even though the initial tissue damage from her back injury has healed, she still suffers from significant pain, and none of the interventions tried to date have resulted in sufficient relief. Pain has changed Donna's life. Prior to her back injury, she and her husband, Jim, were part of a ballroom dance club, and Donna was a faithful member of the local chapter of the Sweet Adelines Singers. She sang in the church choir, volunteered at the library, and was admired widely for her beautifully kept home and her fabulous dinner parties. Since her back injury, Donna has become somewhat of a recluse. Her pain has severely curtailed her daily activities around the house, her participation in community events, and her interest in hobbies*

that she used to enjoy. As the pain lingers on, she has become despondent and depressed, gradually giving up on ever having a normal life again. Her pain, and all that comes with it, is having a negative impact on her relationship with her husband as well. She has become what some specialists in pain management refer to as "a pain person." Her entire life revolves around her back pain. Donna's personal physician has referred her to the Backpain Clinic at Roseville Rehabilitation Center for a 4-week inpatient program intended to provide an intensive transdisciplinary approach to address Donna's physical, emotional, and social functioning.

In Part I of this chapter, we will follow Donna through her course of therapy, including referral, assessment, treatment, documentation, evaluation, and issues related to professional ethics.

REFERRAL

The first step in the treatment process is referral, which facilitates access to health care providers. Requests for services, including music therapy, may come from various sources, including physicians, psychologists, occupational therapists, physical therapists, speech and language pathologists, teachers, parents, social workers, and, occasionally, clients themselves. In a hospital setting, referral for music therapy services is generally initiated by a physician. In a public school setting, the referral may be generated by parents, the school psychologist, or the interdisciplinary team, as part of the student's Individualized Education Program. A request for music therapy in a nursing home may come from a staff member, physician, family member, or the activity director.

Upon admission to Roseville Rehabilitation Center, Donna goes through a battery of tests and interviews conducted by different members of the treatment team. Dr. Kim, the physician, administers a medical exam to determine if there is any remaining tissue damage or abnormality contributing to her back pain. Then, the psychologist conducts an evaluation to identify any psychological factors (such as depression or personality traits) associated with Donna's condition. Jon, the physical therapist, assesses Donna's functional movements (e.g., walking, sitting, turning her torso, etc.) to identify any maladaptive patterns of movement and to determine her level of fitness and activity prior to and after her injury. Brenda, the occupational therapist, is reviewing an assessment of everyday activities at home that Donna and her husband filled in prior to her admission at the center. Florencia, the social worker, interviews Donna to learn more about her lifestyle and interests prior to the onset of back pain, as well as the impact of pain on her life. The initial assessments identify that dance and music have had an important role in Donna's life, so music therapy is identified as another important treatment modality for Donna. Matt, the music therapist, will develop treatment goals and objectives for Donna's inpatient therapy and to facilitate her transition back into her community.

ASSESSMENT

An **initial assessment** is completed prior to the start of treatment. It provides an overall view of the client's history and present condition. According to the American Music Therapy Association's Standards of Clinical Practice (*AMTA Member Sourcebook*, 2007), assessment should be included as a general procedure prior to commencing services with a client. An assessment is an analysis of a person's abilities, needs, and problems (Cohen & Gericke, 1972; Lipe, 2001; Punwar, 1988). As the example above indicates, assessments often include nonmusical categories of psychological, cognitive, physiological functioning, communication, and social skills, as well as musical skills, music preferences, and response to music (Douglass, 2006). In addition to completing their own assessments, music therapists may refer to assessments conducted by other health professionals (physician, physical therapist, occupational therapist, social worker, etc.). Assessment information can be acquired by interviewing the client and/or family members; testing, observing, and documenting how well the client does in cognitive, physical, or other tasks; viewing the client's interactions with others; or reviewing the client's records. Ideally, assessment data are gathered in multiple ways (Douglass, 2006).

Assessment tools take a variety of forms, including tests, surveys, or measures of specific abilities most relevant to the therapeutic needs of the client (Bruscia, 1987; Douglass, 2006; Fraenkel & Wallen, 2000; Gantt, 2001; Hanser, 1987; Lowey, 2001; Standley, 1996a). The format and content of assessment tools vary considerably from one facility to the next, depending upon the age and type of population served, the policies of a given facility, state or federal requirements for documentation, length of treatment, and time available for assessment (Brunk, 2001; Brunk & Coleman, 2000; Cole, 2002; Douglass, 2006; Scalenghe & Murphy, 2000). The music therapist may evaluate musical interests and abilities as well as strengths and weaknesses in nonmusic domains that are amenable to assessment by musical stimuli (e.g., auditory perception, memory, auditory discrimination, gross and fine motor coordination, and social and emotional behaviors (Hanser, 1987).

There are three primary types of assessment currently used by music therapists: (1) an **initial assessment**, completed at the beginning of the therapeutic process to identify client strengths and weaknesses, and to help formulate treatment goals; (2) **comprehensive assessments**, completed when a client is referred for music therapy services only (as opposed to music therapy being one of many services provided by a treatment team); and (3) **ongoing assessment**, which tracks functional levels and progress through the treatment process (Douglass, 2006).

Why Is Assessment Important?

There are several reasons why music therapists need to know how to administer assessments. One of the most important reasons is that the information learned from an initial assessment helps to determine the nature and scope of treatment, including whether the client is suited for music therapy, and, if so, what treatment goals and techniques are appropriate.

A second reason for assessing client needs is to provide a reference against which progress during treatment can be measured (**ongoing assessment**). In other words, we can't tell how far we have gone if we don't know where we started. If ongoing progress is not satisfactory, the therapist may modify the treatment plan. At the end of treatment, a final evaluation helps to determine improvement since the initial evaluation.

Third, the continued growth and development of the music therapy profession is dependent upon the ability to accurately assess, monitor, and evaluate treatment (Douglass, 2006; Isenberg-Grezeda, 1988). According to Cohen, Averbach, and Katz (1978), no profession, whether it is music therapy or another discipline, can legitimately attain true professional stature without a viable assessment system, not merely the completion of an assessment form. Such an assessment system must underscore the uniqueness of music therapy and contribute to the fulfillment of an individualized client treatment, training, and habilitation plan.

Areas of assessment. In order to determine a treatment plan, the team will assess the strengths and needs of the client in the following areas: (1) **medical**, which includes past medical history and current health status; (2) **physical**, which includes range of motion, gross and fine motor coordination, strength, and endurance; (3) **cognitive**, which includes comprehension, concentration, attention span, memory, and problem-solving skills; (4) **emotional**, which includes appropriateness of affect and emotional responses to various situations; (5) **social**, which includes self-expression, self-control, and quality and quantity of interpersonal interaction; (6) **communication**, which includes expressive and receptive language skills; (7) **family**, which includes assessment of family relationships and needs; (8) **vocational/ education**, which includes adequacy of work skills and preparation for the workplace; and (9) **leisure skills**, which includes awareness of recreational needs, interests, and

434 - PART THREE — PROFESSIONAL ISSUES IN MUSIC THERAPY

participation in meaningful leisure activities and knowledge of community resources. In addition, there may be specific music therapy assessments that address among other things musical background, interests, and skills.

Donna's interdisciplinary treatment team has completed an initial assessment during her first few days in the back pain program. The types of assessment conducted are outlined for each functional area.

Medical. *The doctor has conducted a lengthy interview with Donna and her husband to obtain a history of the pain problem, how it started and progressed, and interventions tried to manage it. This includes a record of dosage and frequency for pain and sleep medications used since the initial injury. A medical examination including x-rays and various tests has been completed to determine any physical conditions contributing to Donna's back pain. The doctor has identified no physiological abnormality that accounts for the extent of discomfort that Donna currently suffers, thus specific medical treatments to correct physical conditions are not indicated. Donna's exam indicates that she is slightly overweight (possibly due to her sedentary lifestyle), which adds to her back problems, and she has regular bouts of insomnia.*

Physical. *As a result of back pain, Donna's normal movement patterns (such as walking, sitting, standing, bending, and reaching) have been compromised. She has a self-protective walk (very slow and with a distinct limp), which has reduced the efficiency and speed of her movements, and she has lost muscle tone, flexibility, and endurance as a result of her sedentary life. In addition to analyzing the structural aspects of Donna's movements, Donna is asked to fill out several pain scales (such as those described in Chapter 11) to indicate the type and extent of pain that she experiences during different types of movements and tasks. She has also completed a shuttle walk test, which determines the rate at which she walks. These assessments provide a baseline for measuring progress in treatment.*

Cognitive. *Donna's psychological testing indicates intelligence within the normal range. She has difficulty concentrating (short attention span, poor memory, and poor problem-solving skills) that appears to be related to pain and depression.*

Emotional. *The psychologist has conducted an interview as well as administered several standardized assessments, including the Minnesota Multiphasic Personality Inventory (MMPI), the Beck Depression Inventory*

(BDI2), and a medical outcomes survey (SF-36). These assessments have been administered to better understand her current mood state as well as personality traits, which may suggest particular approaches for helping Donna control and manage her pain. These evaluations indicate a significant level of depression, resentment, and anger, and she has developed a sense of helplessness and dependency not atypical for patients with chronic pain (Sarafino, 2006). The evaluations also indicate that Donna would be a suitable candidate for specific types of intervention that are part of the treatment options at Roseville.

Social. The social worker's interview reveals that Donna has withdrawn from most of her social activities (ballroom dancing, Sweet Adelines Singers, attending church, etc.) since her back injury. Donna reports feeling lonely, but she makes few attempts to leave the confines of her home or to invite friends to visit. The evaluation indicates that Donna would like to re-establish involvement in dancing and singing, and the one thing that brings her some consolation is listening to her favorite music, which she sometimes uses to help her sleep.

Communication. Donna has no medically-based difficulties with communication, though she finds it difficult to speak with others in a straightforward manner regarding personal matters. Her communication problems are more closely aligned with psychological and emotional functioning than any physical limitation.

Family. Both the social worker and psychologist have met with Donna and her husband, Jim, as well as with each individually. Jim has expressed considerable frustration that Donna's back problems have essentially "taken over" nearly every aspect of their life. Donna's pain is so prevalent that their life revolves around that, and he has become responsible for all household chores in addition to all of his usual responsibilities. He wants his "real wife" back.

Vocational/Education. Donna's career as a homemaker has been disrupted by her pain. She has difficulty with or delegates almost every task required to run a household (e.g., cleaning, laundry, shopping, cooking, etc.) and she has essentially given up any sense of pride in how her home is maintained or decorated. An occupational therapist has met with Donna to discuss her household duties with her and to discuss a plan of action for re-establishing her capabilities in this aspect of her life. In *conjunction with the physical therapist, they have assessed the level of pain that Donna experiences in various functional tasks.*

Leisure skills. *Interviews with the social worker and the music therapist reveal that Donna and Jim used to be quite social. They enjoyed ballroom dancing nearly every week, and they often entertained guests in their home. Now, Jim occasionally meets with friends on his own, but then he feels guilty for leaving Donna home alone. Donna used to be a regular participant in the local chapter of Sweet Adelines, but she gave that up after her back injury made it difficult for her to stand or sit comfortably for any length of time during choral rehearsals and performances. Now, about all she does is watch TV, listen to music, and try to sleep. On a more positive note, Donna seems motivated to start dancing and singing again, and the team notes that Donna derives pleasure and comfort from listening to music.*

Music therapy assessment. *Matt, the music therapist, will refer to the assessments by the other team members as well as completing his own assessment in order to develop a treatment plan. Through his music therapy assessment, he determines prior musical background and interests as well as preferred musical styles and forms of participation that will be motivating and relevant to Donna's life. Because music will be used as part of Donna's exercise and relaxation programs, Matt has given Donna a questionnaire to determine her favorite musical styles, and to identify musical selections that might be suitable for relaxation sessions as well as to promote exercise. He has also interviewed Donna about her participation in the ballroom dance club, Sweet Adelines Singers, and her church choir in order to learn more about the practice schedule and required physical skills needed to participate successfully in each.*

Assessment Tools

Although the format and content of assessment tools will vary depending upon the type of disability and the focus of the person doing the assessment (e.g., physician vs. social worker), good assessments have in common the characteristics of being reliable and valid (Douglass, 2006; Fraenkel & Wallen, 2000). Reliability refers to the consistency with which a test measures a behavior or behaviors. To be reliable, a test must measure a behavior consistently. Validity, on the other hand, has to do with how well a test really measures what it is supposed to (Fraenkel & Wallen, 2000). For example, a bathroom scale is intended to measure one's weight, and therefore is valid if it measures how many pounds you weigh (as opposed to some other things such as your waistline circumference or your current mood). If a scale is reliable, you could step on the scale several times within a few minutes (without any major changes such as attire, food intake, or energy expenditure) and you should get a very similar reading of weight.

Music therapy assessments have been published for use with a variety of populations, including persons with developmental disabilities (intellectual disabilities and autism), children in special education, persons with behavioral-emotional disorders, children who have been hospitalized, hospice patients, and older adults (Adler, 2001; Bitcon, 1976; Boxill, 1985; Braswell et al., 1983, 1986; Bruscia, 1987; Cassity & Cassity, 2006; Cohen et al., 1978; Cohen & Gericke, 1972; Coleman & Brunk, 1999; Douglass, 2006; Groen, 2007; Hintz, 2001; Layman, Hussey, & Laing, 2002; Loewy, 2000; Maure-Johnson, 2006; Nordoff & Robbins, 1977; Wasserman, Plutchik, Deutsch, & Takemoto, 1973; Wells, 1988; Wigram, 2001; York, 1994). These tools vary in format and content in order to be useable and useful with the varied developmental levels, communication abilities, therapeutic needs, and treatment foci associated with the various populations and placements (e.g., educational, hospital, rehabilitation, etc.). The drawback for some of these tests is that reliability and validity have not yet been fully established. In such cases, caution must be used when interpreting the results.

As indicated previously, Donna's team is using a variety of assessment tools to evaluate her progress, including interviews, x-rays, charting of medication usage, psychological tests, pain scales, questionnaires, measures of Donna's walking and other functional movements (Sarafino, 2006), and observational tools. The treatment team now uses these initial assessments to develop a treatment plan that will address the various aspects of Donna's condition.

TREATMENT PLAN

Once the **initial assessment** data have been gathered and analyzed, the next step is to establish a treatment plan. In some treatment approaches, each specialist develops his or her own plan more or less independently. In care plans that are **multidisciplinary** in nature, each team member will focus on and report in team meetings on particular aspects of the client's needs that are considered closest to his or her disciplinary scope of practice (e.g., the physician focusing on medications, and the physical therapist focusing on functional movements such as standing and walking).

Some treatment teams have an **interdisciplinary** approach, in which each team member takes primary responsibility for particular treatment goals, but there is collaboration in the development of treatment goals and how those goals will be attained. This particular clinic uses a **transdisciplinary** approach, and therefore several specialists may collaborate on particular goals and objectives (Hobson, 2006). For example, the physical therapist and music therapist will collaborate on the exercise program, the psychologist and music therapist will collaborate on the relaxation program, and the music therapist and social worker will collaborate on the leisure skills program. Ongoing assessment will be gathered by each caregiver over the period of rehabilitation to evaluate Donna's response to treatment.

Therapeutic Goals and Objectives

The essence of a treatment plan lies in therapeutic goals and objectives, which are based on established treatment priorities. A goal may be defined as a broad statement of the desired outcome of treatment. Thus, the treatment team, in consultation with Donna, has developed the following treatment goals for Donna's four-week back pain rehabilitation (Sarafino, 2006):

Treatment goals for Donna:

1. *Reduce Donna's experience of pain, including psychological components (such as depression and helplessness)*
2. *Decrease or eliminate the use of medication for pain*
3. *Improve physical and lifestyle functioning (including her level of activity at home, physical exercise, and participation in the community)*
4. *Enhance her social support and restore her family life to pre-injury level of interaction and satisfaction*

Each team member will be contributing to one or more of these treatment goals.

Whereas goals are broad statements of desired changes in client behavior, objectives are more specific and short-term. A goal is broken down into a series of short-term objectives. Each objective describes an immediate goal, which is measurable, and may be viewed as a small step in the process of attaining a final goal. The extent of improvement anticipated within a specified time frame will vary depending upon the status of the client at the time of initial assessment. If clients show either slower or more rapid improvement than anticipated, the objectives may be changed to reflect more likely treatment outcomes. Various members of the treatment team will focus on particular objectives and maintain ongoing assessment of progress throughout her treatment program. Listed below are examples (not intended to be comprehensive) of (1) objectives that could reflect each of Donna's goals, and (2) assessment tools that could be used to measure ongoing progress:

Goal 1. *Reduce Donna's experience of pain, including psychological components (such as depression and helplessness)*

Objectives:
   a. Reduce levels of pain experienced during walking, sitting, household chores, and at bedtime by 40%
   b. Establish a regular program of exercises for strength, flexibility, and relaxation that will support the back in everyday activities
   c. Achieve lessening of depression and perceived helplessness

Ongoing assessments:
   a. Visual analog scale [see Chapter 11] for self-report of pain each day before and after walking, before and after relaxation exercises, before and after occupational therapy, and each evening at bedtime
   b. Complete 20–30 minutes of strength, flexibility, and relaxation exercises 5 days per week
   c. Pain diary
   d. Beck Depression Inventory

Goal 2. *Decrease or eliminate the use of medication for pain*

Objectives:
   a. Donna will demonstrate the use of 4 methods of cognitive pain strategies for reducing discomfort: progressive relaxation techniques, distraction, guided imagery, and pain redefinition, and be able to give examples of situations in which each can be applied in her everyday life.
   b. Donna will learn healthy patterns of movements and accommodations to reduce discomfort during functional activities in the household and leisure activities

Ongoing assessments:
   a. Therapist observation of Donna's use of each strategy, paired with measures from pain scales
   b. Monitor dosage and frequency of pain medication

Goal 3. *Improve physical and lifestyle functioning (including level of activity at home, physical exercises, and participation in the community)*

Objectives:
   a. Increase length of treadmill walking by 50% each of 4 weeks

440 - PART THREE — PROFESSIONAL ISSUES IN MUSIC THERAPY

    b. *Increase velocity of walking on shuttle walk test by 30% by end of 4 weeks*
    c. *Increase strength and endurance using weight-bearing exercises*
    d. *Complete 8 of 10 of the list of functional home activities by week 4*
    e. *Develop ergonomically suitable movements for completing two ballroom dances, and complete 10 minutes of ballroom dances with spouse (foxtrot and waltz) by week 4*

Ongoing assessments:
    a. *Chart duration of time spent on treadmill and weight-bearing exercises each week*
    b. *Measure distance walked in 1-minute increments*
    c. *Evaluate strength and range of motion in physical therapy clinic*
    d. *Structured observation of functional activities*
    e. *Chart length of time in ballroom dance practice*

Goal 4. *Enhance Donna's social support and restore her family life to pre-injury level of interaction and satisfaction*

Objectives:
    a. *Donna will accompany Jim to a ballroom dance club event for at least 15 minutes by week 3*
    b. *Develop strategies for sustained standing and sitting during choir rehearsals*
    c. *Donna will increase tolerance for standing during choir practice by week 4*

Ongoing assessments:
    a. *Checklist of attendance at sessions and social activities*
    b. *Pain scales and entry in pain diary to assess physical comfort during sitting, standing, and dancing*

Now that the treatment goals, objectives, and assessment tools have been established, Matt, the music therapist, has developed specific music therapy interventions that will be used to help Donna meet her objectives. As you have learned in previous chapters, music can be an effective therapeutic tool for the psychological, social, and physical challenges that Donna faces. Music is an excellent medium for exploring and expressing emotions. Music also has a strong social component, bringing people together in a variety of circumstances. From a physical standpoint, music can be an effective stimulus for use in cognitive pain management (as a distraction or to promote relaxation), and it can promote efficient movements and persistence in exercise. Consequently, there are many ways that music therapy can contribute to Donna's treatment goals and objectives. For some of the treatment objectives, Matt will work with Donna to select and create music recordings for use in her physical therapy and relaxation routines. For other treatment objectives, Matt will work with Donna to re-establish healthy behaviors that involve music participation. The list below summarizes the interventions that Matt will contribute to the treatment goals and objectives.

Music as a stimulus to reduce discomfort. (related to Goals 1 and 2)

Matt integrates information gathered from Donna's questionnaire to develop lists of music selections that Donna can use as part of relaxation and to promote sleep. Matt will confer with Donna about the final choice of songs, will prepare an easily-used CD, and will instruct Donna on how to use music for distraction and to promote a relaxation response. He will practice these skills with her during several sessions and provide written instructions that she can refer to after discharge.

Music to promote efficient movements and persistence. (related to Goals 1, 2, and 3)

Matt will develop an initial list of tunes that Donna enjoys (as indicated through her preference questionnaire) and that are appropriate in tempo and beat for the exercise program devised by the physical therapist. Donna can use her individualized exercise music during physical therapy as well as after discharge.

Music in group therapy. (related to Goals 1, 2, and 4)

Donna will participate in group music therapy during which lyric analysis, writing music, and group discussion will be used to help Donna with expression of feelings and modulation of her mood. This group will also provide an important form of social support as she practices new adaptive behaviors.

Music and leisure skills. (related to Goals 3 and 4)

Matt and the physical therapist will meet with Donna to analyze the kinds of movements required for successful participation in ballroom dancing and choirs. Matt provides input on the requirements of prolonged sitting and standing in choral rehearsals, use of breath support, etc., and he also outlines the primary movements required for the foxtrot and waltz, two of the dances most commonly played in the ballroom dance club. The physical therapist then suggests healthy movement patterns or accommodations that will allow Donna to persist in these social activities.

Matt will develop recording of ballroom music and choir selections that Donna can use in practicing these skills. Matt will also assist Donna in maintaining her participation checklist for ongoing assessment.

DOCUMENTATION OF PROGRESS

Monitoring progress throughout a client's therapeutic process is one of the most important aspects of a therapist's job (Ottenbacher, 1986). It allows the therapist to make adjustments in the treatment plan if progress is not occurring and it ultimately measures the success or failure of a treatment program.

As we have learned, objectives are carefully written to reflect precisely what the client needs to do to meet the treatment goal. Because the behavior can be observed by the therapist, it can also be accurately recorded and matched against a baseline, or level at which the behavior was occurring before treatment was begun (initial assessment). A baseline measure is important to obtain, because it indicates the severity of the problem and serves as a reference point for later evaluation of treatment effectiveness (Hall, 1974). Oftentimes a treatment team will meet to discuss a client's progress on each goal, and the various health professionals will report on progress or lack of progress in their areas. If the client is not making reasonable progress, then the team either will discuss possible modifications in the chosen interventions, or will modify the objectives based upon the present level of functioning.

Organizations must maintain accurate and complete records on the diagnosis, treatment, and care of all clients. This information provides a chronological account of the client's treatment and is considered a legal document (Miller, 1986). A client's record also contains information used to monitor quality (effectiveness of treatment), cost effectiveness, and efficiency. In some cases, music therapy progress reports are used to justify charges to school budgets, insurance companies, Medicare, and Medicaid (Lewis, 1989; Punwar, 1988). On a more immediate scale, the record establishes an important communication link among all caregivers involved with the client.

The submission of regular and accurate written reports is a fundamental responsibility of all music therapists. Although reporting requirements and formats vary greatly among organizations, most reports contain assessment data, goals and objectives, treatment plans, progress notes, and a final report at time of discharge or discontinuation of services. The information must be written in a clear, concise manner using nonjudgmental, objective terminology. In the case of private practice, the music therapist bears primary responsibility for documentation and determining appropriate dissemination of data to authorized agencies or individuals (Reuer, 2007; Wilhelm, 2004).

EVALUATION AND TERMINATION OF TREATMENT

When a client has met his or her treatment goals, or when the treatment team decides that the client has derived the greatest possible benefit from therapy, treatment is discontinued. In some circumstances, treatment centers or insurance coverage stipulates a typical length of treatment for a specific type of illness or condition. Thus, when setting objectives, there is an expectation that a particular level of improvement should be feasible within that predetermined length of treatment.

At the time of discharge or discontinuation of treatment, the music therapist writes an evaluation of the entire music therapy process, including the initial goals that were set and progress that was made. The therapist may include recommendations for further treatment or other services.

> *Donna has completed the 4-week back pain program and has met most of her goals. In Matt's summary, he recommends continued use of music to promote relaxation and exercise in her own home. He has also, with Donna's permission, contacted the choir director of Sweet Adelines to discuss some of the accommodations that were developed to help Donna with the physical requirements of choir rehearsal. Donna and her husband have attended two events of the ballroom dance club, the first time for 15 minutes, and the second time for 30 minutes. Although she is not without pain, she can now tolerate her discomfort and is more effective at maintaining a more normal level of social activity. Donna and Jim hope that, with persistence in her pain management and physical exercises, she will be able to eventually return to full participation.*

Donna's case study is just one example of the treatment process. Treatment protocols and assessment tools vary considerably depending upon the nature of the condition and the unique needs of each client. Hopefully, this case example helps you to see the general process that takes place in clinical practice.

The next section of this chapter focuses more on the therapist and the professional and personal qualifications that contribute to professional effectiveness.

Approaches Developed within the Field of Music Therapy

Two approaches that developed primarily within the field of music therapy are **Nordoff-Robbins Music Therapy** and the **Bonny Method of Guided Imagery and Music**. These psychotherapeutic forms of music therapy use a combination of the spoken word and music to elicit changes in client behavior. Depending upon the clientele and primary goals, as well as the therapist's own personal philosophy, some sessions use predominantly musical communication, and music is considered by some therapists to be inherently therapeutic—that is, no verbal processing is essential. These approaches to music therapy are intensely personal, frequently conducted on an individual basis, and used with a variety of clientele. Goals are usually broad and aimed at personal growth, self-actualization, and building self-worth in clients.

Nordoff-Robbins Music Therapy. Nordoff-Robbins Music Therapy developed from a unique partnership between Paul Nordoff, a composer, and Clive Robbins, a special education teacher. From 1959 until 1976, the year of Nordoff's death, the two collaborated on what they called "active" music therapy. Clive Robbins later worked for many years with his wife, Carol, to continue the team approach to therapy. Active music therapy primarily uses improvisation to attain therapeutic goals and is founded on the idea that all persons, no matter the level of (dis)ability, have inborn musical ability and creativity. The tapping into the client's innate musical ability leads to personal growth and development (Kim, 2004).

Internationally located facilities offer training programs and internships for music therapists interested in the Nordoff-Robbins approach. Students take classes in improvisation, musicianship, assessment, and theory of group music therapy. Each student must complete a prescribed set of clinical experiences under supervision, learn to document client progress, and complete an internship of 38 weeks. There are three levels of training available for those therapists who either have a master's degree or are enrolled in a graduate program in music therapy (Nordoff-Robbins Center for Music Therapy, 2008).

Nordoff and Robbins initially practiced music therapy as a team, one playing the piano while the other worked directly with the client. In current practice, therapists may work individually or, in the case of larger groups, work in pairs. Depending upon their needs, clients may be seen in individual sessions or a group setting, or may participate in both. The primary instrument used by the music therapist is either a piano or guitar. Participants engage in music making, playing high-quality instruments of various kinds, including pitched and percussion instruments. Singing and movement can be incorporated into the session to add variety and enhance communication between therapist and client. Nordoff-Robbins music therapists apply their techniques to a wide range of adults and children, including those with developmental disabilities or socioemotional problems, older adults, and clients in medical settings (Aigen et al., 2004).

Nordoff-Robbins music therapy emphasizes the concept of **self-actualization** and the meaningfulness of human destiny. Fundamental to this approach is the belief that within every human being is a musical self (sometimes referred to as the "music child"). The music serves as the primary clinical medium and agent of change. There is no specific format or procedure for a session; improvisation (and sometimes precomposed pieces) is used to begin a musical dialogue between participant and therapist. This form of communication is an important concept in active music therapy, with the therapist accepting whatever the client presents musically. This helps the adult or child to gain musical competence through using different rhythmic patterns, dynamics, and harmonies, and, ultimately, to improve expressive skills, self-confidence, and self-esteem. Nordoff-Robbins practitioners strive to build an effective relationship between themselves and their clients with the ultimate goal of helping the person to attain an improved quality of life (Aigen et al., 2004).

Clinical goals and objectives aim to develop the client's individual potential as opposed to working toward cultural expectations of "normality." Rather than establishing short-term behavioral objectives, clinicians generally focus on long-term therapeutic growth characterized by expressive freedom, creativity, self-confidence, and other human qualities associated with self-actualization (Aigen et al., 2004). Assessment does not typically focus on specific target behaviors; rather, sessions are recorded and then reviewed by clinicians, who study significant musical and nonmusical responses, changes, musical relationships, and teamwork. These observations are documented in a narrative style, which is referred to as "indexing the session" (Aigen et al., 2004).

For further information on the Nordoff-Robbins approach, the following are recommended sources: *Creative Music Therapy: A Guide to Fostering Clinical Musicianship* (Nordoff & Robbins, 2006); *Music Therapy for Handicapped Children* (Nordoff & Robbins, 1992); *Improvisational Models of Music Therapy* (Bruscia, 1987); *Paths of Development in Nordoff-Robbins Music Therapy* (Aigen, 1998); *Music Centered Music Therapy* (Aigen, 2004); *Healing Heritage: Paul Nordoff Exploring the Tonal Language of Music* (Robbins & Robbins, 1998); *Here We Are in Music: One Year with an Adolescent Creative Music Therapy Group* (Aigen, 1997); *Being in Music: Foundations of Nordoff-Robbins Music Therapy* (Aigen, 1996).

The Bonny Method of Guided Imagery and Music. Helen Bonny, the founder of Guided Imagery and Music (GIM), developed the idea of using classical music to stimulate and sustain a dynamic process through the imagination, which facilitates both self-exploration and what Abraham Maslow termed "peak experiences" in persons seeking self-awareness. Based on **humanistic** and **transpersonal** theories, GIM practitioners subscribe to the idea that the combination of music and **imagery** can help a client expand **self-awareness** that leads to a more healthy state of being (Bonny & Savary, 1990).

In an era where the drug LSD (lysergic acid diethylamide) was used in clinical research to enhance peak experiences for the purpose of self-actualization (with obvious drawbacks), Bonny proposed substituting music for the drug. Her subsequent research concluded that music, when properly applied, could intensify and safely contain imagery, thus aiding uncovering and working through detrimental thoughts, emotions, and feelings. By 1974, music and session protocols were in place leading to this form of music therapy practice (Burns & Woolrich, 2004).

GIM therapists use a combination of carefully selected and sequenced classical music to evoke and catalyze images, which may represent the participant's conscious and unconscious feelings from past and present events. As the music plays during individual sessions, the therapist facilitates an ongoing dialogue with the client as the imagery emerges, which fosters focus and engagement with the experience. Through the skillful use of music and imagery, the individual experiences a cathartic release of emotions, which leads to a transformation in the perception of the past events and the ability to view them from a new perspective. This cognitive reframing can then lead to positive behavior change and a renewed sense of self-worth (Burns & Woolrich, 2004). Therapeutic goals include creativity, self-exploration, spiritual insight, and cognitive reorganization (McKinney, 2007b).

The type of classical music used in GIM sessions is designed to challenge and expand the client's comfort level while providing sufficient structural support within which to explore images that arise during the GIM session. According to Goldberg (1992), music may evoke affective or feeling responses, which in turn evoke images. The music therapist chooses music that matches the client's affect, energy level, and issues. The arrangement of musical elements (dynamics, melody, harmony, rhythm, and orchestration) must suggest certain emotional qualities fitting client needs. The titles of many of the music programs for GIM suggest themes, such as Positive Affect, Relationships, Transitions, Affect Release, and Emotional Expression (Bonny, 2002). It is important to note that the music therapist's role in GIM is not to solve the client's problems but to guide, support, and serve as witness to the individual's process toward self-understanding and change. Persons who are most appropriate for GIM are those diagnosed with certain types of behavior or emotional disorders, those with chronic illness, or those seeking a better understanding of self. Individuals with psychosis are not appropriate candidates for GIM (Burns &

Woolrich, 2004). Facilitation of this approach requires advanced training in GIM as well as in counseling, psychotherapy, or music psychotherapy.

Desired clinical outcomes may include improved interpersonal relationships and lives that are more manageable and meaningful (Körelen & Wrangsjö, 2001). Research studies conducted with healthy adults as well as persons with depression or chronic illnesses (such as rheumatoid arthritis or cancer) have documented the following: significant decrease in emotional distress (including anxiety and depressed mood); significant improvement in relationships, and manageability and quality of life (Burns, 1999; Körelen & Wrangsjö, 2001; McKinney, Antoni, Kumar, Tims, & McCabe, 1997); reduced pain and improved physical functioning (Jacobi & Eisenberg, 2001–2002); and reduced blood pressure (McDonald, as cited in McKinney, Antoni, et al., 1997). Studies examining the potential use of GIM to reduce stress and enhance immune function (psychoneuroimmunology) have reported significant changes in neuro-endocrine responses associated with stress (McKinney, 2007a; McKinney, Antoni, et al., 1997; McKinney, Tims, Kumar, & Kumar, 1997).

For additional information, the following sources are recommended: *Music and Consciousness: The Evolution of Guided Imagery and Music* (Bonny, 2002); *Music and Your Mind: Listening with a New Consciousness* (Bonny & Savary, 1990).

Music Therapy Approaches Reflecting or Based upon Psychological Philosophies, Theories, or Models

Music therapists work with a variety of clientele, some who have as their primary diagnosis a behavioral-emotional disorder, and others who may have behavioral or emotional problems that accompany another primary diagnosis (e.g., learning disabilities, intellectual disabilities, some chronic illnesses, etc.). Consistent with a biopsychosocial model of health care, treatment should incorporate the psychological and social needs of the individual. Toward this end, music therapists often work collaboratively with other health care providers, including psychologists, social workers, and child life specialists, to address psychosocial issues.

While music therapists often feel more comfortable with particular approaches, they may need to select music therapy interventions that are congruent with philosophies, theories, or models of psychological functioning that have been adopted by their client's treatment team or the facility's overarching mission or philosophy. In this section, we have provided a summary of several prominent philosophies, theories, or models associated with the field of psychology, but which have informed and shaped music therapy practice as well. These include **behavioral therapy, cognitive behavioral therapy,** and **psychodynamic therapy.** In addition, an **eclectic** approach, which is the use of techniques from several different approaches, will be presented at the end of this chapter. You may recall reading about these terms in

Chapter 8. You may find it helpful to review that information in conjunction with reading this next section.

The Behavioral Approach to Music Therapy. The behavioral approach to music therapy is defined as the use of music in association with the therapist to change unhealthy patterns of socially important behavior (such as drug abuse) into more appropriate skills (abstaining from using drugs) (Standley, Johnson, Robb, Brownell, & Kim, 2004). Behavior is changed through a highly structured environment using **classical** or **operant** conditioning principles developed by psychologists, most notably B. F. Skinner and Albert Bandura. Behaviorism examines human behavior through **empirical methods** (quantifying observable and measurable behaviors) rather than focusing on thoughts and internal emotional conflicts. Behavioral psychology is the philosophical and theoretical basis for understanding human behavior. **Applied Behavior Analysis (ABA),** which is often used in educational and clinical settings, helps to link research with clinical practice. ABA consists of a variety of creative approaches and procedures that reflect behavioral theories to influence behavior change. These approaches and procedures have been validated through over 40 years of scientific research and are widely used in the United States (Standley et al., 2004; Sulzer-Azaroff & Mayer, 1991).

Procedures derived from behavioral therapy (including ABA) have been used to assess and treat a wide range of clinical entities, including persons with physically disabling conditions and behavioral-emotional disorders, and, in particular, adults and children with intellectual disabilities and autism spectrum disorders (Sturmey, 2002). Behavioral therapy can be used to modify a host of maladaptive behaviors, including self-injurious or self-stimulating behaviors, anxiety and phobias, depression, eating disorders, smoking, and antisocial behaviors (Corey, 2001).

Techniques common to behavioral therapy include **positive** and **negative reinforcement** of behavior, **punishment**, **extinction** of **undesirable** behaviors, **token economies** to strengthen socially desirable behaviors, and **shaping**. These are just of few of the terms that are commonly used in behavioral therapy and ABA. You can read definitions of these terms in the book's glossary and learn more about these techniques in other books and chapters that focus on behavioral therapy.

Techniques such as **reinforcement** and **shaping** can be easily integrated into music therapy sessions. In a general sense, music therapists often use these techniques to help clients participate successfully in the therapy session. Music therapists may use praise, award stickers (such as stars or happy faces), or other sorts of reward to reinforce appropriate behavior. But one of the special and powerful tools that music therapists have to offer is *music itself*. Most people find some sort of music beautiful and engaging. For example, adolescents often consider music central to their social and emotional life, and they will, on their own, spend hours a day listening to favorite music. Many research studies have shown that listening to or playing music can be a very powerful **reinforcement** that can be used to increase a target behavior. For example, a child with a behavioral disorder who is often verbally aggressive may "earn" the chance to take guitar lessons from the music therapist if he doesn't use offensive language throughout the day.

Music therapists also use techniques such as **shaping** in order to help clients develop new and challenging skills. For example, when first learning to play piano or guitar, most people sound pretty awkward and inept. Using principles of behavioral therapy, the music therapist can shape or gradually guide the client's skills toward a desirable level of competency, which in turn can support self-confidence.

Another therapeutic intervention that has emerged from the behavioral tradition is the pairing of relaxing music with special relaxations techniques (progressive relaxation or autogenic relaxation). The music eventually becomes **conditioned** with relaxation. These are only three of a panoply of ways in which behavioral principles integrate readily with music therapy interventions.

Since the formation of the National Association for Music Therapy in 1950, there has been a strong link between music therapy and behavioral therapy. The *Journal of Music Therapy* has published numerous research studies dating back to the 1960s and continuing today using behavioral strategies coupled with music therapy interventions (Gfeller, 1987). The field continues to grow through empirical research and development of new techniques that lead to more effective treatment.

The following resources provide more information on applied behavioral analysis and behavioral music therapy: *Principles of Behavior Modification* (Bandura, 1969); "Applied Behavior Analysis" (Hanser, 1995); "A Meta-analysis on the Effects of Music as a Reinforcement for Education/Therapy Objectives" (Standley, 1996b); "Four Decades of Music Therapy Behavioral Research Designs: A Content Analysis of *Journal of Music Therapy* Articles" (Gregory, 2002).

Cognitive-Behavioral Music Therapy. As noted in Chapter 8, cognitive therapies are based upon the premise that what we think about an event, object, or person has an enormous influence on what we feel and how we act (Corey, 2001). Cognitive approaches emphasize the importance of cognitive (mental) processes as determinants of behavior. The influence of behavioral therapy in this approach can be seen in the use of many techniques designed to alter maladaptive behaviors in conjunction with modifying irrational thoughts (Scoval & Gardstrom, 2002).

Cognitive-behavioral therapy is designed to help the clients replace undesirable, irrational thinking with healthier cognitive patterns. Cognitive-behavioral therapists do not delve into a person's past or probe internalized emotional conflicts; instead they focus on the client's current life situation and work toward a more satisfactory way of handling problems and seizing opportunities for positive growth. A music therapist may use this theoretical approach with persons having a variety of emotional and social problems, including anxiety disorders, substance abuse, eating disorders, and mood disorders. Cognitive-behavioral therapy has also proven useful to treat chronic pain and sleep disorders. Cognitive-behavioral therapy requires that the client be capable of insight and verbal communication; thus, this approach may not be suited for persons who are out of touch with reality (psychotic) or who have serious intellectual deficits (Corey, 2001). It is effective for use with groups or individuals.

The role of the music therapist who works within this therapeutic framework is almost like a coach or educator who encourages and supports the client in taking responsibility for his or her own changes, specifically to learn to adjust cognitive processes (thinking differently) and associated behaviors. Typically, a therapist will use a number of approaches to change feelings and behavior, such as role playing, rehearsal, and modeling. For example, within a structured music therapy intervention (such as playing instruments together), the music therapist may have members of the group rehearse or role play behaviors that are problematic in their everyday lives (Bryant, 1987). A very withdrawn person who is shy and reclusive may practice taking a leadership role in the musical ensemble. Or the music therapist might model (demonstrate) appropriate ways of communicating or behaving. The therapist may ask clients to complete assignments outside the session, and then keep a diary of specific thoughts and feelings that arise during situations. This provides practice and experimentation with new ways of responding to uncomfortable situations identified in therapy.

Cognitive-behavioral music therapy practice includes the components of music and verbal processing. Music therapists use guided listening strategies including lyric analysis, song writing, and relaxation experiences, which are described in Chapter 8. These experiences can help the client to identify issues in the song's content that have relevance to their personal situation (Bryant, 1987). Paring preferred relaxing music with an **autogenic** or **progressive relaxation** (a technique adopted from behavioral therapy) script can help clients with pain management and focus attention away from an unpleasant medical procedure (Standley et al., 2004). Music has also been effective in reducing stress in teachers as well as in adolescents who suffer from post-traumatic stress disorder, and in reducing cravings in persons suffering from alcohol abuse.

A recent study by Silverman (2007) indicates that music therapy practitioners use cognitive-behavioral strategies more frequently than other approaches with persons who have behavioral emotional disturbances. This is an important finding given that about 21% of music therapists work with this clinical population. According to Cassity (2007), the use of cognitive-behavioral therapy has grown over the past few decades and will continue to increase, as a philosophical orientation in psychiatric care and, consequently, also in music therapy.

References that provide more information about cognitive-behavior therapy and music therapy include: *Rational Emotive Behavioral Therapy: A Therapist's Guide* (Ellis & McLaren, 1998); "The Use of Rational Humorous Songs in Psychotherapy" (Ellis, 1987); "A Cognitive Approach to Therapy Through Music" (Bryant, 1987); and "The Use of Cognitive-Behavioral Music Therapy in the Treatment of Women with Eating Disorders" (Hilliard, 2001).

The Psychodynamic Approach to Music Therapy. This approach is related to psychodynamic theory of psychology, which had its origins in the theories of Sigmund Freud, as well as theories of later psychodynamic therapists (e.g., Jung, Adler, etc.) that extend or modify Freudian theory. These theories are described in detail in many psychology textbooks and courses. Briefly, the psychodynamic model is based upon the belief that human behavior is strongly influenced by unconscious psychological processes, such as internal conflicts, impulses, desires, and motives, of which we are largely unaware on a conscious level. Early childhood events are believed to have lifelong effects on our psychological states. A number of psychodynamic therapies have developed out of psychoanalytic principles, but all are concerned with explaining the motives behind why people think, feel, and behave as they do. Therapy is aimed at helping the individual gain insights or increased awareness of unconscious conflicts, in order to develop more adaptive and satisfying behaviors and relationships (Wilson, O'Leary, Nathan, & Clark, 1996).

Several models of psychodynamic music therapy are based upon psychodynamic theory. Among the pioneers of psychodynamic music therapy are Florence Tyson, an early American practitioner of this form of music therapy, Juliet Alvin (who used the term *psychodynamic music therapy*), and Mary Priestly (associated with a model of therapy known as Analytical Music Therapy); Alvin and Priestly were both British music therapists. As is true within the field of psychology, there are several approaches to psychodynamic music therapy. They differ on matters such as the role of music within therapy, the nature of the patient-client relationship, professional training methods, and therapy techniques. Some music therapy approaches used by psychodynamic music therapists include vocal and instrumental improvisation, song writing, patient-selected music, music imagery, and the Bonny Method of Guided Imagery and Music (described earlier in this chapter). It is important to note that some of these techniques are also used by music therapists who do not consider themselves to be psychodynamic therapists. These techniques are not inherently associated with psychodynamic principles, but they can be facilitated in such a manner that therapeutic goals associated with psychodynamic principles are addressed (Isenberg-Grezeda, Goldberg, & Dvorkin, 2004).

Psychodynamically-based music therapy is used to help patients develop insights into unconscious drives, motives, and conflicts that negatively impact present functioning. The relationship between the therapist and the client is fundamental to the treatment process and is used to help the patient gain insight into old relationships and patterns of behaviors, including defenses and resistance to change. Music and/or verbal interaction are the essential elements of change. According to Ruud (1980), music acts as a stimulus in which the abstract nature of music detours intellectual control and provides access to unconscious conflicts and emotions. These conflicts and emotions can then be expressed through music. In addition, musical activity can help clients to attain a stronger ego (sense of self) and improved self-esteem.

There has been debate regarding the role of music versus the role of the patient-therapist relationship in music psychotherapy. Bruscia (1998) has suggested four levels of engagement between the patient and therapist that fall on a continuum from exclusively musical interaction (in which therapeutic issues are accessed, worked through, and resolved through musical engagement), to predominantly verbal interactions in which the therapeutic issues are accessed, worked through, and resolved verbally, but music experiences are used to facilitate or enrich the discussion (Isenberg-Grezeda et al., 2004).

This type of music therapy practice requires extensive and advanced training in psychodynamic music psychotherapy therapy, exceptionally strong skills in musical improvisation on the part of the therapist, and a commitment to more extended therapy and capacity for insight on the part of the client.

For additional information, the following sources are recommended: *Music Therapy* (Alvin, 1975); *The Dynamics of Music Psychotherapy* (Bruscia, 1998); *Essays on Analytical Music Therapy* (Priestly, 1994).

Music Therapy Approaches Reflecting Biomedical Models

A large number of music therapists works with clientele whose primary diagnoses involves a disease or condition that requires medical treatment and/or specific forms of neurologic rehabilitation (e.g., strokes, Parkinson's disease, cancer, COPD, etc.). While music therapists often address the psychological and social needs of persons with medical problems (see Chapter 11), music therapists also collaborate with physicians, nurses, physical therapists, and other health-care providers to treat or ameliorate the physical, biological, or neurological aspects of the disease or condition. Those sorts of conditions and music therapy interventions are described in many chapters of this book, in particular Chapters 6, 7, 10, 11, and 12.

While music therapists may have personally preferred music therapy approaches, their choices of music therapy interventions should also be congruent with philosophies, theories, or models adopted by their client's treatment team or the mission or philosophy of the hospital, clinic, or rehabilitation center where they work. In some facilities, this may be a biomedical orientation to treatment. This section describes music therapy approaches that emphasize a biomedical approach, that is, from a brain and behavior perspective. Some core aspects of a biomedical perspective are (1) the focus on the neurobiological foundations of the human nervous system, (2) a strong emphasis on music perception and active music participation as a form of stimulation that activates physiological and neurophysiological processes in the body (which include affect and cognition as part of neural behavior), and (3) the belief that the unique structural and cultural properties of music can be harnessed to access brain and behavior functions to facilitate and to promote healing and rehabilitation.

Throughout this book are examples of music and biological functioning. In Chapter 2, the long history of music as an influence on human functioning and health is presented. Chapter 3 outlines many ways in which music influences physical functioning, including neurological processes. Chapters throughout the book illustrate the link between physical functioning and various aspects of music listening and involvement.

In recent years, there have been several notable connections between music and physical well-being that have been documented through clinical research. As Chapter 11 notes, preliminary studies consistent with **psychoneuroimmunology** (an interdisciplinary field that involves the bidirectional relationships between the mind, brain, and immune system) indicate that stress-related hormones and neurotransmitters can suppress immune functioning. Music in conjunction with stress reduction and relaxation can reduce levels of these hormones and neurotransmitters (McKinney, 2007a).

Therapeutic application of music (such as rhythm and melodic patterns) have been associated with improved neuromotor, speech/language, and cognitive functioning for persons suffering from neurologically-based conditions such as stroke, Parkinson's disease, multiple sclerosis, traumatic brain injury, or cerebral palsy. The following music therapy model, **Neurologic Music Therapy (NMT),** developed by Michael Thaut, focuses on utilizing musical stimuli for a variety of neurological disorders. Michael Thaut has provided an overview of NMT in the following paragraphs.

Neurologic Music Therapy (This section contributed by Michael H. Thaut). The study of the neurobiological basis of music ability is inherently linked to the study of music's influence on brain function. In other words, when we study the biology of music in the brain, we inevitably recognize a reciprocal relationship in musical behavior: The brain that engages in music is changed by engaging in music. Although much has been learned since the early1990s about the effect of music on brain structure and function, a transformational framework, a new theoretical model, explains how musical responses can be generalized and transferred into nonmusical therapeutic responses. This scientific model called the **Rational Scientific Mediating Model (R-SMM**—for more information refer to Chapter 10), searches for the therapeutic effect of music by studying if and how music stimulates and engages parallel or shared brain function in the following areas, based on the psychological and physiological processes in music perception: cognition, speech and language, motor control, and emotion. Therefore, one can also describe the paradigm shift in this model as a change from an interpretive "social science" model to a perceptual "neuroscience" model.

Since about 1990, there has been a large body of research conducted in the neurosciences of music. This research—by enabling a more complete understanding of the neurobiological basis of music—has led to the development of "clusters" of scientific evidence for the effectiveness of specific interventions of music within therapy, rehabilitation, and medicine. In a comprehensive effort by researchers and clinicians in music therapy, neurology, and the brain sciences, these "evidence clusters" have been codified into a system of therapeutic techniques subsequently termed *Neurologic Music Therapy* **(NMT)**. This codification—which began in the late 1990s—has resulted in the development of clinical techniques that are standardized in applications and terminology as well as supported by evidence through scientific research. Because the system of techniques is research-based, it is dynamically open-ended in terms of future development and knowledge.

Five basic definitions articulate the most important principles of neurologic music therapy:

- NMT is defined as the therapeutic application of music to cognitive, sensory, and motor dysfunctions due to neurologic disease of the human nervous system.
- NMT is based on a neuroscience model of music perception and production, and the influence of music on functional changes in nonmusical brain and behavior functions (R-SMM).
- Treatment techniques are evidence based; they are based on data from scientific and clinical research and are directed toward functional nonmusical therapeutic goals.
- Treatment techniques are standardized in terminology and application and are applied to therapy as therapeutic music interventions (TMI), which are adaptable to the patient's functional needs.

- In addition to training in music and NMT, practitioners are educated in the areas of neuroanatomy and physiology, brain pathologies, medical terminology, and rehabilitation of cognitive, motor, speech, and language functions.

Clinical applications of NMT are subdivided into three domains of rehabilitation: (1) sensorimotor rehabilitation, (2) speech and language rehabilitation, and (3) cognitive rehabilitation. In each domain, NMT can be applied to patient treatment within different clinical fields and disciplines, such as inpatient and outpatient neurologic rehabilitation, neurogeriatrics, neuropedioatrics, and neurodevelopmental therapies. Depending on the patients' needs, the therapeutic goals are directed toward functional rehabilitative, developmental, or adaptive goals. Within this framework, the primary major area of therapeutic rehabilitation not fully covered is psychiatric rehabilitation. However, as the understanding of the nature and the mechanisms of psychiatric disorders progresses, our understanding of effective rehabilitation strategies will improve. Within an emerging framework of neuropsychiatric models, it will be possible to design effective treatment techniques in NMT, most likely within the domain of cognitive rehabilitation (Unkefer & Thaut, 2002).

More detail about Neurologic Music Therapy is discussed in Chapter 10. Therefore, only two additional concepts will be specifically mentioned here due to their particular significance for music in rehabilitation.

1. *Technique standardization.* In current music therapy practice, there is considerable variety in how various therapy approaches are named, with some terms being essentially activity descriptions and some being borrowed from other fields. This lack of standardization can make communication among professionals difficult. Therefore, standardization can provide an important foundation for establishing treatment goals and intervention protocols that can be more consistently recognized by other health professionals and insurance companies.

In Neurologic Music Therapy, two parameters of technique definition are introduced to allow for the development of standardized descriptions and applications. The first parameter is based on the functional goals of the therapeutic music exercise—for example, to improve range of motion of arms, enhance declarative memory, train selective attention, or facilitate speech encoding in a patient with expressive aphasia. The second parameter is based on the mechanism in music that facilitates the therapeutic change, such as rhythm as a sensory timer for motor control, or musical pattern perception as a mnemonic device to enhance learning and recall through metrical organization of verbal materials; or singing to access alternative neural pathways to encode verbal output. Based on standardized descriptions, techniques can be uniquely and consistently defined in a way that separates them from each other. The actual design of the therapeutic exercise, on the other hand—within its standardized structure—draws on an unlimited number of musical resources and experiences to be translated in highly creative yet logical designs into a functional therapeutic experience for the client.

2. *Assessment.* Assessment is an essential component for implementing "best practice" standards embraced internationally by many rehabilitation professions to ensure quality care for patients. Assessment is a complex process that all professions wrestle with, and music therapy is no exception. Within NMT, assessment evolves out of a simple question: What do music therapists assess that is unique to their professional role in facilitating best treatment options for the patient? A second issue is that assessment plays the critical role in helping to select which treatment is the right one for the patient's diagnostic status and which treatment option has the greatest likelihood of success.

This process, however, can be effectively applied only when well-defined and standardized treatment techniques exist, and when something is known about treatment success rates. This knowledge can be obtained by clinical research investigating techniques and elements of their mechanisms. Without standardized treatment techniques and a comprehensive evidence basis that is grounded in scientific mechanism and outcome research, meaningful development of assessment procedures remains difficult. In NMT, assessment is aided by standardization of goals and interventions. Outcome data are available and will continue to shape the future of this model.

Additional information regarding NMT can be found in the following sources: "The Neurosciences and Music" (Avanzini, Faiena, Minciacchi, Lopez, & Majono, 2003); *Oxford Handbook of Music Psychology* (Hall, Cross, & Thaut, 2008); "Rationales for Improving Motor Function" (Hummelsheim, 1999); *Retraining Cognition: Techniques and Applications* (Parente & Herrmann, 1996); *Rhythm, Music, and the Brain* (Thaut, 2005); *Music Therapy in the Treatment of Adults with Mental Disorders: Theoretical Basis and Clinical Interventions* (Unkefer & Thaut, 2002).

Eclectic or Integrative Approach

An **eclectic** or **integrative** approach to therapy means that therapists draw freely on techniques from all types of therapy without necessarily accepting the theoretical frameworks behind them. This represents an overall trend away from exclusiveness or narrowness of adhering to a particular system or theory, with the goal of more efficient treatment (Baruth & Huber, 1985; Corey, 2001). According to Corey (2001), a trend toward eclecticism has been motivated by a proliferation of therapies throughout the 20th century, along with recognition that no single theory is comprehensive enough to account for the complexities of human behaviors, especially when taking into consideration the diverse characteristics and problems of client types. In addition, socioeconomic realities such as insurance reimbursement and short-term health care models are problematic with regard to some theoretical approaches that required long-term commitment, and result in gradual change or recovery. Furthermore, there has been limited evidence to differentiate among some therapy approaches with regard to effectiveness, paired with recognition among professionals regarding commonalities across different approaches. By accepting that each theory has its strengths and weaknesses, and by adopting an integrative perspective, therapists have the opportunity to more closely match therapeutic interventions with the needs and goals of individual clients (Baruth & Huber, 1985; Corey, 2001).

An integrative approach to therapy should not be a random selection of one's personally favorite techniques. It is important for the therapist to consider which theories provide the best basis for understanding cognitive, emotional, behavioral, and biophysical dimensions, and then reflect on therapeutic approaches that are the best fit for the client's presenting problems, cultural background, and individual personality. An integrated approach requires a solid understanding of different therapy approaches (obtained through formal study, continuing education, ongoing observation, review of research literature); the characteristics, needs, and strengths of different types of clients; self-reflection on one's own abilities; clarity regarding the mission of the agency in which one practices; and the knowledge, skill, art, and experience to determine what techniques are suitable for particular problems and circumstances (Corey, 2001).

In a survey of music therapists who work in psychiatric facilities, Silverman (2007) found that the largest proportion described themselves as having an eclectic philosophical orientation toward psychiatric treatment. Cassity and Cassity (2006) have advocated for a multimodal model of therapy for persons with behavioral and emotional disorders, which systematically addresses various domains of human functioning (e.g., behavior, affect, sensation, cognitions, etc.). Eclecticism or integrative therapy is commonly used within the field of music therapy, and its use is likely to increase.

This textbook has presented a wide range of approaches to therapy that reflect an extensive set of therapeutic techniques, some that are more or less suitable for a particular type clientele. Given the wide variety of clients served by music therapists, some level of eclectism is likely to remain an important part of music therapy practice.

CONCLUSIONS

Over an entire career, music therapists are likely to work within different clinical settings and with a variety of clientele who differ in age, clinical needs, background, and beliefs. Furthermore, a therapist who is aware of societal changes will seek input through professional collaborations, advanced studies, professional conferences, and information on scientific and clinical advances available through books and journals. As a result of life experiences, therapists also evolve in their understanding of themselves, the human condition, and their own personal responsibility to their clients and colleagues. All of these factors speak to the importance of being a lifelong learner who evolves personally as well as professionally with regard to music therapy approaches and the clinical contract with our clients.

SUMMARY OF PART II

In Part II of this chapter, you have learned about common music therapy approaches used to treat adults and children with disabilities. Also introduced were terms commonly used to describe music therapy approaches; terms such as *method, philosophy, theory,* and *model,* though having distinct meanings, are sometimes used interchangeably by music therapists. The field of music therapy was originally developed by musicians, educators, physicians, and psychiatrists who initially used an intuitive approach to music therapy practice that served the profession well for a time. But it was not until the mid 20th century that an emphasis was placed on the importance of research. As more research was carried out, the field of music therapy began to develop and mature at a rapid pace. In addition to better scientific knowledge about the way music influences cognitive, physiological, and socioemotional function, changes in society (including multiculturalism and the deinstitutionalization movement) have shaped today's practice in music therapy.

We also learned that not all approaches work equally well with all persons with disabilities, leaving it to the music therapist to select the most appropriate methods to meet client needs. Prominent approaches discussed in this chapter included educational models, approaches developed within the field of music therapy, and music therapy practice based on psychological philosophies. Finally, music therapy integrated with biomedical models and the increasingly popular eclectic approach to music therapy practice was discussed. Music therapists need to remain sensitive to the various factors that influence therapy effectiveness, and on-going developments in the field regarding best practice.